THE ROMANCE OF WATER

THE ROMANCE OF WATER

HERBERT WENDT

TRANSLATED FROM THE FRENCH BY
J. B. C. GRUNDY

LONDON
J. M. DENT & SONS LTD

© Librairie Hachette 1963
© Translation, J. M. Dent & Sons Ltd 1969
Translated from *Le Roman de l'Eau*, Hachette, Paris
Printed in Great Britain at
The Aldine Press · Letchworth · Herts
for
J. M. DENT & SONS LTD
Aldine House · Bedford Street · London
First published 1969

TRANSLATOR'S NOTE

I wish to record my thanks to Miss Pamela Watson
of the publisher's staff for the great help she has
given me in the editorial arrangement of this book.

J. B. C. GRUNDY

SBN: 460 07717 1

CONTENTS

v

70 - 2994

LIST OF ILLUSTRATIONS

vii

Fig. 1(*a*) is from *Wealth from the Oceans* by Tony Loftas (1967); Figs. 1(*b*) and 2 are from *Planet Earth* by Ronald Fraser (1961); Fig. 3 is from *Life in the Deep* by Maurice Burton (1958) ('Progress of Science' series, Phoenix House).

H₂O OR THE DISCOVERY OF WATER

It is written in Genesis: '. . . the same day were all the fountains of the great deep broken up, and the windows of heaven were opened'. . . 'And the waters prevailed exceedingly upon the earth; and all the high hills, that were under the whole heaven, were covered.' The elemental power of water calls to mind the floods and disasters underlying the various Creation myths. Water is life, abundance, God's blessing all in one. 'Be praised, O Lord, because of the water,' St Francis of Assisi proclaims. 'It is so needful, pliant, precious and fragile.'

What is water? It is a liquid without smell, colour or taste, a compound of hydrogen and oxygen which boils at the temperature of 100° C., and whose freezing point is zero centigrade.* Water is indispensable: more than seven-tenths of the globe's surface is covered with water and nine-tenths of animal life is found in it. Lower animals and vegetable life contain 90 per cent water, and higher animals, including man, between 60 and 70 per cent. Ceaselessly water irrigates the human body, nourishes its cells; it is the prime mover in those manifold and complex physical processes which we call Life.

Falling from the sky as rain, water nourishes the soil, passes through animal and vegetable creation, unites into streams and rivers and lakes, vaporizes, forms clouds, condenses and falls again in droplets, a vital circuit constantly begun again. A waterless globe would be no more than a mass of dead rock.

Thus it is hardly surprising that, two thousand five hundred years ago, there was born the idea that water, the prime source of all life, was the basic substance from which other forms of matter derived; an idea which from that time onward has never ceased to fascinate poets, philosophers and scientists. Today we all realize that this notion, by no means misconceived, accords in part with the fact that hydrogen, the element H with atomic weight of 1·00813 and

---

* Boiling point 212° Fahrenheit, freezing point 32° Fahrenheit. To convert Centigrade to Fahrenheit multiply by ⅑ and add 32.

of such prominence in the modern world, is indeed the fundamental ingredient of matter.

This theory of water as the primary source of all things was propounded first by Thales, a Greek, who did not know what hydrogen was—less still had he any idea of nuclear fusion. He lived about 595 B.C. at Miletus, a coastal town in Asia Minor, and historians are unanimous in regarding him as the father of philosophy. The degree to which Thales and the other pre-Socratic thinkers of Miletus were philosophers in the modern sense is a matter of opinion. The Greeks called them physiologists, meaning naturalists. This they truly were—thinking and theorizing scientists like Galileo, Laplace, Darwin and Einstein.

A fortunate age! The various sciences and speculative disciplines were not yet divided by impassable gulfs. The wide-ranging curiosity of Thales led him to study the nature of water, and to see in it the basis of everything. He could do so with impunity, for nobody had then thought of requiring scientists to keep to their facts and leave philosophy to the philosophers. In the same way, no one desired the philosopher to stay in his world of ideology and not disturb the scientists at their tasks. The result was that Miletus, a port and commercial town at the mouth of the Meander, became the cradle of western physics and philosophy.

We learn a good deal about Thales from scattered pieces of evidence. Various entertaining anecdotes reveal him as a shrewd politician, an astute merchant and a successful speculator in oil, though others reproach him for professional aloofness. One story in particular recounts that once, while gazing at the heavenly bodies, he fell into a well, amid the jeers of the bystanders. Adept at geometry, he calculated the height of the pyramids during a journey in Egypt and brought back to Greece the mathematical knowledge of the Egyptians. He held that all matter was animate, and he may well have suspected the existence of magnetism and electricity. From all points of view he seems to have had a truly encyclopaedic mind.

As has been mentioned, the pre-Socratic Greeks were first and foremost naturalists and rationalists. In seeking the prime substance they were looking not for some abstract principle but for tangible matter. Philosophers of the period could choose among four, the traditional elements of ancient chemistry: earth, water, fire and air. These were not, of course, 'elements' in the sense of modern chemistry, immutable components of matter, for their form changed and could be changed. Must one of them have been progenitor of the other three? If so, which? Thales unhesitatingly chose water.

The partisans of earth and fire and air protested. The rather futile debate as to which element took precedence need not detain us here. But for the Greek researchers, thinkers and poets, water continued to hold outstanding interest: no animal life is possible without blood, no plant without sap; the earth's disk floats upon the primordial waters of Oceanus; it was from water that the gods arose, into it that the earth once sank. After Thales a second physiologist from Miletus, Anaximander, propounded the surprisingly modern and evolutionist theory that all terrestrial animals, including man, derived from marine creatures.

'What is water?' was also the question asked in the Middle Ages by the alchemists of Europe and the Arab world as, amid the fumes of sulphur, they sought in their sanctums the 'philosophers' stone' and tried to transmute base metals into gold. Yet it would be wrong to ridicule those wizards and their disciples, for the chemists of today descend from them in a direct line.

For a whole millennium the cauldrons and retorts of the alchemists glowed and hissed. Countless salts, metals, liquids, mixtures and tinctures, bases and substances, simmered upon wayward fires. Did those materials derive, as the Greeks had maintained, from a small number of basic elements? The alchemists replied in the affirmative and, like the Greek physiologists, believed in the transmutability of the elements. They too, emulating Thales, were searching for prime matter, the root of everything. And most of them inclined towards water.

Boiling turned water into steam, frost made it ice. Salts could be obtained from sea water, and did not miraculous mercury suggest a metal in liquid form—or a metallic liquid? Some of the alchemists even supposed that all salts, ores, metals, minerals and crystals had emerged from water which had been subjected to colossal pressure and incalculable heat in the centre of the earth.

Even on the threshold of modern times many of the best minds still considered that the systematic distillation of water would produce soil and that quartz was evidently crystallized water. It was only in the second half of the eighteenth century—between 1766 and 1783 to be precise—that four scientific inquirers noted independently that water was not an element but a composite substance. Admittedly, none of them deduced the consequences of his discovery; that remained to a fifth man, a master of chemistry, a few years later.

Throughout the eighteenth century men of science had been inquiring into the properties of gases and liquids and into the nature of combustion. Combustion was believed to depend upon the action of an agent which was named 'phlogiston', and for over a century this theory prevailed. It was firmly believed in by the first of the men we have referred to, Lord Henry Cavendish, grandson of the second Duke of Devonshire. He was a wealthy amateur of the kind in which England has been so prolific; of original ideas and to some extent a misanthropist, he dedicated almost his whole fortune to experiments in chemistry and physics. This was just at the time when the classical belief in earth, air, fire and water was being replaced by the concept of elements—fundamental substances which defy analysis. Such was the case of gold, of silver, copper, iron, sulphur, phosphorus and chlorine, but not of earth. Were fire, air and water like that too?

Henry Cavendish was particularly interested in the composition of the atmosphere and in 1766 he submitted to the Royal Society a paper entitled 'Factitious Airs', in which he touched on hydrogen and its explosive effect when mixed with air. Cavendish has been named as the discoverer of hydrogen but he did not make this claim himself and indeed mentions that the explosive effect was known to Robert Boyle and others. Cavendish thought that this gas was in fact 'phlogiston'. He continued his experiments for many years and eventually reached the conclusion, about 1782 or 1783, that water was 'dephlogisticated air combined with phlogiston'. Meanwhile, in 1774, our second inquirer, Joseph Priestley, had isolated oxygen—which was none other than 'dephlogisticated air'.

Joseph Priestley was a Dissenting minister and an outstanding amateur chemist. Like Cavendish he was responsive to all problems; his inability to accept the official doctrine of the Church caused him much difficulty, and it was only in his hours of leisure that he could take up the side-issue of oxygen and combustion. A man of liberal ideas, Priestley was known to be a supporter of the French Revolution and on the second anniversary of the Revolution a mob burned down his house and chapel, among others. He fled from Birmingham to London, thence to America. This scientific non-conformist ended his eventful life on a remote farmstead in Pennsylvania in 1804.

He had settled at Birmingham in 1780 and had immediately joined the Lunar Society there, with many of whose members he had been in correspondence for several years. These included many men of inquiring spirit, among them James Watt, inventor of the condensing steam engine, who had a very practical interest in the nature of water and steam and their properties. Cavendish and Priestley certainly corresponded with each other and it was thus that in 1783 all these men were forming ideas on the exact nature of water and the part played in its constitution by 'phlogiston' (hydrogen), and 'dephlogisticated air' (oxygen). In January 1784 Cavendish communicated to the Royal Society his finding that water was a combination of these two elements, much to the annoyance of Watt, who felt that *he* had arrived first at the proper conclusion. Both men, however, were too great to remain at loggerheads for long over a question of priority, and as Watt later said: 'It matters little whether Cavendish or I discovered the composition of water; the great thing is that it *is* discovered.'

Meanwhile the Swedish chemist Wilhelm Scheele had independently established the main constituents of the atmosphere, and reached the conclusion that there were two predominant gases, one of them aiding combustion, the other preventing it.

It required the genius of the fifth man, Antoine Laurent Lavoisier, to appreciate the full consequences of these discoveries and arrive at the true nature of combustion. Lavoisier, who was also in touch with members of the Birmingham Lunar Society, lived in Paris, that Mecca of the natural philosophers of the time. On the very eve of the French Revolution Lavoisier described in his *Elemental Treatise on Chemistry* the marvel of combustion. Rejecting the phlogistic theory he revealed the true nature of the process: combination of a substance with the oxygen of the air, the proof of which is said to have cost him over 50,000 *livres*. In addition Lavoisier set down the fundamental principles of the conservation of matter, and his many deductions and observations earned him the title 'father of modern chemistry'.

In Paris there is a sealed tube containing 45 g. of the water synthesized by Lavoisier, and this carefully preserved relic is doubly precious. For Lavoisier had the misfortune to be not only a scientist. He was a civil servant too: a head tax-collector, inspector-general of explosives, member of the board set up to establish the new weights and measures, director of the tobacco monopoly and, finally, secretary of the treasury. Large sums thus passed through his hands, affording sufficient grounds for the revolutionaries to treat him as a profiteer of the *ancien régime*. He was arrested on the pretext that tobacco, bad enough before, had under his control become unsmokable. Arraigned before the tribunal Lavoisier was condemned to death. The defence dwelt upon his scientific merits, but the judges rejected their arguments with the lapidary phrase: 'The Republic has no need of scholars!' On 8th May 1794 the father of modern chemistry died upon the guillotine.

Nevertheless it was presently realized that France had need of scholars, and that in the long run individuals such as Lavoisier were of more use to humanity than politicians and ideologists. Eleven years after the death of Lavoisier two of the greatest savants of the time, Louis Joseph Gay-Lussac, physicist and chemist, and Alexander von Humboldt, traveller and naturalist, proved that water contains two parts of hydrogen to one part of oxygen.

Thus water is neither elemental in the ancient acceptation of the term nor an element in the chemists' sense, but a composite substance. It is a true chemical compound, whereas air and earth are mere mixtures and fire is a chemical process. The nineteenth century had just parted company with the brilliant speculations and the pipe-dreams of antiquity and the Middle Ages. Henceforth every substance was studied, decomposed, enclosed in rigid formulae, and a list of elements was drawn up—a list, to use contemporary terms, of the 'primordial and fundamental substances which cannot be decomposed further'. The atomic epoch was beginning. Chemists no longer regarded water as the *fons et origo* of all. Hydrogen, its chief component, had snatched first place.

At the beginning of the nineteenth century William Prout, an English chemist and physiologist, was already maintaining that even the new chemical elements, apparently fixed and immutable, could be decomposed and that, at least in theory, it was possible to strip them down, to split them and reach the final unit, which was the hydrogen atom. Prout's theory met with polite incredulity.

It is not to our purpose here to trace the developments in theory and technology which led to the first splitting of an atom in 1919 and then to the complexity of present-day nuclear physics, but one important discovery must be mentioned.

In 1932 the American chemist Harold Clayton Urey discovered that there is, in addition to normal water, a 'heavy' water (with the formula D_2O); and he identified the hydrogen isotope D, deuterium, with an atomic weight of 2·0147, of which ordinary water contains a proportion of about 0·02 per cent. Shortly afterwards a second hydrogen isotope, tritium, was created artificially in a nuclear reactor: it is not found in ordinary water. 'Heavy water' would be of no special interest to us—unlike fish, for whom a stronger mixture of D_2O is fatal—were it not that deuterium and tritium have one surprising property. When subjected in a nuclear reactor to a temperature above fourteen million degrees C., by nuclear fusion they transmute into helium and give off a vast amount of energy in the process.

This is the kind of temperature prevailing inside the Sun, and the source of solar energy is very probably the continuous transmutation of hydrogen into helium. Terrifying possibilities arose: would man succeed in reproducing artificially the sequence which takes place in the heart of the Sun? Only three years after Urey's discovery Frédéric Joliot-Curie did not hesitate to prophesy: 'We have every reason to bring forward the possibility that scientists may go on to atomic mutations of an explosive nature.'

The H-bomb was already on the horizon.

In the American 'atomic city' of Los Alamos, in the 1950s, the phantasm took shape. It was not without grave misgivings that the project was undertaken. Some protested that the explosion of a hydrogen bomb might start a chain reaction of world dimensions: the hydrogen within the atmosphere and the waters of the Earth would be transformed into helium, the planet would become a flaming star and disappear into the void. Albert Einstein gave warning in these terms: 'The spectre of universal ruin takes ever clearer shape upon the horizon.' Edward Teller, the father of the H-bomb, nevertheless brought his project to fruition, and on 1 November 1952 a ball of fire of a diameter of three and a half miles arose above the island of Eniwetok in the Marshall Islands. There was a crater two hundred feet deep: man had brought off for the first time what was the prerogative of the Sun—with the one distinction that at Eniwetok there had been only destruction and nothing had been created.

The phenomena which take place in the Sun are to be distinguished from the nuclear reaction in a hydrogen bomb only by the slow pace at which they follow each other. The energy released does not destroy: on the contrary, it produces other energies.

Nuclear physicists have long dreamed of reproducing this process in slow motion, of making artificial suns which would serve human nature instead of threatening it. Deuterium, the heavy hydrogen which exists freely in nature, would thus become the main source of energy mastered by man. Alas, history teaches us that it is never learning but always power politics which exploit a new discovery. If things were otherwise we could study calmly from now on the unsuspected possibilities of the use of hydrogen and forget the nightmare vision of the mushroom over Eniwetok.

There is a long thread linking Thales of Miletus and Edward Teller, the primordial element of water and the H-bomb.

The word water connotes sea, river, ice, rain, snow, blood and sap, fecundity and floods, boons and perils. It is of water that many of the chapters of the history of creation, of our planet and its inhabitants, speak. We can well understand how Thales describes the apparently omnipotent water as 'the beginning of all'. Sumerians and Babylonians too invented a definition which is no less pleasing and accurate: Water is the most precious gift the gods made to man.

PART ONE

WATER, SPACE, TIME

All is born of water, all is sustained by water.
GOETHE

CHAPTER ONE

THE FLOOD

THEORIES about the creation of the Earth are among the most tempting forms of speculation and the most fascinating mental exercises in which man has indulged for thousands of years, and in all the legends water plays a vital role. The Sumerians and Babylonians thought of the universe as an immense sea whence, like some circular island, the Earth's disk had emerged. Homer tells of Oceanus, the river of life and the creator of the universe of the gods, the human world and all else. The Bible puts it more clearly:

And the earth was without form and void; and darkness was on the face of the deep. And the Spirit of God moved upon the face of the waters. . . . Let the waters . . . be gathered together unto one place, and let the dry land appear. . . .

The majestic picture of worlds begotten by a primordial sea has no doubt long been consigned by scholars to the realm of mythology; but even in modern Creation 'myths' water surges, boils and becomes steam, rain falls from the sky and vaporizes in contact with a burning globe, and is transformed afresh into cloud. For millions of years before the flood this mighty cycle of cataclysm persisted. In 1755 Immanuel Kant laid down a hypothesis postulating a nebula rotating on its own axis as the origin of the planetary system. Forty years later the astronomer Simon Pierre Laplace conjured up a vision of the primitive Sun as a gigantic cluster of gases girt with primitive vapours which gradually solidified and became planets. Physicists and astronomers of our own time, smiling at the theories of Kant and Laplace, have launched a dozen others. But whether our planetary system was the product of some primordial explosion or of the collision of two cosmic masses, whether it arose from the collision of the Sun with some cosmic cloud which it had attracted and engulfed or even from 'eddies' in a vast mass of cold dust and gas, at some moment the Earth whirled into the universe.

When did this happen? In 1654 James Ussher, an Irish bookman and Bishop of Armagh, inferred from the table of generations in the Old Testament that the Earth had been created in 4004 B.C.

11

Shortly before the French Revolution Georges Louis de Buffon, the most eminent naturalist of his time, concluded from his observations of a white-hot ball of metal cooled slowly that our globe was at least 74,800 years old. In the latter half of the nineteenth century the geologists carried this figure to a hundred million years, and increased it to two thousand million in the first half of the twentieth century.

There are in fact rocks to which the latest methods of dating assign an age of more than 2,500,000,000 years, an estimate which presupposes that the Earth had already cooled before the start of that period. It seems likely that the period of incandescence before cooling—the 'astral era' of our globe—began between three and a half and five thousand million years ago. At the time of writing, any estimate, even one based upon astronomic, physical or geological data, is instantly open to question.

The spinning Earth followed its course, wrapped in gaseous clouds and shaken by streams of molten magma. Enormous quantities of gas disappeared into space, others stayed within the atmospheric confines or within the core of the sphere—especially (fortunately for us) oxygen, hydrogen and carbon dioxide. From 1,000° C. the temperature dropped to 500° and then to 374·2° C. At this point the drama reached its climax: in obedience to the strict laws of chemistry, when that 'critical' temperature was reached, the oxygen and hydrogen combined, and H_2O was born! Chemists have sketched a terrifying picture of that inchoation; according to them mighty explosions and tempests of fire marked the union of the elements of water.

Above the Earth, bloated, chaotic, riven and racked as it was, hung a pall of thick vapour. It cooled, the vapour condensed, and rain fell on the peaks and plateaux and still warm rocks. So it went on for hundreds of millions of years. Half way down the water vaporized, cooled again, fell again, changed once more into vapour. But a day came when the temperature of the Earth's crust had lowered to the point where drops of rain were no longer transformed into mist: the water stayed upon the Earth, filtering into the crevices of the ground. From that moment it rained without ceasing, and a trillion and a half tons of water poured down. The seething water collected in the valleys and hollows produced by the outpouring of magma upon the Earth's crust and formed turbulent and billowing seas, from which rose clouds and mists.

The deluge overwhelmed the face of the Earth and levelled its surface, previously dotted with craters like those of the Moon. The water defined the first continental blocks, gnawed at the rocks, scoured out the sea basins, and carved the courses of innumerable rivers into *terra firma*. So began the Archaean period, the first stage in the 'mythical epoch' of geology.

The composition of the water itself became modified. Falling from the sky as pure H_2O it was enriched by the salts and minerals from the rocks over which it passed, carrying them off in solution to become the salt water of the sea. This has been a continuing process, for at later periods the soluble minerals in sea water have been used and transformed by marine fauna.

The waters of the various oceans contain an average of $3\frac{1}{2}$ per cent of salts: sodium chloride and magnesium chloride, sulphates of magnesium, potassium and calcium are the most abundant, with traces of many others. Modest as are the proportions represented by the minerals when concentrated and solidified, their total weight would amount to forty-seven billion* tons; or, spread evenly over the Earth, they would constitute an even layer more than one hundred and sixty feet thick.

Besides these main constituents, ocean water includes in solution thirty-six other elements—iodine, phosphorus, arsenic, copper, aluminium, iron, silver, gold, uranium, to mention only the best known. It is believed that marine gold would amount to four times that of the deposits on land. Similarly the amount of uranium in solution in sea water is estimated at a million tons—quite enough to feed a large number of atomic piles for thousands of years. Hence the hopes aroused in our epoch, so greedy for raw materials, of exploiting the treasures of the ocean. But we must go back to the Earth's Archaean period to discover how these minerals first reached the oceans.

If we are to believe the astonomers, who use spectrum analysis for the study of the chemical composition of the planets of the solar system, the Earth was an unusually successful creation: its adequate supply of water seems to give it an advantage over its neighbours. At present we are limited to conjecture about the conditions prevailing on the three most distant planets, Uranus, Neptune and Pluto. But we know that the temperature is always several hundred degrees below zero and that the atmosphere,

* Throughout, one billion = one million × one million.

especially that of Uranus, is composed almost entirely of methane. If there should be water on these planets, it would be frozen in floes and seas of ice.

The giant planets Jupiter and Saturn are probably gaseous masses revolving round a solid nucleus and surrounded by a dense atmosphere made up largely of methane and ammonia. There should be sufficient hydrogen to suggest the presence in the atmosphere of water in some form. Saturn's curious rings are, according to some, a collection of particles, the relics of former moons; others think that they consist of ice crystals. There is no point of comparison between that planet and Earth. Although the satellites of Saturn and Jupiter are favoured by science-fiction writers, a realistic observer cannot think of them as inhabited by living beings in the normal sense of the term.

There remain the Earth's three closer neighbours, Mercury, Venus and Mars. We need give our attention only to the last two, for Mercury, only four times the size of the Moon, has no atmosphere and, since it takes as long to rotate on its own axis as it does to complete its solar orbit, always has its same side towards the Sun, and thus lacks the alternation of day and night. On one side the temperature reaches about $400°$ C.; on the other, plunged in eternal darkness, it is about minus $100°$ C.

Venus, for her part, hides behind a dense gaseous envelope, which was the subject of investigation by the U.S. space-craft *Mariner V* and the Russian space-craft *Venus 4* in the autumn of 1967. The atmosphere of the planet appears to consist of a high proportion of carbon dioxide together with nitrogen, but the possibility of the presence of other gases has not been entirely ruled out. At a height of about twenty-five miles from the surface of the planet the atmospheric temperature was recorded as between $127°$ C. and $175°$ C. However, the shape of the planet itself remains unknown.

The best known of all the planets is Mars, whose external appearance calls to mind that of Earth, a resemblance which has stimulated the imaginations of utopians and seers. Mars has polar caps, probably of ice or frost, and there are dark markings which have been interpreted, but not established, as a rudimentary flora. The highly rarefied atmosphere of Mars contains carbon dioxide and possibly traces of oxygen, and the surface temperature is on the whole below that of Earth, with more extreme differences between day and night. Vast areas are taken up by reddish and ochreous deserts above which rise clouds of dust. Information about the so-called 'canals' and 'seas' of Mars is still imperfect, but at the utmost it seems unlikely that the amount of water on the planet exceeds that of the English Channel.

The planets closest to Earth are on the whole unrewarding. The Moon, our satellite, is even more disappointing, for it has no atmosphere, no water, no wind, no seasons and no life. It is, however, of great interest to anyone who favours the bold theory of George Darwin.* He held that the Moon is simply a mass detached from Earth, and that the resulting cavity was filled by the waters of the Pacific Ocean. A kindred theory postulates the impact of an enormous meteor upon the molten globe before the era of the flood, with identical consequences—the Moon and the Pacific. But most modern authorities are agreed that the Moon was once an independent minor planet and was attracted and captured by Earth.

The Pacific Ocean has existed since the earliest geological periods. Whether, with Bacon the philosopher, Buffon the zoologist, Pickering the astronomer and Wegener the geophysicist, we believe in the theory of continental drift—a theory which has taken hard knocks but which has been returning to favour in recent years—or whether on the other hand we accept that the basis of the continents was determined very early in Earth's history, the fact remains that the globe's earliest sea is, on all historical-geological maps, what we now call the Pacific.

The preparation of maps of this kind is a most exacting task, for Earth's distant past has left behind only a litter of fragments: buried shelves and boulders, submerged rock tables, plains, depressions and sea beds overlain by layers of later sediment. It is by means of such distorted and fragmentary material that geologists try to establish the sites of ancient seas and land masses. The maps drawn by different schools of geology vary greatly but are agreed upon one matter: throughout the geological epochs there has existed a Pacific Ocean, at one time covering both the Far East and a portion of North America. Geologists tell us that there were two major land blocks in the succession of geological eras. The southern continent has been called Gondwanaland from the name of a district in Central India where its strata were first recognized. It included what is now South America and stretched across the

* Sir George Howard Darwin (1845–1912), second son of Charles Darwin.

southern Atlantic, Africa, southern Asia, the area occupied by the Indian Ocean, parts of Australia and the Antarctic. To the north was another major land mass, or masses, one part of which was given the name Laurentia from the St Lawrence River, since it was identified first in part of what is now Canada. Geologists claim to have identified traces of this northern continent from North America to the high latitudes of the Far East, via Scandinavia and northern Siberia.

Between those two continents, changing over long periods of time both in extent and in outline, was the sea which has been given the name of Tethys. It is now represented by the Mediterranean, although at times in the remote past it extended from the Atlantic eastwards into the Pacific. Tethys, who gave her name to the Mediterranean of classical antiquity, is in Greek mythology the consort of Oceanus, and thus the mother of all things. This charming symbolism is also expressive of a scientific fact: many of the great upheavals which moulded Earth's present features took place along the line of what was the bed of Tethys. Mountains reared up, volcanoes burst forth, waves scoured the *terra firma*, and the waters spread across its surface. And while the Pacific justified its name for aeons and underwent little change, new seas, new shores, new lands sprang from the womb of Tethys. In them the fate of the globe was sealed; the world as we recognize it was gradually taking shape.

CHAPTER TWO

THE DROPLET ASSAILS THE ROCK

WHEN the flood was over, the Sun rose upon a bare and lifeless planet. Volcanoes smoked above the emergent ground. The land itself seemed alive; never tranquil, it raised and lowered itself, bent and straightened, gave up vast areas to the ocean and won back new ones from the waters. Two primordial elements, in the sense given them by the Greek physiologists, water and earth, were locked in a mortal conflict that has never ceased.

The water continued the levelling and destruction begun by the great rains. Little by little it cleared itself a channel, undermining stone, destroying gigantic mountains in the course of millions of years, sweeping their remains downstream and dropping them into marine basins. From the beginning of the history of the world this terrible despoiler has brought about more destruction than all the other erosive forces put together.

Until men had understood the immense span of time represented by the geological epochs, geologists could not explain this sly and pitiless war of attrition between water and land, let alone the nature of earth's counter-offensive, equally slow and pregnant with consequences. The discovery of 'geological time' started one of the greatest revolutions in the world of science.

Reluctance to propound an interpretation of Earth's history at variance with the biblical narration of one simultaneous Creation hindered for centuries the development of geology as a science based on observable fact. Some, confronted with this problem, suffered agonies of conscience; others, more outspoken, had often found themselves dangerously close to heresy. At the end of the eighteenth century geologists generally were divided into two main camps: the Catastrophists and the Uniformitarians.

Broadly speaking, Catastrophists believed that the geological and geographical features of the planet were attributable to sudden and recurrent 'catastrophes', fearful upheavals accompanied by widespread floods, on the last of which Noah launched his Ark. Predominant among Catastrophist doctrines was Werner's 'Neptunist' theory. Abraham Gottlob Werner, son of a mining engineer, early became interested in minerals, and in 1775, when only twenty-five years old, he obtained a teaching appointment at the Mining Academy at Freiberg in Saxony. Eloquent and forceful, he made Freiberg the most famous geological college of his time. Werner declared that *all* rocks, and granite earliest among them, had been laid as sediments by oceans which once covered the entire globe and had subsequently diminished in extent; hence the term Neptunism, since Neptune was god of the oceans. Volcanic activity Werner ascribed to 'spontaneous combustion' of coal seams not far below the surface; it had played no part in the story of Earth's formative periods.

Uniformitarianism, on the other hand, which was largely the concept of James Hutton, a Scot, declared that Earth's history was very long and continuous, that agents of erosion and land-building had been the same in the most distant past as they were at the present time, and that changes were not due to sudden unrelated cataclysms but to a uniformity of processes.

Adherents mainly of the Catastrophist school were the so-called Vulcanists, who were nevertheless prepared to admit that basaltic rocks were of volcanic origin and thus could not be included among rocks laid down as sediments by ancient seas. Advocates of Uniformitarianism were sometimes referred to as Plutonists, since in addition to basalt they declared granite also to be of igneous origin and stressed—over-stressed—the importance of subterranean heat in consolidating sediments; hence their name, derived from Pluto, god of the underworld.

Hutton's published work was not very readable, and his conclusions were contested even when more lucidly expounded by John Playfair in *Illustration of the Huttonian Theory*, 1802. It remained for another Scot, Charles Lyell, born in 1797, the year of Hutton's death, to bring about the general acceptance of the fundamental ideas of Uniformitarianism.

Charles Lyell studied law, but while still an undergraduate at Oxford pursued his interest in geology and became a Fellow of the Geological Society of London, which had been founded in 1807. He became its joint secretary in 1823, and later abandoned law entirely in order to devote himself to the study of geology. In 1830 there was published the first volume of his *Principles of Geology*, in which, and in the subsequent volumes, 1832 and 1833, he extended and revised Hutton's ideas, establishing the principles of Uniformitarianism as a true basis of geological science. Lyell was appointed Professor of Geology at King's College in 1831 and lectured there in 1832 and 1833. But influential as his lectures were, he preferred to devote his energies to travel and writing, developing his ideas from direct observation. The Royal Society awarded him a medal in 1834 and he became President of the Geological Society in 1835; the teachings of *The Principles of Geology* were established, if not unanimously accepted. For facts concerning changes in Earth's features in historical times Lyell was to some extent indebted to the German geologist Karl von Hoff, the first two volumes of whose *History of the natural changes of the Earth's surface* had appeared in 1822 and 1824; but von Hoff's later volumes (1834, 1840, 1841) in turn owed something to Lyell's *Principles*.

Lyell's work played a part also in revolutionizing the natural sciences; for a slow and continuous evolution of Earth itself must logically set the pace for that of its inhabitants, its fauna and flora. When young Charles Darwin embarked on a voyage round the world in 1831 he took with him Lyell's book, and it was through the eyes of Lyell that Darwin looked at the rising and declining continental masses and studied the multi-millenary contest in which water has been pitted against land. From it he made practical deductions which contributed to his famous theory of evolution and so gave biology a new outlook.

In the light of increasing knowledge geologists have been obliged to modify Charles Lyell's doctrines to some extent. Nevertheless it was from Lyell that we first received some notion of the length of geological periods and of the slow, remorseless and secret struggle, aeon upon aeon, between land and water.

That struggle proceeds without man's full awareness of it. Tides and undertows gnaw at the dry land, carrying off sand at one point and depositing it elsewhere. Great rivers and their tributaries hollow out their beds, break into cascades and sweep precious top-soil down to the lower courses of their valleys and to the sea. In the mountains frost splits the rock, glaciers deepen valleys and carry debris to lower levels. Day after day enormous quantities of water evaporate from the seas and fall again upon the land. If the water vapour escaped into space instead of returning to the earth as rain, the level of the oceans would drop by about three feet each year, and in some four thousand years the billions of tons of water which the seas contain would be no more than a memory.

If other forces were not active as counter-agents to the destructive effects of water, the levelled continents would long since have disappeared beneath seas a mile deep. The power opposing water is almost as fluid and remorseless. Volcanic eruptions originating in the endless turmoil beneath the Earth's mantle, earthquakes, the effects of the slow drying out and lifting of land once submerged beneath water or sheets of ice—these agents have continuously set up stresses in the Earth's crust, raising new continents and mountain-high plateaux.

It is now a commonplace that throughout geological time the restless Earth has elevated marine basins and transformed them into mountains. The marine sediments, whether of debris carried into the sea from the land or of the chalky remains of countless shellfish, which formed regular layers on the bottom of the sea, were petrified under the immense pressure. In the course of time terrestrial movements thrust these marine rocks upwards, so distorting and bending them in some cases that we can almost believe that the stone broke upon the mountains like waves.

From classical antiquity onwards naturalists and philosophers have sought to explain the discovery in the Alps, and even at sixteen or seventeen thousand feet in the Himalaya, of fossilized sea shells and petrified marine mud. Scholars and thinkers such as Leonardo da Vinci in the fifteenth and Bernard Palissy in the sixteenth century had been puzzled by these phenomena. Leonardo correctly interpreted shells found far inland as evidence of former seas, but did not take the matter further. Palissy was one of those whose convictions brought him into conflict with theological doctrine, and he died in the Bastille. Collectors such as John Woodward in the seventeenth century were unshakably convinced that these petrifications were relics of the biblical Flood; but Voltaire, the old rogue and eternal sceptic, shrugged his shoulders and explained that the pilgrims of yore who climbed the passes used to throw away the remnants of their food, which had finally turned into stone.

Geologists and palaeontologists divide Earth's past into eras and periods, although they do not all agree about the limits of each within a few million years. The earliest era is variously termed the Azoic and Proterozoic ('without life' and 'first life'), the Archaean, or the Pre-Cambrian, and ended between 500 and 600 million years ago. It was succeeded by the Palaeozoic ('ancient life'), or Primary, era (whose earliest period is termed the Cambrian). The Mesolithic ('middle life'), or Secondary, era began about 200 million years ago and in turn gave way, about 70 million years ago, to the Caenozoic ('new life'), which covers both the Tertiary era, ending about a million years ago, and the Quaternary era. The first period of the Quaternary was the Pleistocene ('most recent'), during which the Ice Ages occurred; and the period in which we live, beginning 10,000 to 12,000 years ago, is called the Holocene ('wholly recent'). The named periods of each era lasted for varying lengths of time, but each is marked by its own geological characteristics and by fossils which permit the determination of the periods when, for example, the sea submerged a particular part of the present-day continents.

We owe the concept of systematic dating and identification of rocks by their stratification and contained fossils to a self-taught genius, William Smith. Smith, born at Churchill in Oxfordshire in 1769, was educated only at the village school but learnt the elements of geometry and of surveying from borrowed books. He established himself as a surveyor, notably for canals, and became renowned as a civil engineer, which took him to all parts of the country. He was thus able to pursue his interest in geological formations and to observe how the same rock strata could be identified at different places by their fossils. His first geological map, of the area around Bath, was published in 1799; for years he worked patiently on producing a stratigraphical map of the whole of England and Wales, which was published in 1815; in 1816 his book *Strata Identified by Organised Fossils* was published, followed the next year by *The Stratigraphical System of Organised Fossils*. Although the Geological Society was slow to recognize the value of Smith's work (which earned him the nickname 'Strata' Smith), his ideas were fairly widely known by the time Charles Lyell in turn was formulating his 'principles'. Smith's work brought order and method into geology and it is from the early years of the nineteenth century that the nomenclature of the geological periods originates. Meanwhile in France and Germany others had been groping towards similar ideas. We cannot name all the individuals and their particular contributions to a general expansion of knowledge, but of especial note are Jean Baptiste de Lamarck (1744–1829) who studied the fossils of rocks in the Paris region and is considered now to be the founder of invertebrate palaeontology, and Georges Baron Cuvier (1769–1832), who worked in particular on the comparative anatomy of living and fossil specimens and is known as the founder of vertebrate palaeontology. Smith and Cuvier considered that fossils were evidence of a series of separate creations, but Lamarck's detailed work led him towards a theory of evolution.

Let us return, after this digression into the realm of geology, to the primeval ocean. Many hundreds of millions of years before the start of the first geological period which can be identified by fossils occurred an event of incalculable dimension. Life appeared in the warm and mineral-rich waters of the early seas.

CHAPTER THREE

THE BIRTH OF LIFE

IN 1953 Harold Clayton Urey, the discoverer of heavy water, invited Stanley Miller, one of his graduate students, to make an unusual experiment. In a hermetically sealed and sterilized glass vessel Miller mixed the gases methane, ammonia and hydrogen (which Urey, following the ideas of the Russian A. I. Oparin, believed were constituents of Earth's primitive atmosphere) and water vapour. An electrical discharge was passed through the circulating mixture for seven days. The result was astounding: the reaction which had taken place produced organic substances: amino-acids, complex compounds which are integral constituents of proteins and present in all living matter.

As the result of his experiment Miller had obtained scarcely more than a milligram of amino-acids; and since these are not living matter, the American chemist had not succeeded in creating *life* in a glass vessel. Nevertheless his success in synthesizing organic acids was full of implications: had he come near to creating the conditions which had given rise to the first form of semi-living organisms in a primeval sea a thousand or two thousand million years ago?

What were those organisms like? Possibly—some biologists would say probably—they resembled viruses such as are known today. Viruses, the cause of many diseases, occupy a position between living and non-living matter. They are too small to be seen except with an electron microscope, and it was the brilliant work of an American biochemist, W. M. Stanley, in 1935 that proved them to consist of a speck of nucleic acid cloaked in protein. All living cells are made up of these two groups of chemical substances.

Viruses are incapable of independent existence, except briefly, and survive only as parasites in the cells of higher organisms; they do not breathe or show organic development. Biologists therefore do not class them as 'living'. There are, however, similar micro-organisms, bacteriophage viruses, which can move independently. It is tempting to assume that the first 'living' organisms resembled the free-moving bacteriophage viruses and that the parasitic viruses

22

represent a later adaptation when higher forms of life had come into existence.

To the ancient myths of creation biologists have added their findings upon the origins of life. It revealed itself somewhere in the warm, marginal waters of a primeval sea, so rich in nucleic acids, carbon dioxide, potassium, calcium, sulphur and phosphorus; in due course were born unicellular and defenceless organisms sensitive to light which, belonging to neither the animal nor the vegetable kingdom, fed upon inorganic matter. In the course of time, perhaps due to intensification of sunlight or to cosmic radiation, mutant molecules appeared and the organisms developed into the first single-celled plants.

A blue-green alga is generally accepted as representative of the first vegetal life. Although lacking a true cell nucleus it is impregnated with the green substance chlorophyll, which means that it is capable of photosynthesis—that is, of transforming, with the aid of light, atmospheric carbon dioxide and hydrogen from water into carbohydrates. This change is accompanied by a release of oxygen—a vital factor, for by releasing free oxygen into an atmosphere previously deficient in it the process of photosynthesis slowly created conditions essential to the development of a varied flora, and subsequently of marine and terrestrial fauna dependent in turn on available oxygen and abundant plant life for food. The text books say it was about fifteen hundred to two thousand million years ago that the oceans were invaded by algae, and indications of organic matter have been found in rocks over two thousand million years old in southern Africa. But these conclusions may have to be reconsidered: in 1967 a Swedish chemist discovered that an alga of the type known as *Chlorella*, taken from the mud of stagnant water, is capable when grown in a strictly controlled atmosphere of 100 per cent methane of producing by photosynthesis an atmosphere containing 6 per cent oxygen in a matter of days. Such an isolated experiment cannot be considered as proof, but it raises the question of the possibility of the existence of such forms of life, and of an atmosphere containing free oxygen, at an earlier geological period than is generally considered probable.

The first traces of primitive life have definitely been identified in rocks of Pre-Cambrian date. By the dawn of the Cambrian period invertebrate sea creatures with hard 'shells' had come into existence, as fossil finds testify. We are justified in being astonished at the great diversity and complexity of flora and fauna which have developed from single-celled forms in the teeming seas since the transition to the Palaeozoic era a mere five hundred or so million years ago.

At first this life was passive, at the mercy of the waters. Later the organisms grouped themselves in colonies, became many-celled, acquired a digestive system and the organs required for breathing, motion, reproduction; they learned to 'swim' and to move directionally. The microscopic algae gave birth to dense seaweeds and water grass; the minute animal forms gave rise to echinoderms such as sea urchins, arthropods, molluscs. In manuals of natural history this chapter of evolution seems to follow a simple and logical sequence, but the complex evolutions of which the Cambrian seas were the theatre are among the obscurest secrets of the world's history. Over half of the forty divisions of animal life, as now classified, have the sea as their only habitat. The majority of the remainder are represented in the sea, in fresh water and on land. Barely a tenth have broken all contact with the liquid element. Marine existence embraces a great variety of forms, adapted to surface waters or deep sea, reefs or strands, rock pools or brackish shallows; in the water there is room for all.

The basis of every higher form of marine life is phytoplankton, which drifts in the uppermost waters of the ocean. These single-celled plants 'feed' on the mineral salts in sea water by means of photosynthesis and form enormous trails, especially in cold seas. Phytoplankton may be said to play the part in marine life that grass plays in the economy of dry land farming. In the spring, when the longer hours of daylight warm the surface waters, the plant plankton flourishes and sailors say that the sea 'blooms', and it is a fact that the ocean is touched with green over vast expanses. The cycle of the phytoplankton is complicated, but broadly speaking the spring blooming depletes the mineral salts available and thus the plankton declines as autumn approaches. Upwellings and currents due to temperature differences restore the level of nutrient salts in the surface waters during the cold days of shorter sunlight which follow, and lead again to abundance of plankton in the spring. Drifting with the plant plankton and living on them are the zooplankton, microscopic animal forms which in turn provide food for larger kinds of marine fauna, and so on up the scale to the fish we ourselves eat and to the marine mammals.

Plant and animal plankton take many different forms. Among the phytoplankton the diatoms, the most numerous, form from the sea's minerals an external cell wall of silica. The microscope reveals them in astonishing variety—pillbox shape, rectangular, irregular; other kinds form chains or spheres, are star-shaped, anchor-shaped, have whip-like flagella. The zooplankton, Radiolaria and Foraminifera for example, are no less varied and strange. Included among the zooplankton are fish eggs and fish of various kinds in their early stages of growth, when they too must drift with the currents, unable yet to swim where they will.

At different periods in the Earth's past billions of planktonic plants and animals lived and died, and their remains sank to form sediments in ancient seas, there to undergo a chemical and physical transformation due to pressure. Over millions of years of geological change these viscous deposits became trapped under layers of impervious rock. Today forests of derricks rise in those places where petroleum was thus created.

Plankton has had a further share in the Earth's geological formation. The remains of planktonic plants and animals lie in thick layers on the floors of our oceans. The 'star performer' is unquestionably a foraminifer known as *Globigerina bulloides;* some thirty-five million squares miles of sea bed are covered with a mud called the Globigerina Ooze, which, if the findings of the Swedish research ship *Albatross* are accurate, in places reaches a thickness of some twelve thousand feet.

Plankton allows us to imagine what life was like in early Palaeozoic seas: vast masses of algae, now expanding, now receding, and with them a fantastic pullulation of animalcula. It is true that zooplankton makes up hardly more than two or three per cent of the whole, but precise calculations have established that over a thousand million tons of a single species, *Euphasia superba*, are born and grow each year in the Polar seas.

By the end of the Cambrian period, about four hundred and twenty million years ago, all the main divisions of the invertebrates were represented in the seas. Cambrian rocks are well exemplified in the British Isles (the term Cambrian comes from the Roman name for Wales). Britain and most of Europe lay beneath an ocean which has been named Poseidon—roughly a more extensive Atlantic, although the seas were at that time retreating. In Poseidon's waters were molluscs, worms, starfish, sponges, and especially a group of arthropods called trilobites, the commonest fossil representative of that age. But still lacking, if we read the record of the rocks correctly, were vertebrate marine fauna and any kind of terrestrial animal life.

CHAPTER FOUR

THE PARTING OF THE WAYS

A WELL-READ biologist discussing the origin of the world's first creatures might mention a curious and original work which appeared in 1749; a book nowadays of interest only to a few specialists, but which in the eighteenth century provoked sharp controversy, even engaging the censor's watchful eye. Written sixty years before Lamarck and a century before Darwin, the book in fact contains the first evolutionist theory propounded since the Greek physiologists—in brief, that the animals of the land were descended from those of the sea.

Its title, *Telliamed*, is merely a partial anagram of Benoît de Maillet, a respected French diplomat who evidently wished to remain anonymous. As a further precaution de Maillet entrusts the task of outlining his theory to a fictitious Indian philosopher, giving him as partner a French missionary with the duty of contradicting him. The author took steps to make sure that his thesis, revolutionary in that age, would not be made public until after his death; otherwise he would plainly have become the butt of his contemporaries, and might even have been sent to the Bastille. As his country's representative in Egypt and Abyssinia he could not afford such risks.

The process of development which had, according to de Maillet, led to the conquest of the land, is somewhat naïve. He thought that fish cast upon the shores by waves might have been forced to live in mud pools which were drying out. Unable to get back to their natural element they had to adapt themselves to their new circumstances; fins mutated gradually into limbs, gills into lungs, scales into feathers and hair. Finally, the transformation was so complete that those creatures were able to leave the marshes and take to the land.

We might regard this as an evolutionist's tale for children, but a couple of centuries ago such a proposition bristled with heresy. We do not know the reasons which prompted Benoît de Maillet to draw up his theory of adaptation to environment. Had he observed on the swampy banks of African rivers how lung-fish, at the onset of the dry season, make burrows in the mud where they remain, breathing air, for months if necessary? Had he seen amid the mangroves the mud-skipper, a fish that will actually drown if submerged for too long and which seeks its insect food on land? Whatever the cause, de Maillet is the spiritual heir of Anaximander and the Greek physiologists, and his thesis that all vertebrate animals are descended from fish wins him a place in the pantheon of inspired dilettanti.

The geological period in which the first fish-like creatures appeared is called the Ordovician. It was a very troubled time; there was much volanic activity and the ocean was again advancing, forming new shallow seas at the edges of the land masses. As the oceans encroached and then withdrew they left behind a host of shallow basins of slimy brackish water, deficient in oxygen. Conditions in the succeeding geological period, the Silurian, were similar, but with less volcanic activity and the emergence of new land areas. The two periods together cover rather more than a hundred million years, from the end of the Cambrian to about 312 million years ago. During that stretch of time vertebrate fish evolved and plants invaded the land.

Those waters were, it seems, veritable incubators. Yet, in comparison with the open sea, such places seem inimical to the development of life. Many of the lagoons were sulphureous, and it may have been the lack of oxygen in the water of those noxious pools that obliged some of their denizens—trilobites, crustaceans, sea scorpions—to adapt themselves to breathing air, thus taking the first step towards living on land. We do not know whether the first vertebrates were among them, and it is quite possible that the first branching off of the Vertebrata took place in fresh water. In pools of sweet or briny water the early vertebrates, perhaps resembling worms, insignificant, jawless, with a skeleton of cartilage, could have been safe from the predatory creatures in the open seas. During the Silurian period these ostracoderms, as they are called, developed bony plates on their heads and bodies, though the backbone was still of gristle; the round mouth enabled them to suck in their food.

In the nineteenth century many palaeontologists averred that the Silurian fossils of the ostracoderms were the remains of trilobites and crustaceans. Expeditions undertaken by the Norwegians between 1906 and 1925, however, brought to light in Ordovician beds at Spitzbergen a hundred or more fossil ostracoderms, and Swedish, Norwegian and British specialists investigated these thoroughly. It was revealed that they were neither crustaceans nor fish, in the proper sense, but distant relatives of the river lampreys which are today found in streams, rivers and estuaries.

Fossils of the first true fish belong to the next period, the Devonian. Many of these, the Placoderms, were powerfully armoured, but others were covered with scales, and all had true jaws. Their evolution and development in a great diversity of forms enabled them to leave the lagoons; some emigrated to the rivers, others to the open sea.

The Devonian period is marked by earth movements which slowly elevated land formerly under the sea, with a consequent drying out of marshes, swamps and the margins of sea inlets, sometimes intermittently, as droughts or seasonal heavy rain alternated. If they were to exist in the receding waters, the aquatic fauna must possess an organ for utilizing the oxygen of the air. Such was the origin of the air bladder with which some of the Devonian fish were endowed. In addition, certain of the scaly fish developed paired fins with which they could crawl back into the water if they were stranded. Excluding the sharks and rays typical of the open sea, and the lampreys and their kind, all true fish living today have an air bladder; for most it is not an organ for breathing but a delicate apparatus for maintaining equilibrium.

Zoologists distinguish two main groups of bony fish (Osteichthyes); Actinopterygii ('ray fins') and Crossopterygii ('tassel fins'). The Teleostean branch of the ray fins includes the vast majority of fish living today—over twenty thousand species—while another branch includes archaic types such as sturgeon. Living species of the tassel fins are far less numerous—one branch includes the lungfish while another has one solitary living representative. But the importance of the Crossopterygians in the story of evolution is overriding; from the now extinct branch of Osteolepidae during the Devonian there developed the first amphibians, and hence all land animals, including man.

A series of finds in the middle and upper layers of Devonian rocks in Britain and Canada has enabled us to envisage the process which took place within the swamps. Air-breathing Crossopterygians, with fins at the end of a rudimentary leg, left the pools as they were drying up and, anticipating the amphibians, ventured on to the land in search of lakes and ponds more suited to their way of life. Gradually they became more adapted to terrestrial life and developed into amphibians. The most extraordinary link in this admittedly incomplete chain is a fossil found in a layer dating from the Upper Devonian, on the shores of Escuminac Bay in Canada. The British ichthyologist T. Stanley Westoll has named this creature *Elpistostege*, which means 'promising head'. It fulfils, indeed, its promise, for it shows in material form an instant of evolution fraught with great consequences. In development its skull comes between that of the Crossopterygian fish and that of the Labyrinthodonts, the most ancient amphibians known.

The story of the Crossopterygians holds a further surprise. Instead of leaving the water, certain species settled in sheltered bays. One group, the coelacanths, went on living in the seas and lagoons into the Mesozoic era together with other more highly developed and progressive forms of animal life; their petrified remains are to be found mainly in the Jurassic schists. The coelacanths were large fish with bodies covered with broad scales, powerful jaws and dorsal fins bristling with spikes. Then, in the Cretaceous period sixty million years ago, this family died out.

So it was believed, at any rate, until 22 December 1938, when a momentous event took place. Fishing near the mouth of the Chalumna River in the Indian Ocean off East London in South Africa, the crew of the trawler EL 8 fetched up from a depth of two hundred and fifty feet a living coelacanth. Five feet long, this fish had a steel-blue body and fins like truncated limbs. It was taken—dead by this time—to the Curator of the East London Museum, Miss Courtenay-Latimer, who, puzzled by this unidentifiable specimen, consulted the ichthyologist Dr J. L. B. Smith. Dr Smith was dazed by the implications of the find; it unmistakably recalled the coelacanths of the Mesozoic which experts had unanimously pronounced extinct for about sixty million years. Dr Smith immediately set about scientific investigations but, the war years intervening, it was not until 1952 that another specimen, hooked by fishermen off the Comoro Islands, came into the scientist's hands. There was no further doubt about it: the coelacanth was a 'living fossil', last witness of the Devonian revolution.

The find of the coelacanth, or more precisely of *Latimeria chalumnae*, is rightly considered as one of the twentieth century's greatest discoveries in the domain of zoology. For even though the coelacanth is not a direct ancestor of man, it recalls unexpectedly and astonishingly that time when, leaving behind the half dried lakes and marshes, the pools invaded by mud, other Crossopterygians forsook the liquid element and took those first steps which resulted in the conquest of the land by living creatures.

CHAPTER FIVE

THE TURNCOATS

IN A BOOK concerned with the story of water the geological history of the Earth can only be outlined. The periods following the Devonian are therefore dealt with somewhat summarily; but they are full of interest, taking further the unending processes of mountain building and erosion, the reshaping of continents and seas, with changes of climate bringing now warm, humid conditions, now drought or ice ages. Those environmental circumstances were fraught with consequences for plants and animals, which showed a dramatic increase in number and kind on land and in water; some land animals even turned back to an aquatic existence.

The credit for establishing life so firmly upon the continents is due not to the animals but to the flora. Plants clung to the rock and disintegrated it, changing it into soil and retaining it, preventing rain from washing it away. In the Carboniferous period the continents were largely covered with dense, steamy, evergreen forest; giant ferns, scale trees, climbing and creeping plants buried their roots in a spongy soil, growing, dying, falling, decaying then sinking into the swampy earth where, little by little, their remains turned into coal. Insects swarmed and large amphibians crawled across the marshes, harbingers of the era of the reptiles which were to dominate the earth in the times to come.

The Permian period, which closed the Palaeozoic era about two hundred million years ago, saw a climax of mountain-building and a drying up of inland seas; there were extensive deserts, and

Gondwanaland, the southern continent, underwent considerable glaciations, while in the northern land-masses coniferous trees developed. The age of reptile predominance began. Less clumsy than the amphibians on land, they developed great size and variety of form. Among their number eventually came a group showing the first mammalian features.

In the Triassic, Jurassic and Cretaceous periods of the Mesozoic era the continents and seas gradually approached limits resembling those of today. The sea of Tethys broke through the continental bridges, one arm extended south towards the 'Austral Sea'. Gondwanaland was disrupted; and by the end of the era Australia had become an isolated land-mass. In the woodlands and swamps of the Cretaceous the reptiles luxuriated for the last time before the extinction of the giant kinds; reptilian forerunners gave rise to the birds, and the first inconspicuous mammals appeared.

What was taking place in the oceans during the hundred and forty million years of the Mesozoic era? The vital current which brought such powerful life to the continents was equally dynamic in the oceans. In the shallow seas of the Jurassic period enormous reefs of coral were taking shape. The predatory Cephalopods increased in size and their spiral shells, notably those of ammonites, rank among the most impressive and admired fossils of the Mesozoic. Selachians, the shark family, shared with marine reptiles mastery of the high sea; the Teleosteans, for their part, were conquering inch by inch all the different levels of the ocean. The reptiles, large and small, bristling with defences and protected by thick armour, provided with redoubtable jaws whether herbivorous or flesh-eating, had not broken all ties with the water; by this period too several groups of them had returned to the sea which they were never again to leave.

Some descendants of those reptiles, leading a partly terrestrial, partly aquatic life, are with us today: the sea turtles of tropical waters, for example, which lay their eggs in coastal sands, thus confirming their land-dwelling ancestry. Such reptiles readapted to marine life; they did not take a step backwards in evolution. Among the most familiar and popular fossils of entirely aquatic reptiles are the Ichthyosaurs ('fish-lizards'). These gave birth to living young, a safer way of perpetuating the species than laying very vulnerable eggs, and one that freed them from all necessity of returning to the shore. Fossils of Ichthyosaurs have been found in large quantity in the Jurassic deposits of Germany. It is just possible that the ooze which had accumulated in certain bays—in what is now Swabian Jura, for instance—caused the death of a large number of Ichthyosaurs which, pursuing prey, may have found their way into those gulfs and died trapped in mud. There is no other way of explaining the abundance in these shallow basins of fossils of a creature ideally adapted to life in the open sea.

The Plesiosaurs, wittily described by William Buckland (whose Oxford lectures stimulated Charles Lyell's interest in geology) as 'a snake threaded through the shell of a turtle', were creatures of coastal waters, paddlers rather than swimmers. With their exaggeratedly long necks, rounded bodies and sharp teeth these fossil reptiles too enjoy a certain popularity. It is justified, for mythical sea monsters are often made to look like a Plesiosaur, which seems also to have suggested the reconstructions of the Loch Ness monster.

The limbs of the Mosasaurs, which predominated in the Cretaceous period (from about 130 to about 70 million years ago), were more perfectly adapted to marine life. Long and slender and apparently lacking armour in the skin, this reptile fits admirably the role of 'sea serpent'. The Mosasaurs spread into all the seas of the globe and remained for millions of years the unchallenged masters of the oceans. Palaeontologists ask themselves—and nobody has yet provided a satisfactory reply—why those reptiles, highly specialized marine monsters, fell victim at the end of the Cretaceous to a bone degeneration which led to their disappearance.

These several examples show that the ocean, origin of all life, was from that time onward not forgotten even by creatures which had adapted themselves to land conditions. Anyone who visits the Galapagos Islands will see the crested lizards which, a century ago before the stupid destruction of the unique fauna of the islands, lived in their hundreds on the rocks of the shores, feeding on seaweed. No one has described these aquatic lizards better than Charles Darwin, who visited the Galapagos in September 1835:

> [*Amblyrhynchus cristatus*] lives exclusively on the rocky seabeaches, being never found, at least I never saw one, even ten yards in-shore. . . . When in the water this lizard swims with perfect ease and quickness, by a serpentine movement of its body and flattened tail—the legs being motionless and closely collapsed on its sides. A seaman on board sank one, with a heavy weight attached to it, thinking thus to kill it directly; but when, an hour afterwards, he drew up the line, it was quite

active. . . . The nature of this lizard's food, as well as the structure of its tail and feet, and the fact of its having been seen swimming voluntarily out at sea, absolutely proves its aquatic habits. . . .

But, as Darwin explains a little later on, there is a contradiction between the above and the fact that when hunted this lizard takes refuge not in the sea but higher up the rocks. With the instinct of a biologist Darwin surmises where the explanation of this anomaly may lie:

> Perhaps this singular piece of apparent stupidity may be accounted for by the circumstance that this reptile has no enemy whatever on shore, whereas at sea it must often fall a prey to the numerous sharks. Hence, probably, urged by a fixed and hereditary instinct that the shore is its place of safety, whatever the emergency may be, it there takes refuge.

Present-day reptiles are the humble descendants of the giants of the Mesozoic. New reptilian species followed one after the other for a hundred and eighty million years. Then, comparatively suddenly, they died out. Scientists explain their disappearance as due to over-intense specialization, to abrupt mutations, epidemics, degeneration. What is certain is that the age of the reptiles was over at the beginning of the Tertiary era and that the bones of the major reptiles were already fossilized. From now on another class of vertebrates, the mammals, taking new and odd forms often as heterodox as those of the Mesozoic reptiles, was to have first place.

In the zoological sense the Tertiary era is still with us, for the onset of the Ice Ages, rather less than a million years ago, upset but briefly the climates of tropical and sub-tropical zones: the abnormalities were on the whole no more than the result of excessive rain. In the tropics and sub-tropics the warm climate still has characteristics of the Tertiary—virgin forest and savanna, herds of large mammals. Many forms of animal life which are Tertiary relics have taken refuge there: elephant, rhinoceros, tapir, hippopotamus, okapi, giraffe, sloth, ant-eater, pangolin, lemur, anthropoid apes.

For a great stretch of time from the early Tertiary the climate of the whole world was more temperate than it is today, with widespread tropical and sub-tropical vegetation. The oleander, the vine, the cypress, the magnolia flourished in Arctic areas; Europe and North America were covered with palms, bamboo, tree-ferns and sultry rain-forests. In other words, the expansion of mammalian life in the Tertiary had the advantage of relatively favourable conditions.

Of the numerous lands that the sea had invaded in Cretaceous times many were elevated by earth movements and dried up, some of these beds being subsequently submerged and again raised. Stresses in the Earth's crust gave birth to imposing mountain ranges: Alps, Pyrenees, Apennines, Carpathians, Atlas, the Caucasus, the Andes and the Himalaya. Towards the end of the Tertiary era the map of the globe was more or less what it is today. But a land bridge linked Siberia to North America where the Bering Strait now is, and the Baltic did not yet exist. Only fragments were left of the Sea of Tethys which had formerly stretched across half the world: the Mediterranean, the Black Sea, the Caspian and the Aral.

It was on the Tertiary continents that deciduous trees and flowering plants, insects, birds and mammals attained their heyday; what of the oceans? The deep blue waters of the Tertiary seas were traversed by cold and warm currents and populated by a fauna which lived henceforth at all depths of the oceans, from the shores to the open sea. For the first time animal life ventured even into the marine chasms, although the final conquest of the great deeps by fish is relatively recent.

A large kind of foraminifer, called nummulite, with a characteristic round, flat shell, was very numerous among the marine fauna of the beginning of the Tertiary. Those creatures proliferated with unusual rapidity in the seas, but had died out by the Miocene period. From the Pyrenees to the Altai, mountain chains of later Tertiary formation consist partly of nummulitic limestone. Their fossils are widespread, and it was nummulitic limestone that served for the construction of the Egyptian pyramids.

As early as the Upper Cretaceous some primitive birds had already returned to the seas. Among the best known from fossils, numerous in the chalk of Kansas, is *Hesperornis regalis*, over six feet from beak to tail and provided with spiky teeth. *Hesperornis* had lost the power of flight, and its feet and legs were highly adapted for swimming. It was probably a diving bird and would have been clumsy on land. Penguins of the height of a man are known from fossils of the early Tertiary, all in the southern hemisphere and on the verge of the Antarctic zone where the climate was still more or less temperate. We may be justified in assuming that the progressive reduction in size of these swimming birds shows an adaptation to increasingly severe conditions with the approach of the Pleistocene ice ages, for the inability to fly would have inhibited migration; however, the largest living penguin is the Emperor penguin of the Antarctic, while the smallest is the Galapagos penguin.

Oddly enough, water has at all periods had a great hold upon birds, so closely dependent on the air. The largest concentrations of birds are to be found upon the cliffs, islets and coasts of the northern seas. Gannets, gulls, divers, puffins nest upon the ledges in steep rocks and hunt the teeming fish, crustaceans and molluscs swept along by the currents. Powerful fliers such as the albatross and the great petrel wheel above the open sea, resting even in stormy weather upon the tops of the waves. Frigate-birds, cormorants, pelicans skim the tropical waters, and divers and puffins but newly out of the egg indulge in the joys of swimming.

Several groups of mammals have returned even further towards the reconquest of water. Predatory otters were no longer content to colonize ponds, lakes and rivers, and one of their offshoots chose a maritime life. Sea otters, furred animals which frequent the seaweed-grown shores of the north Pacific, were hunted almost to extermination; they feed upon mussels and sea-urchins. Seals, elephant seals, sea lions, walruses, those master hunters of the open sea, apparently stem from a land-dwelling carnivore, but many species return to land only in the breeding season. The entirely sea-living manatees and dugongs, which inhabit tropical and sub-tropical coastal waters where the aquatic plants on which they feed are abundant, and the now extinct Steller's sea-cow of the north Pacific (exterminated by the early nineteenth century through being over-hunted by that predator, man), derived probably from an early swamp-dwelling elephant. But for both these groups the fossil record is very incomplete.

Man, creature exclusively of the earth, has always been intrigued by the mammals whose habitat is the sea. In the guise of tritons, sirens and leviathans they play a considerable part in the legends and myths of littoral peoples. Sailors' tales and stories revolve more closely round one particular family of mammals. Dubbed 'monsters, marine demons and midnight apparitions' by the Swedish bishop Olaus Magnus, they have haunted many a medieval chronicle. In old drawings and engravings they appear as fantastic monsters with crocodiles' heads, fearsome fangs, beak-shaped jaws and formidable talons. Perhaps these pictures explain the survival of the myth of sea monsters; for species of the cetaceans, the whales, to which many of these drawings refer, are in fact of vaster size than any land animal which has ever lived, including the dinosaurs.

The natural history of the cetaceans is no less exciting than such hair-raising descriptions. It is thought that these mammals, both the toothed whales and the whalebone whales, descend from a primitive carnivore. But no fossils to complete the family tree have yet been found, and the earliest known reveal toothed whales of formidable size fully adapted to marine life by early Tertiary times. The whalebone whales developed later, and dolphins and porpoises (which are toothed whales) not until late in the Tertiary era. It needs a good dash of palaeontological imagination to establish a relationship between such colossi as the blue whales, which may be up to 100 feet long and weigh over 140 tons, and a small flesh-eating land animal.

Cetaceans provoke many other questions among scientists. Sperm whales are able to reach a depth of three thousand feet and to remain submerged for an hour without breathing. The variations of pressure and the release into the blood-stream of toxic gases which such dives entail would kill any other kind of mammal. Even now the way in which these whales tolerate enormous pressures and the lack of oxygen remains a mystery.

Paradoxically the largest, including the blue whale, feed mainly on a shrimp-like member of the zooplankton called krill. Instead of teeth the whalebone whales have in their enormous mouths close-set blades of baleen (the so-called 'whalebone') thickly fringed on the inside with hairs. The whale gulps in tons of water and anything that may be floating in it, closes its mouth and forces the water out with its tongue; the fringed baleen acts like a fine sieve, retaining the krill. These whales must follow their drifting source of nourishment in the south polar seas, routes well known to whale hunters. Since the invention of the harpoon and the introduction of factory ships several species of whales have been hunted almost to extermination.

Zooplankton has existed since Palaeozoic times, but it was not until hundreds of millions of years later that the largest of all animals, able to utilize this source of food directly, appeared. Similarly with the squids, cephalopod molluscs related to extinct forms such as belemnites. Squids first appear in the fossil record of Mesozoic times; they developed considerably in size, and the living giant squid is a veritable sea monster, up to 60 feet long including its tentacles. Possibly the Jurassic ichthyosaurs preyed upon them, but it is the modern toothed whales that really exploit squids as a source of food. Harpooned sperm whales frequently bear round scars inflicted by the suckers at the end of the squid's tentacles, and to judge from these and remains found in whales' stomachs (a squid over thirty-four feet long and weighing 405 pounds was recovered from such a source in 1955) a battle between almost the largest living vertebrate and the largest living invertebrate must be titanic indeed.

Opportunities to observe such a struggle, or to see a living giant squid at all, have been few. The very existence of the giant squid was denied by naturalists until little more than a century ago, although it is undoubtedly to be identified with the 'kraken' of legend, and was real enough to sailors and fishermen. A graphic description of a fight between sperm whale and 'kraken' was given in 1861 by the commander of a French sloop, Lieutenant Bouyer, who managed to haul part of the 'mythical' creature on board his ship. Probably the first experienced naturalist of recent times to examine fresh remains of a giant squid was Prince Albert of Monaco, in 1895. Founder of the oceanographic museum at Monaco, the Prince was very interested in whales and contributed a great deal to our present knowledge of them. Much remains to be discovered about whales, but the most urgent question is whether, even with international control, our present policy of hunting these remarkable creatures for commercial purposes will allow the major species of the whale to survive long enough for naturalists of the future to study them.

CHAPTER SIX

THE ICE AGES

THE LAST stage of this journey through Earth's history brings us to the Pleistocene, a period very strongly and clearly marked by the influence of water. Early geologists already had an inkling of this and tried to correlate the evidence of the rocks with the biblical Flood.

Rounded boulders, mounds of debris and erratic blocks found over wide areas of Europe and North America seemed to constitute proof that a fearful force of water had torn massive rocks, fragments and clay from the mountains and deposited them in the plains. The proposition that the transporting agent might be ice, even as glaciers or sea ice, was slow in gaining acceptance and, as with the discovery of the composition of water or the recognition of the significance of fossils, for example, stemmed from the ideas of many individuals—Hutton, Playfair, Ignace Venetz (a Swiss engineer), von Hoff, Lyell, even Goethe. Foremost is Jean G. F. de Charpentier, who in 1834 read to an audience in Lucerne a paper 'On the probable cause of the transportation of the erratic blocks of Switzerland', citing former extensive glaciers as the 'cause'. Charpentier's theory immediately won adherents, notably the brilliant Swiss naturalist Louis Agassiz, who undertook an exploratory journey in the Alps and in 1840 published his *Studies of Swiss Glaciers* postulating extensive recent (geologically speaking) glaciation of northern Europe: in brief, an Ice Age.

Geologists now recognize four Ice Ages beginning about 600,000 years ago, each interrupted by one or more interstadials, temporary halts to the encroachment of glaciation, and divided from one another by warmer periods, or Interglacials. The last Ice Age ended, according to the latest dating methods, about 10,000 or 12,000 years ago, although geologists are by no means agreed about these dates. Was it the 'last' ice age? Or are we living in an interglacial period, which will end in a thousand or ten thousand years with a further glaciation? We have no means of knowing.

The Ice Ages affected the whole world, for while in the northern hemisphere 'solidified H_2O' stretched only across northern Europe, Asia and America, the remaining parts of the globe suffered a change of climate, with areas of arid tundra fringing the ice sheets and torrential rains in the tropical zones, probably heaviest during the comparatively warmer spells.

Whether, or to what extent, these climatic conditions played a part in that significant event, the emergence of modern man, we cannot say. It is fascinating to speculate that the necessity to adapt to life in bitter conditions might have compelled primitive man to devise means for his protection—to wear clothing, master fire, find shelter, invent ways of killing animals for food. For while we accept scientific findings which seem to prove that the branching off of the human stem from a tree of ape-like ancestors took place in some tropical zone, we need not assume that man's 'inventions' always originated in more clement periods when living was easier. Certainly modern man, *Homo sapiens*, appeared in Europe during the first interstadial of the last Ice Age, seventy to a hundred thousand years ago. *Homo sapiens*, of a type called Cromagnon, apparently displaced the earlier species called Neanderthal man, also a cave dweller in some areas at least. The gaps in the story are tantalizing, but deep in European caves is the evidence of man with an identifiable culture, man who produced on the walls of his caves pictures perhaps of some magical significance, the first glimmerings of art.

The sequence of climatic changes due to ice ages was so slow and took place over such a long stretch of time that there was no sudden catastrophe. Many kinds of animals and plants had time to adapt. Mammoths and Woolly Rhinoceros existed in the steppes, cave bears wintered in their dens, musk-ox and reindeer grazed the mosses and lichens of the tundra. During warmer spells these animals migrated slowly northwards, leaving room for forest-dwelling creatures such as hippopotamus, the giant straight-tusked elephant and the sabre-toothed 'tiger' as a warmer type of flora too extended northwards. The fossil record of these changes in the Pleistocene period is remarkably clear.

At its greatest extent ice covered in the northern hemisphere some twenty million square miles of land—four times more than the area of the present polar ice cap. Nor was its effect confined to the land, for so much water locked up as ice meant a lowering of sea level, producing 'land bridges' for man and beast connecting, for example, Britain to the continent. At the end of the Pleistocene man crossed such a bridge from Asia into America.

As to the causes of the Ice Ages, scientists are not agreed, but they must have been complex and may have involved such factors as a displacement of the poles, an alteration in the Earth's orbit round the Sun, or other cosmic changes—there are plenty of theories. For the effect on the Earth's surface, however, water was the dominant factor, and water and climate are closely connected. Water as ice is still a formative agent, whether it actually covers land and sea as great sheets of ice, carves the features of high mountains as glaciers, or breaks down rock through the action of frost.

The polar ice caps of today produce at their edges icebergs which may reach the size of islands or, especially in the Antarctic, flat-topped 'mountains' which can attain a length of twenty-five miles and on which explorers can camp. These icebergs are of frozen fresh water; they usually move in groups and follow regular routes towards the open sea, some travelling over a thousand miles in the seas of high latitudes until they are melted by warm currents. The sea area off Newfoundland is a notable iceberg grave, and the mingling of cold fresh water with the warm Gulf Stream is an important factor in the cycle of planktonic life, and hence of fisheries. The table-top bergs of the Antarctic deceived many early explorers. In 1840 the American explorer Charles Wilkes reported the dis-covery in the south of the Indian Ocean of a territory which he christened Termination Land, and for sixty years it appeared in atlases although nobody but Wilkes and those with him had seen it. It was only in 1902 that the German Antarctic expedition, led by Erich von Drygalski, established that the alleged Termination Land was only an iceberg. In the same area Drygalski encountered mountains of ice, some over 200 feet high, with knife-edge clefts, which looked very much like islands.

The largest drift of floating ice recalled by seafarers brought alarm to the Cape Horn latitudes between April 1892 and January 1894. For over a year and a half thousands of icebergs blocked the seaways. In most cases these Goliaths are no great danger to ship-ping, but their invisible submerged portions are a menace. In the North Atlantic, on 14 April 1912, one of them caused the loss of the British trans-Atlantic liner *Titanic* on her maiden voyage. This disaster, with its 1,517 victims, induced the American Hydrographic Office to organize an international watch on icebergs; today, with radar, echo-sounders and air patrols, the peril has greatly diminished.

Quite as treacherous as the fresh-water icebergs calved by the polar glaciers is frozen sea water itself which, in the form of ice floes or pack ice, clutters the polar seas and bars the way to explorers. However, sea ice is less hard than that of glaciers and the steel cladding of the modern ice-breaker can deal with pack-ice barriers up to twenty-five feet thick.

The ice floe too is at the mercy of ocean currents. Fridtjof Nansen, whose vessel, the *Fram*, remained prisoner of the ice from 1893 to 1896, described the voyage which took him with the drifting floe from the coast of Siberia to the Pole, then on to Greenland and into the North Atlantic. It was almost the same route as that taken forty years later by the Russian ice-breaker *Sedow*. The venture of the Soviet ice-expert Papanin, who embarked with three companions upon a sheet of ice a couple of miles in circumference and a dozen feet thick at the North Pole, and let himself drift southward along the east Greenland current, was far more dangerous. Two hundred and forty-three days later two Russian ships rescued the four men, who abandoned their shattered floe.

The larger part of the floating ice melts in the ocean. Every year the Atlantic alone absorbs some twenty million tons of water—as much as the contents of the Baltic—which reach it in this way. There are also floes, and even groups of floes, which never reach the open sea; imprisoned in the zone of eternal ice they drift slowly round the Pole. As airmen of the American meteorological service observed in 1946, these ice floes are formed of fresh water, not of salt; they break off in slabs of perhaps forty square miles from the coasts of Ellesmere Island in northern Canada and revolve round the North Pole, carrying with them reindeer antlers and other debris from the land.

One such ice island, named Arctic Research Laboratory Ice Station II, established in 1961 and manned by twenty-one American scientists, drifted thus across the Arctic Ocean, its occupants busying themselves with research and with meteorological and oceanographic observations until the ice began to break up in the Greenland Sea in 1965. Floating ice, once so feared by sailors of the northern waters, has thus become the henchman of the glaciologist, who has still so many problems to unravel. It was not by chance that glaciers and polar ice were intensively studied during the International Geophysical Year of 1957–58.

PART TWO

THE COSMOS OF THE MAIN

*. . . To make the weight for the winds;
and he weigheth the waters by measure.*
JOB, xxviii, 25

CHAPTER ONE

WINDS, TIDES AND WAVES

THE GREEKS personified that river of life which they believed to surround the earth as the venerable giant Oceanus, bestriding marine animals or riding over the crest of the waves with his wife Tethys in a chariot drawn by fish. Coast-dwelling peoples, seafarers and discoverers of later times also personified the ocean. In it they saw not only a limitless mass of water but also a living organism, both friendly and hostile, cause of fear and anguish, worthy of affection and love, guardian of secrets, inspiration of countless songs and hymns and dreams and ambitions. The ocean is indeed a living organism in the sense that it breathes, is traversed by warm and cool currents and does battle with the land, falling upon it with waves, stones, shingle and grains of sand. It is a creature wearing many masks and faces, as abounding in surprises and contrasts as are human beings.

Of the 196,836,000 square miles of the Earth's surface 70·8 per cent is sea, and 77 per cent of these waters has not yet been properly explored. The total volume of sea water is estimated to be 1,800,000,000 cubic yards. This mass is set in motion by winds, which cause waves and currents, and by the attraction of the Sun and Moon, and it regulates the world's water economy. Behind these rather bald statements lie cosmic forces and phenomena of almost frightening magnitude, among them the union of those two ancient 'elements', air and water. For the sea is not only water laden with mineral matter: it also contains in solution the chief components of air, without which no life in the oceans would be possible. The proportion of oxygen in sea water is higher than that of the atmosphere, the averages being 34 and 21 per cent. However, in the cold seas of high latitudes, storm-swept and abounding in algae, the oxygen content may be as much as three times the average, while in tropical waters and in the great ocean deeps the quantity may be well below it. It was formerly believed that sea water at great depths lacked oxygen, but it is now known that currents provide this indispensable element even in the dark abyssal waters.

The atmosphere plays another vital role in the regime of the oceans: sea, waves and wind belong together. A motionless realm of water is unimaginable, a dead, oppressive waste. Air in motion is the motor which keeps the seas perpetually moving. Winds are air currents caused by differences in pressure and temperature arising from unequal heating by the Sun—and unequal radiation from land and sea—and from the rotation of the Earth. This transformation of heat into motion is a kind of climatic power-station.

Thus, contrary to the belief of the ancient Greeks, the chief winds do not escape from a bag at the whim of Aeolus. They blow as the climatic power-station dictates. In outline, it works like this: at the Equator the air is strongly heated by the Sun, rises, and is replaced by air flowing in from north and south; the heated air flows toward the Poles, cools, descends, and divides, some flowing back towards the Tropics and some continuing towards the colder zones. There is thus a continuous circulation of air, but its course is modified by factors such as the distribution of land masses and sea, the Earth's daily rotation and, of course, seasonal changes, so that even a map showing only the chief wind zones of the world reveals a complicated network of air currents.

A typical wind zone map shows cold air blowing outwards from the Poles, then zones of westerly winds—the 'Roaring Forties' of the southern hemisphere, where there is very little land to deflect them—and beyond these the Trade Winds blowing towards the Equator; between the westerlies and Trades, at latitudes where the warm air currents flowing out from the Equator have cooled and are descending, are zones of calm or very light winds (called the Horse Latitudes in the northern hemisphere), while at the Equator are the zones of complete calm called the Doldrums.

In the days of sailing ships seafarers feared these calms even more than the storm winds, for ships often drifted for weeks with limp sails, especially in that part of the North Atlantic which the Spaniards called the 'Golfo de las Yeguas', the Sea of Mares. This name and the corresponding English 'Horse Latitudes' are supposed to derive from the fact that when ships were here becalmed, the horses on board, being transported to the New World, soon died for lack of water and fodder, and their carcases—and perhaps living animals too—were thrown overboard. It is thus with a retrospective shudder that historians recount the journey of Mem de Sa, newly appointed governor of Brazil, when he proceeded in 1557 to take up his post. It took him eight months to reach Bahia (Salvador) from Europe, and on the way forty-two men died from hunger or exhaustion. There are many instances of this kind.

Bahia, the goal which Mem de Sa finally reached, lies in the zone of the south-east Trade Winds. It was not by chance that the conquerors of the east coast of South America made their chief harbours at some distance from the Equator; the climate and above all the prevailing winds helped to make Bahia, Rio de Janeiro, Montevideo and Buenos Aires into centres of shipping and trade between Europe and South America.

But the seemingly regular pattern of windy and calm areas is all too often suddenly and violently disturbed by cyclonic storms, which arise chiefly within the Tropics. Called hurricanes, typhoons or cyclones in different parts of the world, these are low-pressure areas from a few miles to several hundred miles across, within which winds are spiralling rapidly. The whole system moves forward, and where rotation and forward movement are in the same direction the wind speed may be 200 miles per hour. The nearer the Equator the smaller and more severe the cyclonic storm; in higher latitudes 'cyclonic' conditions produce gales, squalls, rough seas, but comparatively little damage. Smallest and most violent of all are the funnel-shaped tornadoes in which wind speeds have been estimated at 500 miles per hour. A tornado picks up debris and dust as it travels over land in a narrow, twisting path, while over the sea it becomes a waterspout. These cyclonic storms leave a fearful trail of destruction where they pass over land, and at sea cause huge waves and can wreck ships in their path. The courses of hurricanes and typhoons are closely watched by weather stations so that as much warning as possible can be given of their approach.

Nevertheless, despite their spectacular and dangerous nature, the effect of storms upon the sea is far weaker than that of the regular winds which blow in the same direction in the same areas almost from one end of the year to the other. The steadiest influence is that of the Trade Winds blowing in towards the Equator; deflected by the rotation of the Earth, they blow in the northern hemisphere from the north-east and in the southern from the south-east. The north-east and south-east Trade Winds have played an essential part in the history of navigation by sailing ships and in geographical discovery; furthermore they are mainly responsible for the North and South Equatorial currents which flow from east to west.

Such steady winds are the prime cause of all marine currents. Blowing regularly and reliably they propel before them masses of water which are replaced by surface water flowing in or by water welling up from the deep. The two-fold impulse of the wind and the Earth's rotation gives the currents considerable power.

The study of surface and deep-water currents is indeed one of oceanography's main tasks. For the ancients these movements of water held something mysterious and terrifying, and a trace of this ancestral awe is to be found in Edgar Allan Poe's tale *The Descent into the Maelström*, in which the remarkable currents of the Lofoten Islands are described:

> I perceived that what seamen term the *chopping* character of the ocean beneath us, was rapidly changing into a current which set to the eastward. Even while I gazed, this current acquired a monstrous velocity. Each moment added to its speed —to its headlong impetuosity. In five minutes the whole sea as far as Vurrgh, was lashed into ungovernable fury; but it was between Moskoe and the coast that the main uproar held its sway. Here the vast bed of the waters seamed and scarred into a thousand conflicting channels, burst suddenly into frenzied convulsion—heaving, boiling, hissing—gyrating in gigantic and innumerable vortices, and all whirling and plunging on to the eastward with a rapidity which water never elsewhere assumes, except in precipitous descents.

This is of course the vision of a writer fascinated by horror, but it is none the less true that serious scholars still talked at the time of mysterious forces and the effects of suction operating in the depths of the ocean. Only slowly has man perceived how the ever-active sea breathes and circulates.

The chart of the sea currents is as complex as that of the winds; for as we shall see the currents come up against the land masses, are deflected by the continental shelves, split, run into counter-currents. Movement of cold currents along the ocean floors must also be reckoned with. Welling up, they enrich the surface waters with minerals from the sea bed, and especially where cold currents encounter warm ones plant and animal plankton are abundant and all sea life flourishes. Such results are especially well known to man where the warm Gulf Stream, flowing northwards, encounters the cold Labrador Current flowing southwards in the rich fishing grounds off the Newfoundland coast; or where the cold, north-flowing Peru Current enriches the surface waters of the Pacific coast

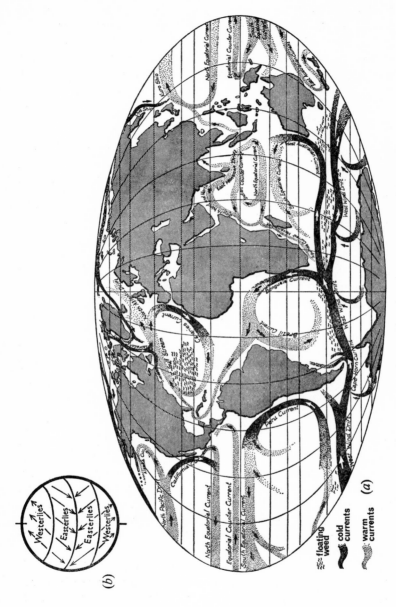

Fig. 1: (*a*) Ocean currents of the world; (*b*) prevailing winds.

of South America, indirectly providing Peru's chief export, the
fertilizer guano, for the abundance of fish attracts thousands of
birds to the islands and cliffs. Should the Isthmus of Panama ever
subside, the consequences of a drastically altered pattern of ocean
currents would be almost unimaginable. Loss of the Gulf Stream
(which will enter this story again) would certainly result in a colder
climate for western Europe, and indeed there would be world-wide
changes in conditions.

The people of the Mesolithic Age who settled several thousand
years ago on the shores of northern Europe noted that the sea
provided for their wants with unfailing regularity and abundance.
Twice daily the tide covered the beaches; twice daily, as it withdrew, the waters left upon the sand or in rock pools shellfish and
other sea creatures in sufficient quantity for the shelly remains of
countless meals to form mounds which, much later, would be
investigated and analysed by archaeologists. We do not know if
Stone Age men puzzled over the rhythm of the oceans; but others
did a good deal later, and they remarked that the regular movements of the seas were governed not only by terrestrial factors but
also by a far stronger force derived from outside the Earth: the
tides.

Compared with the influence of the tides, that of the winds seems
very modest. For the effects of the most violent hurricane scarcely
penetrate beyond six hundred feet below the surface; even the
currents attributable to the consistent Trade Winds hardly affect
the bulk of the waters, the ocean deeps. But, at whatever level it
may be, the smallest drop of sea water is subject to the law of tides.

Scientists studying tides ought to bow with reverence to the
physiologists and naturalists of antiquity. In ancient Greece all
passably educated people knew already that the ebb and flow were
ordained by cosmic powers. Slight as is the average tide of the
Mediterranean, the regular alternation of high and low was enough
to suggest to Greek philosophers a lunar explanation. They noted
that the flow was especially high at full Moon and were not unduly
surprised; for was not the Moon the cause of so many of the
wonders of Nature?

When Pytheas of Massilia (Marseilles), the first literate explorer
of northern waters, reached the coasts of Norway and the northern
seas, about 330 B.C., he observed the fullness of the tides and the

fury of the surf, which could not but impress a man from the Mediterranean. Pytheas attributed these unwonted prodigies to the attraction of the Moon, whose bright golden orb, wrapped in mist, shone above the sea of Thule. Educated men such as Aristotle, Pliny and Caesar completed this tidal theory with the statement that the seas responded to the double attraction of Moon and Sun, and that the Moon played the larger part despite its smaller size.

Strangely enough, such knowledge became blurred as the scholarship of antiquity receded from men's memories. In the seventeenth century distinguished scientists, among them Galileo and Descartes, did not conceal their perplexity regarding tides. Only after Newton's publication, in 1687, of the Law of Universal Gravitation and a lunar theory of tides did the world of science renew contact with the tradition of Greek and Roman thought on this point. Universal gravitation means that every particle of matter in the Universe exerts gravitational force on every other particle, so that each drop of water on Earth, theoretically at least, is subject to the attraction of all the heavenly bodies. In practical terms, the influence of the planets and the remoter stars is cancelled by that of the Moon and Sun.

By virtue of that part of Newton's Law which states that the force of attraction between any two bodies, or particles of matter, is directly proportional to the product of their masses, the water of the oceans ought to be influenced more by the Sun than by the Moon, for the mass of the Sun is 332,291 times that of the Earth, while the mass of the Earth is eighty-one times that of the Moon. But the law also states that the force of attraction is inversely proportional to the distance between the two bodies, and while the Moon is 'only' an average of 238,857 miles from the Earth, the Sun is 93,004,000 miles distant. This explains why the rhythm of the tides is controlled by the phases of the Moon. Twice a month, however, when the Moon is in a straight line between Earth and Sun, the attractive forces of Sun and Moon are added together, hence the spring tides; and twice a month, when Sun and Moon are on directly opposite sides of the Earth, the influence of the Sun reduces the effect of the Moon, hence the neap tides. There are two tides a day because the tide-generating force, as it is called, is strongest at the point of the Earth's surface where the Moon is overhead and at the antipodes of that point, weakest at the points half way between those two.

The position of the Moon in its elliptical orbit round the Earth—and therefore its exact distance—latitude, the inclination of Earth's axis and other complicated factors determine the height and time of tides at any given place; nevertheless, tides can be very accurately predicted—from a practical point of view one of the most useful contributions made by astronomy and mathematics. The Earth's physical features play an obvious part in local modifications of the tides. In the southern hemisphere, where there is comparatively little land to impede the movement of water, the difference between high and low is on average not more than two feet. But coastlines and the nature of the ocean bed have a considerable effect on height and velocity of tides in the northern hemisphere. In the English Channel, a twenty-foot tide at Cherbourg becomes a thirty-foot tide at Calais, while in the narrow Bay of Fundy the rise is up to fifty feet. In the Lofoten Islands the rising tide produces dangerous whirlpools due to the particular coastal features, recalling the phenomenon so superbly described by Edgar Allan Poe in *The Descent into the Maelström.* The legend of Scylla and Charybdis certainly originated in such an eddy or vortex which filled the seamen of antiquity with dread.

On the sea shore the incoming tide is often accompanied by breakers and surf, even in fair weather. The crests of waves move faster than their bases, which are impeded by the drag of the sea bottom, topple forward and break in foam on the shore. In wild weather with an onshore wind and a rising ride, breakers frequently thunder over esplanades and sea defences, flinging sand and pebbles inland. But in all conditions the combination of tides and currents ceaselessly changes the coastline, carrying sand from one point to build sandbanks, and eventually perhaps islands, at another; forming sandbars across harbours and scouring deep channels elsewhere. Even in very calm weather an incoming tide running abruptly against cliffs can be quite dramatic, and with high winds water and spume may be flung spectacularly a hundred or so feet over a cliff top. The erosive force can be tremendous, for in addition to sheer pressure and the wearing effect of stones and debris, the impact suddenly compresses the air in minute pockets in the rock, helping to break up the stubborn face of the land so that it more easily falls prey to the undermining forces, crumbles and slips or crashes into the sea.

The joint action of very high wind and very high tide can have disastrous results. The long list of cataclysms which have laid waste the coasts of the North Sea alone during the past few centuries is dolefully explicit. On All Saints' Day 1170 the inrush of the sea cut off from the mainland the islands of Wieringen and Texel and changed the Zuider Zee, formerly a fresh-water lake, into a great inlet; on 17 November 1218 the sea invaded the Jade Bay in Oldenburg; other inundations took place in 1267, 1277, 1287, 1362 and 1377, contributing to the gradual formation of the Dollart Pool near the mouth of the Ems. On 2 November 1570 another flood claimed 41,000 victims on the Frisian shore; in 1634 the island of Nordstrand was carried away by the sea, and a string of low islets formed along the Frisian coast. At New Year in 1855 the island of Alt-Wangerooge disappeared in turn, and the floods of 1953, the most recent catastrophe, devastated coastal areas of the Netherlands and Britain.

Even after a storm has died down the waves it has created continue to travel across the open sea, sometimes manifesting themselves as an apparently inexplicable ground swell in calm weather on a distant shore. There is an entire gamut of waves—soft ripples which scarcely wrinkle the surface, swells running for thousands of miles, crested billows which crash over the decks of ships, rollers which break on the shore or rear abruptly to attack cliffs. The study of waves is a science in which graphs of volume, sinusoids, cycloids and other geometric figures play an indispensable part. Photography, too, has enabled us to observe that wave formation is far more complicated than was once supposed. The front of a wave is not smooth, its crest is not clean and sharp in profile. As the force and direction of the wind alter, the sea becomes choppy, waves cross one another, one swallowing the next; they increase or diminish. Waves reach their greatest height after several days of storm. Then, in the open sea, they chase one another in rapid sequence, rear abruptly but seldom break. This, one of the grandest sights imaginable, can be compared only with the release of subterranean fire in a volcanic eruption. Such a spectacle is seldom seen by the landsman, who is more familiar with the breakers of the seashore, the zone of surf.

In some parts of the world the location and configuration of the land result in a ceaseless roar of surf as long rollers pile up.

Its crashing [writes the explorer Eduard Pechüel-Loesche when describing the surf of the African coasts] reminds one of the roar of thunder or an express train, or the distant sound of an artillery barrage. Every now and then one is aware of a muffled drumming, of whistling, of something like the clash of cymbals; sometimes also the uproar ceases abruptly and an uneasy calm sets in.

Another and more famous explorer, Charles Darwin, on board the *Beagle* in the region of the islands around Cape Horn, describes the spectacle vividly:

> The surf was breaking fearfully on the coast, and the spray was carried over a cliff estimated at 200 feet in height. . . . The sea looked ominous, like a dreary waving plain with patches of drifted snow.

The shore zone between high and low water mark, so strongly affected by the tides, is of interest not only to oceanographers and coast-dwelling people but also to biologists, for it is a unique habitat. Nowhere else is there such a constant alternation between wet and dry, cold and heat, raging breakers and peaceful calm. Nowhere else has such variety of form of animal life evolved to meet the stringencies of the environment. And probably it was in just such relentless marginal zones between ebb and flow that the most fateful event in the history of our planet took place: the adaptation of sea creatures to life on land.

All denizens of this marginal strip are obliged to adapt themselves four times a day. When the tide comes in they live the aquatic life of their brethren of the high sea, but when it ebbs they must protect themselves, sometimes in most complicated ways, from the perils of heat and desiccation. Some creatures cling to the rocks to avoid being drawn in and pounded by the surf and waves, others bury themselves in the sand or mud, bore a shelter for themselves in the rocks, or withdraw into their shells. Even rain can be fatal to these inhabitants of the tidal zones which, with very few exceptions, cannot live in fresh water; those which at low tide are unable to withstand for a few hours the dew or a shower are doomed in advance. Yet the number of creatures which survive both stifling heat and heavy rain is considerable, as can be realized from examination of the rocks at the high-tide line. Even in the slack water of low tide they are covered with molluscs, gastropods and crustaceans heedless of sunshine, cold, rain and hail and moistened by the spray only twice every twenty-four hours.

The tangles of seaweed carpeting the rocky sectors of the tidal zone are an ideal habitat for many of those in bondage to the tidal pattern; the population density of one of these plots is sometimes as much as several hundred thousand to the square yard. Other plants which emerge only at low tide give shelter to annelids, coelenterates, shrimps, ascidians, echinoderms in astronomic quantity. Among these are some which have an incredible resistance to desiccation. The French zoologist Alcide d'Orbigny witnessed a hundred and thirty years ago a miracle of resuscitation. Having collected in the Antilles several specimens of sea snails he placed them on his return to Paris in a drawer together with other specimens. Not until a year later had he time to study them. Since the shells had become dusty, he dipped them in a bucket. Judge of his astonishment when he saw the body of first one, then another, gastropod emerge from its shell. Soon the Antillean snails, all perched upon the edge of the bucket, sat waiting as their instinct bade them for the arrival of the life-giving waters.

The muddy coastal mangrove swamps of the Tropics are a unique world of their own. Supported by their long aerial roots the mangroves, typical of the tropical tidal zones, are the only large land plants which have been able to take hold in the borders between land and sea. The spread of roots and trunks allows them to face the violence of the surf, while air roots take in the atmospheric oxygen which is deficient in the ooze. Mangroves are viviparous in the sense that the ripened seed, instead of falling from the tree, starts to grow a long root while still attached to the parent plant, and when it falls at low tide its root is ready to anchor it to the mud; at high tide the seed may be carried off and drift until it can find a footing in shallow water. Not infrequently these mangrove seedlings are tossed about for hundreds of miles before they lodge.

The impenetrable jungle of a mangrove swamp is an enormous mud trap. Elsewhere in coastal zones the surf withdraws putrescent matter far from the shore, leaving behind sand, boulders or bare rock. The roots of the mangrove retain such particles and make them fast in sticky beds which exude a putrid smell. In this way the mangroves win new areas from the sea, which they transform gradually into marsh and thus into new lands.

In such muddy, root-tangled swamps live varieties of animals no longer pertaining to the marine world and not yet to that of the land; to some degree they are making ready for a change of element. On the mud banks crabs perform grotesque courtship dances.

Gastropods crawl across the marsh, and that singular fish the mud-skipper, *Anabas scandens*, leaves the water altogether to cross from one muddy backwater to another or to pursue its insect food. Well might this unfamiliar terrain with its extraordinary flora and fauna seem to recall a long-past epoch of Earth's history.

CHAPTER TWO

CURRENTS AND CLIMATE

THE BOSTON Customs were complaining about the mail boats which provided the regular service between Britain and her North American colonies. They took two weeks longer to cross the Atlantic from Falmouth to New York than did the Yankee merchantmen sailing from London to the ports on Narragansett Bay farther north. From which it might be concluded that the crews of the mail boats were less competent. However that might be, the inhabitants of Boston addressed a letter in 1769 to the Lords of the Treasury demanding the improvement of the posts.

Nothing happened. When questioned, the captains replied that they could do no more and that the guilty party was a current reported long since by Spanish navigators. The Spaniards, as English sailors had known for a couple of centuries, used two routes for crossing the Atlantic. The southern one, which they preferred, passed by the Canaries and the gentle 'Golfo de las Damas' and came out at the Antilles; the northern one they dreaded, for in addition to regions first of blustering, contrary winds and then of light variable airs there was the strong current flowing steadily north-east. It was this 'Gulf Stream' which delayed the mail packets crossing the Atlantic in higher latitudes.

Their Lordships readily understood that His Majesty's ships could not follow the southern route, that of the Conquistadores, in order to circumvent the Gulf Stream. What they did not understand was how the merchant skippers, with more heavily laden vessels and starting from farther east, reached the American ports a fortnight before the Royal Mail packets. How could this wretched current be avoided? And, more important, where was a chart of it? The captains could throw no light, for the Gulf Stream did not appear on maps.

Then the Treasury decided that, after all, it was none of their business. It was the concern of the Postmaster-General of the Colonies, who came, in point of fact, from Boston where the protest had originated. The complaint of his fellow-townsmen was forwarded to him. This Postmaster-General of the Colonies was nothing less than a genius who, in a lifetime of eighty-four years, invented the lightning conductor and a type of electrical condenser, improved the processes of printing, sponsored a large number of charitable works, edited a collection of popular proverbs, fought against tyranny, slavery and intolerance, and laid down at the age of seventy the moral foundations of American independence. 'He snatched lightning from the skies and the sceptre from the tyrants,' wrote one of his admirers. His name was Benjamin Franklin.

Franklin, who represented the American colonies in Britain and whose revolutionary opinions made him suspect to His Majesty's government, was puzzled by the complaint from Boston; but although he was ready to improve the conveyance of the mail, he was less eager to strengthen the links between his country and Great Britain, as London would have wished, than to develop relations between New England and the rest of the world. Franklin had the good fortune to meet in London Timothy Folger, a whaler captain from Nantucket, a Massachusetts island off Cape Cod. The whalers, as Franklin was long since aware, knew the Atlantic very much better than did the mail-boat captains.

Folger, a distant relative of Franklin, explained to him how it was possible to avoid both the Gulf Stream and the banks and reefs lying off the American coast. He marked the current on a chart, together with sailing instructions, and Franklin forwarded it to the Secretary of the General Post Office suggesting that it be engraved and published for the benefit of British captains. Folger himself was sceptical about their using it, as Franklin recorded in his autobiography:

'We are well acquainted with that stream [said Captain Folger], because in our pursuit of whales, which keep near the sides of it, but are not to be met with in it, we run down along the sides, and frequently cross it to change our side, and in crossing it have sometimes met and spoke with these packets, who were in the middle of it, and stemming it. We have informed them that they were stemming a current that was against them to the value of three miles an hour, and advised them to cross it and get out of it, but they were too wise to be counselled by simple American fishermen. . . .

'When the winds are but light, they are carried back by the current more than they are forwarded by the wind; and, if the wind be good, the subtraction of seventy miles a day from their course is of some importance.'

Eventually the practical experience of the North American whalers and merchant skippers overcame the haughty conservatism of British captains, although it was not until after the end of the American War of Independence that Franklin's chart was published; he had improved it from his first-hand experience during further voyages between Europe and America. It slowly gained acceptance, and as a result captains on the east–west crossing of the Atlantic set a course allowing them to make use of the Labrador current flowing south-west. This route is still followed today.

Mention has already been made of some of the other ocean currents and their effects. There are many of them, warm or cold, strong or weak, and they have long been studied, measured and charted like the winds which give rise to them. Among cold currents, some of them carrying polar waters to the Tropics, are the Humboldt (or Peru), Benguela and West Australian currents in the southern hemisphere, and the Labrador, the Greenland, the Oya Shio, the California and the Canaries currents in the northern. Cold currents reaching the Tropics are warmed and join the strong westward-flowing Equatorial currents, which would encircle the globe were they not impeded by the continents.

But the land masses are there. Across the vast expanse of the Pacific sweep the North and South Equatorial currents, one to be deflected northward along the coasts of Asia as the warm Kuro Shio, or Japan current, and the other southward as the East Australian current. Both mingle in a complicated pattern around the islands and archipelagos of the East Indies, part returning across the Pacific and part passing through into the Indian Ocean. Here the strong influence of the monsoons imposes a seasonal variation on the flow of the northern current, and the southern is again deflected by the mass of Africa to provide the warm Mozambique and Agulhas currents. In the Atlantic the South Equatorial current, encountering the bulge of South America, turns south as the warm Brazil current, but also sends into the Caribbean an arm which enters the Gulf of Mexico, flows out past Florida, and merges with the Antilles current to form the Gulf Stream and thus rejoin the complex circulatory system of constantly interchanging ocean waters.

To the Spanish explorers of the time of the Conquistadores the Gulf Stream was *the* ocean current, *el corriente*, easily distinguishable by its blue waters from the colder, greyer seas defining it on either side. The man who discovered it was none other than Christopher Columbus; he complained on several occasions of the strength of the current off the Cuban coast, and that his ship 'even with a fair wind made scarcely a mile a day'. Narratives by Spaniards and Portuguese confirmed his observations. Already in 1516 Peter Martyr, the great chronicler of the *Conquista*, was answering questions in his book *De Orbe Novo* about the origin and nature of *el corriente*.

Later chroniclers and navigators were of the opinion that the Gulf Stream originated from the Mississippi and other rivers emptying into the Gulf of Mexico, and that it flowed north along the eastern coast of America before bending westward to enter the Pacific, a notion which suggested the famous but for centuries hypothetical North-West Passage. It was with many reservations that opinion began gradually to support the most advanced theories of seafarers who maintained, on the other hand, that the Gulf Stream turned eastward to brush the coasts of Europe, that it was responsible for the mildness of the European climate, and perhaps indirectly also for the fact that Europe, of modest size in comparison with the other continents, had represented an indispensable stage along the path of civilization and progress.

Drawn by the Jesuit Athanasius Kircher in about 1670, the first known chart of the Gulf Stream teemed with sea monsters, lethal whirlpools and legendary creatures. Kircher made the Gulf Stream disappear in the latitude of the Lofoten Islands into the bowels of the earth, whence it emerged as springs and fountains. What is important is that Kircher already knew that a warm current crossed the Atlantic. A hundred years later, thanks to Franklin, the precise course of the *corriente del Golfo* was known. Henceforth the way was clear for the oceanographers of the nineteenth century to establish the full course of the Gulf Stream, or North Atlantic Drift as it is often termed after it has left behind the Newfoundland Banks.

Today we know that this benevolent current soon divides. One arm reaches out south-eastward to the shores of Portugal, ultimately returning, as the cold Canaries current, to the North Equatorial current; another turns northward, encounters the cold, ice-bearing Greenland currents and protectively encircles Iceland. The main current, however, runs strongly north of the British Isles and up the coast of Norway, round the North Cape and into the Barents Sea, finally to succumb to the icy Arctic waters in the region of the west coasts of Novaya Zemlya. Its offshoots warm the western shores of Spitsbergen and the coasts of the North Sea. No other warm current reaches such high latitudes; its influence keeps northern harbours open and moderates the severity of winter in all the lands it affects.

Among those contributing to the increasing knowledge of ocean currents was the great German traveller and scientist Alexander von Humboldt, explorer of South America, whose name is sometimes given to the cold north-flowing current off Peru. Crossing the Atlantic from Spain to Central America in 1799, in company with the French botanist Aimé Bonpland, he took temperature measurements of the waters through which they sailed. He had noted the name ' *Mar de Baga* ', the 'sea of berries' (i.e. the bladders of seaweed) on a chart of 1436. The Carthaginians had already suspected the existence of this 'sea' within the bosom of the Atlantic; the Greeks were aware of the Punic legends and the Arabs of the Greek texts referring to them; and finally the Arab commentaries had fallen into the hands of the Portuguese. It was they who gave this sea the name *Sargaço*, which means no more than 'seaweed'.

The calm, almost currentless Sargasso Sea, in which the seaweed *Sargassum bacciferum* may attain a length of a thousand feet, is a veritable marine jungle of twenty-five thousand square miles, and was regarded by seafarers before the time of Columbus as a trap for ships from which there was no escape and in which crews died of hunger and thirst. Columbus, however, discovered for himself that the seaweed could not hold ships fast; nor did he encounter any phantom vessels. The presence of such a mass of vegetation suggested the proximity of land, but during several weeks of making slow headway in the almost windless Sargasso Sea Columbus saw not the slightest sign of coast or islet. Only after regaining the open sea did his flotilla finally make landfall at one of the islands of the Bahamas.

Although Columbus gave a veracious account, the legends about the Sargasso Sea continued to circulate. For seafarers it was an accursed place of ghosts and monsters. Demons rising out of the thickets of seaweed pulled down with their scaly hands sailors bathing in the warm water; the long yellow streamers of the weed were the hair of nymphs and sirens. And it was rumoured that in the depths were hidden mountains of pearls and gold.

Humboldt noted that the Sea of Sargasso was surrounded by currents which isolated it from the rest of the ocean. But he was wrong when he stated that the Sargasso Sea was relatively shallow and that the seaweed was rooted in its bottom. In fact it floats freely. It was almost certainly torn at first by currents from West Indian shores and carried off into the Atlantic where, reproducing vegetatively, it gradually clustered into marine jungles which are unique.

From how far back does the Sargasso date? The scientists of the Danish research ship *Dana* studied this question for several years. The two main expeditions, of 1928–29 and 1930, confirmed that the seaweed forests of the Sargasso have existed for hundreds of thousands or even for millions of years; for several species of animal typical of coastal waters are found here fully adapted to the special conditions of the floating weed, some resembling the shape and colour of the bladders of the weed. In order to survive, these creatures, which had been dragged from their usual habitat together with the Gulf weed, evolved specialized forms and thus, in the words of Prince Albert of Monaco, 'there gradually developed between the floating streamers a fauna whose mimetic powers and complete adaptation to its surroundings have made it virtually unidentifiable to the untrained eye'.

It was Johannes Schmidt, the oceanographer who led the *Dana* expedition of 1928–29, who first observed that that river-fish, the European common eel, was in fact a product of the Sargasso Sea. Until the middle of the nineteenth century the wildest reports circulated about the way in which eels reproduced themselves. Nobody had seen eel eggs floating in rivers or lakes, or even very young eels, and there was complete obscurity about how the adults reproduced. In 1653 Izaak Walton wrote:

> And others say . . . Eels are bred of a particular dew, falling in the months of May or June on the banks of some particular ponds or rivers, apted by nature for that end; which in a few days are, by the sun's heat, turned into eels.

Other naturalists maintained that eels were engendered by reptiles, or else that they were born of mud. Later, after theories of spontaneous generation had been abandoned, the breeding-grounds of eels were sought upon the seashore. It was not until 1895 that the Italian zoologists Grassi and Calandruccio discovered that certain small, transparent creatures resembling willow leaves in shape and living in the Atlantic, which had previously been known as a separate species, *Leptocephalus brevirostris*, were in fact eel larvae.

For twenty-five years Johannes Schmidt traced the movements of *Leptocephalus* from the research ships *Thor* and *Dana*. In the calm waters of the Sargasso Sea the plankton nets brought up the smallest larvae and also the eggs of eels; here was the cradle of the species. The 'willow leaf' larvae hatched from the eggs drift with the currents, as Dr Schmidt recorded, to reach European and North African shores within two to three years, during which time they change into elvers, the young eels so well known in the rivers where they spend seven to ten years. The slightly different American common eel, breeding to the west of the European variety, has a shorter distance to travel to reach fresh water, and the larvae metamorphose within a year. When they are fully adult the eels leave the fresh-water lakes and rivers and return, by some remarkable but unknown means of navigation, across thousands of miles of ocean to their birthplace. Here they breed and die, and the cycle starts again.

Why do eels carry out, twice in their lifetime, this appalling journey? We do not know, but this question prompts another. Did eels ever live in the waters of a vanished continent, swallowed by the Atlantic, whose shores served them as spawning-ground? Supporters of Atlantis gladly seize on this possibility. In their view, when 'lost' Atlantis sank amid the waves the young eels were forced to drift with the currents and seek the rivers of other continents. At spawning time, however, they returned to the mother waters of the species. For those who regard Atlantis as a fiction—and this includes most experts—the riddle of the migration of the eels remains.

CHAPTER THREE

ATLANTIS AND THE DISTANT ISLES

'A ND before the strait which is called the Pillars of Hercules, there was an island greater than Libya and Asia Minor together.' So begins Plato's description of Atlantis in *Timaeus;* he extols the wealth and power of the islanders, their temples, canals, bronze industry, their civilization, their irrigation system and even their tame elephants. A little later he comes to the point:

> Within the space of one day and night of terror. . . . Atlantis plunged into the sea and disappeared. That is the reason why this ocean is even today treacherous and not to be explored, being obstructed by the muddy shallows which the island cast out as it was swallowed up.

The legend originates in Egypt, where, Plato states, Solon, the wise Athenian law-giver, was said to have learned it from the priests of Saïs. All the same, the fact that Plato seasons his narrative with moralizations, and attributes the downfall of Atlantis to ungodliness and covetousness leaves a suspicion that this tale, designed to impress his contemporaries, was the product of his inventiveness. In spite of this, Atlantis more than any other mythical land has fired imaginations for two millennia, and given rise to some thirty thousand books, in which evidence for and against the existence of Atlantis has been persuasively put forward.

Atlantis has been looked for where Plato placed it, near to the Straits of Gibraltar, and also in many other areas: Africa, Central America, Ceylon, Crete, Sweden, Spitsbergen, Heligoland; and its destruction attributed to earthquakes, meteors, glacial phenomena and the biblical Flood. Various writers have identified the people of Atlantis with the Caucasians, the Mayas, the Guanches, first inhabitants of the Canaries; and they have been credited with the paternity of numerous civilizations scattered between the Indus and the Andes. Even the Stone Age rock engravings have been linked with them. The legend will not die.

The more level-headed seekers of the lost continent confine their attentions to the region of the Pillars of Hercules, and look towards that ocean named after Plato's Atlantis. The more cautious among them point out that there was once a rich trading city in south-west Spain, presumed to have been at the mouth of the river Guadalquivir, whose founders and whereabouts are unknown. When they spoke to Solon of Atlantis were the Egyptian priests referring to the city of Tartessus, the biblical Tarshish of the second millennium B.C.? Or to an African kingdom at the foot of the Atlas which had disappeared by Solon's time? Both hypotheses are plausible. Alas, if either were true it would be the end of many fantasies and more—or less—scholarly opinions about Atlantis.

Let us follow the enthusiasts who seek Atlantis to the west amid the deeps of the Atlantic Ocean, for it is there that the bulk of the clues is gathered. Are we to infer that the Canaries or the Azores are the remains of an engulfed continent? Geologists retort that this is impossible, that the Canaries and Azores are of volcanic origin and there is no trace of a sunken land shelf. Indeed, samples and soundings and submarine photography disprove the existence of a continent in the Atlantic depths. The thickness of the sediments, on the other hand, is evidence of long geological continuity between the west coast of Europe and Africa and the eastern littoral of the New World, while the submarine Mid-Atlantic Ridge is of very ancient geological formation.

Is then the existence of a continent providing a stepping-stone between the Old and the New Worlds, ancient home of the fresh-water eels, a mere hallucination? In that case, reply the atlanti-phils, how does it happen that the legend of a sunken realm figures in the mythology of many of the ocean's coastal peoples? The folk-lore of Ireland, Wales and Brittany tells of a sunken island to the west of Europe; the Mayas, Toltecs and other peoples of Central America, too, retain the tradition of a vanished land in the east from which their forbears are believed to have come. Until the time of the Spanish conquest cartographers were convinced of the existence in the Atlantic of an island which they christened Antiglia. The Antilles have borrowed its name.

How are we to explain, demand the supporters of Atlantis, the existence of an astonishing correspondence in matters of religion and culture between ancient civilizations on either side of the ocean? Might not the Cromagnon men, precursors of the Europeans, and the ancestors of the Palaeo-Americans all have sprung from Atlantis? Megaliths, pyramids, sun worship, astronomy, the lore of the seasons, mummification, belief in magic—these things exist not only at the core of the civilizations of Europe and Asia but also in Central America and on the high plateaux of the Andes. Was there never, in ancient times, a 'bridge' named Antiglia or Atlantis which disappeared into the waters twenty, ten or five thousand years ago and of which the memory is kept alive by the legends and the myths of the Atlantic's coastal peoples?

The discussion may go on for years, for scientists do not want for arguments. They question the value of religious and cultural correspondences and affirm that people of the Americas were, in such matters, just as susceptible to influences arising in eastern or south-eastern Asia, and they maintain that certain manifestations of mind or behaviour are integral to a particular phase of human development. As for legends about sunken continents or vanished islands, these exist wherever man lives near the ocean. Waves and currents are undermining islands or carrying off parts of the coast-line everywhere. In short, the myth of Atlantis is, they say, the manifestation of a pristine fear, one imposed upon man by the sea until he has learned to master it.

Let us leave proponents and opponents to their battle. Ever since *Homo sapiens* has spread over the surface of the globe he has been witness to countless natural catastrophes. One of the most devastating in recorded history took place on 26 and 27 August 1883, when the island of Krakatoa in the Sunda Strait exploded in a most violent volcanic eruption and, blown apart, disappeared beneath the sea. Perhaps as many as 50,000 people lost their lives in the disaster, for the volcanic eruption set in motion a *tsunami* (often called a tidal wave) fifty feet high which moved rapidly outwards in all directions, causing havoc and destruction along the coasts of Java and Sumatra. This seismic sea wave was recorded around the whole world, while the volcanic dust carried high into the atmosphere caused colourful sunsets everywhere for over a year.

Within half a century after the calamity a new island arose from the submarine crater which had swallowed the isle of Krakatoa. A few years went by; then it was colonized by plants and animals, airborne or carried on floating tree trunks. From a symbol of destruction Krakatoa became that of renaissance, showing how life implants itself on arid soils cut off by the sea.

Large or small, all land enclosed by water is by definition an island. It is important to distinguish between islands which are portions of continents cut off by the sea and islands sprung from the ocean bed. The Indonesian archipelago, the Philippines, New Guinea, New Zealand, Madagascar, the British Isles, the archipelago of Japan and many others are related to their neighbouring continents. But there are, besides, innumerable islands which have never been part of a mainland. Like the divinities of the sea, these islands have issued from the womb of the ocean.

Most of them took shape in the following way. One day in Earth's long-distant past, submarine volcanoes erupted, building mountains which reached and then overtopped the level of the sea. Erosion gradually reduced the peaks; the stone crumbled, alluvion accumulated upon the rock, sea birds settled in the crevices, nested and contributed by their excreta to the formation of a layer of humus. The wind brought seeds and insects; worms and other invertebrates landed, conveyed on floating wood. Song birds, birds of prey made a stop on the new land during their seasonal migrations. And in certain cases and by methods still obscure, turtles, lizards and snakes came to complete the range of animals. Such is the genesis of an oceanic island, its fauna and flora coming from outside. The emergence in 1963 of the volcanic island named Surtsey twenty miles south of Iceland has given biologists a splendid opportunity of observing how life gains a foothold on barren territory.

Singularly, several species of terrestrial animals which normally avoid the sea are found on islands isolated in the ocean. The outcome of involuntary migrations is entirely a matter of luck; currents bear away a lizard clutching a piece of wood, or the wind deposits on a stone a young spider hanging from her thread. Later the animal will perhaps be lucky enough to see another of the same species arrive just as fortuitously, which will make possible the perpetuation of the species in new territory. Plants spread more easily, for the birds transport many seeds, while others are borne on the wind or float in the sea.

What sort of ecology is to be found upon such oceanic islands? Tristan da Cunha in the South Atlantic lies about 1,800 miles from the African coast and over 2,000 from that of South America; in the sixteenth century the island was held to be the edge of the world. Yet it is covered with grass and ferns, and many sorts of insects, snails and finches dwell there, as well as one thrush and one rail which cannot fly. Another kind of rail has been exterminated by the rats brought by man. St Helena, also in the South Atlantic, had a splendid vegetation before the arrival of man, but the goats then introduced devoured the young shoots and have destroyed the forests, also effacing an indigenous species of gastropod.

On the St Paul rocks (not of volcanic origin) in the Atlantic just north of the Equator between Africa and Brazil, the fauna is strictly limited to insects and spiders. On Mauritius and other islands east of Madagascar it once included the dodo, a bird related to the pigeon, which was the size of a turkey and could not fly. Easy to catch, it was slaughtered in such large numbers by sailors and settlers that it became extinct in the seventeenth century.

Owing to the Equatorial currents and counter-currents the many islands, archipelagos and islets of the Pacific abound in 'foreign' plants and animals from both south-east Asia and the Americas. Bats, fruit-eating pigeons and iguanas had settled in the Pacific islands long before man, and the Polynesians, who are superb sailors, contributed to the enrichment of the fauna and flora by acclimatizing the sweet potato, the yam, the taro, the pig and the dog, which they brought with them. The isolated Hawaiian group of islands is noteworthy for species of birds not to be seen anywhere else.

Still in the Pacific, there is another group of islands deserving special mention, for the fauna there inspired the theory of the evolution of species set forth by Charles Darwin. The Galapagos archipelago is a volcanic group which rises from the sea on the Equator six hundred miles from the coast of Ecuador. Here meet the Humboldt current, coming from the Antarctic, and the South Equatorial current. Their combined action has helped to endow the Galapagos with an abundant and strangely assorted fauna: penguins from the Antarctic, giant tortoises and lizards from Central America, insects including beetles and even a species of rodent.

Zoologists would like to know how enormous land tortoises managed to cross six hundred miles of the Pacific to reach the Galapagos. It may be that their ancestors were smaller and, imprisoned upon floating tree trunks, were transported from South America by the currents and stranded on some beach of the island group. Another school of thought suggests that in past geological times this archipelago was connected to Central America by now submerged land. At all events, isolated here the tortoises developed to gigantic size. The lizards, too, are monsters—the aquatic one described on page 32 being between three and four feet in length.

Many species of bird, especially of finches, are unique to the Galapagos Islands.

It was in September 1835 that the survey ship H.M.S. *Beagle* arrived at the Galapagos Island with the twenty-six-year-old naturalist on board. Darwin thus had the opportunity to study the remarkable fauna at close quarters:

> The natural history of these islands is eminently curious, and well deserves attention. Most of the organic productions are aboriginal creations, found nowhere else; there is even a difference between the inhabitants of the different islands; yet all show a marked relationship with those of America, though separated from that continent by an open space of ocean, between 500 and 600 miles in width. The archipelago is a little world within itself, or rather a satellite attached to America, whence it has derived a few stray colonists, and has received the general character of its productions . . . we seem to be brought somewhat near to that great fact—that mystery of mysteries—the first appearance of new beings on this earth.

For twenty-four years Darwin reflected upon the 'mystery of mysteries'. Then in November 1859 his book *On the Origin of Species by Means of Natural Selection* was published and immediately caused great controversy. It heralded a new era in natural history, in which the reptiles and birds of the Galapagos Islands played an important role.

Biologists studying the processes of evolution are still greatly interested in the often strange degrees of specialization revealed by creatures of isolated islands. But many species formerly protected by the vastness of the ocean will soon be no more than museum exhibits. During the past four centuries man and his satellites—rats, pigs, goats, dogs, rabbits—have, on reaching the most distant shores, caused the disappearance of several species. And since the oceanic islands are mainly small and their specialized flora and fauna numerically weak, the natural habitat and indigenous species are rapidly destroyed. Like the whales, the giant tortoises and lizards and other species are threatened with the fate of the dodos and the northern sea-cows: extinction.

CHAPTER FOUR

CORAL GARDENS

CORAL reefs are the creation of tiny sea creatures which secrete a protective skeleton binding members of the colony together. These reef-building coral polyps live only in the upper waters, rich in oxygen and sunshine, of seas in which the mean temperature never falls below 21° C. They like the presence of surf and settle on rocky ledges close to the shore. There they create strange edifices, certainly the most beautiful and colourful within the seas, which take the form of mushrooms, fans, columns, feathers, miniature forests. In these underwater gardens live varied and dissimilar animals: sponges, sea anemones, molluscs, shellfish, echinoderms, and multi-coloured fish.

The coral polyps are the greatest builders of the animal world: to their thousands of years' toil we owe the appearance of innumerable islets and islands, banks and barriers which give their characteristic relief to large sectors of the Pacific, the Indian Ocean and the Caribbean. The atolls of the South Seas, the reefs of the Red Sea and off the coast of Ceylon, the coral banks of the Australian Great Barrier Reef and of Madagascar leave far behind the work of man.

These structures have long been of interest to naturalists. They noticed that the coral polyps thrive only in the surf area and just below the surface of warm seas: cold or deep water is fatal to the reef-building kinds. Yet some of the coral masses have a base situated fifteen or twenty thousand feet below their summit, whilst others rise over three thousand feet above the sea. Movements of the Earth's crust explain these anomalies. When a coral coast is lifted up, the drifting spores settle lower; when, on the other hand, it subsides the polyps build at a higher level. Though deserted cliffs and reefs may raise heads like bald blocks of chalk in the middle of the ocean, the polyps living by the surf below will continue building without pause.

Such enormous coral structures are in fact the outcome of a close link between the movements of the Earth's crust and the activities of the tiny polyps, and they prove that modifications of this geological nature are slow and gradual, for if it were otherwise the polyps

69

would have been unable to harmonize the pace of their building with the raising or subsidence of the floor of the sea. This was beginning to be suspected a hundred and twenty-five years ago when Charles Darwin undertook his researches. Naturalists asked why polyps made three quite different kinds of construction: the barrier, the fringe reef and the atoll; and in particular the reason for this last, a ring of coral surrounding a calm lagoon.

Six months after his stay in the Galapagos Islands Darwin took up the study of atolls when the *Beagle* cast anchor off the Keeling Islands in the Indian Ocean.

> The ring-formed reef of the lagoon-island is surmounted in the greater part of its length by linear islets. On the northern or leeward side, there is an opening through which vessels can pass to the anchorage within. . . . The shallow, clear, and still water of the lagoon, resting in its greater part on white sand, is, when illuminated by a vertical sun, of the most vivid green. This brilliant expanse, several miles in width, is on all sides divided, either by a line of snow-white breakers from the dark heaving waters of the ocean, or from the blue vault of heaven by the strips of land, crowned by the level tops of the cocoa-nut trees. As a white cloud here and there affords a pleasing contrast with the azure sky, so in the lagoon, bands of living coral darken the emerald green water.

The attraction of such landscapes had been proclaimed long before Darwin by various mariners and navigators. The atolls were regarded as ideal anchorages, provided their entrances were deep enough. The great migrations of the Melanesians, Micronesians and Polynesians are closely bound up with atolls, which provided a stopping-place with coconuts, fish and sea turtles at hand. The atolls were staging-points upon the route leading the Polynesians to New Zealand, Hawaii and Easter Island.

Darwin was not content with describing the beauty of the atolls; what he wanted to do was to study the process of their formation. Previously it was believed that the coral polyps raised the atolls to protect themselves against the fury of the breakers, but Darwin declared this explanation fanciful. He observed that, instead of taking refuge in the lagoons, the polyps established themselves outside the atolls in the area beaten by the surf. The theory he drew up about the Keeling Islands is both simple and reasonable: the atolls are former islands once edged with coral reefs. As the isles sank the polyps were constrained to heighten their structures in order to remain close to the surface. Finally the isles were completely submerged and all that was left was the circular reef on the site of the vanished coastline.

In Darwin's view the same procedure had given rise to the coral barriers which lie off continental shores: they are evidence of a sunken coast which geographers have but to follow in order to re-establish the relief of bygone epochs.

Another theory has arisen to rival Darwin's: that the Pleistocene Ice Ages were indirectly responsible for the formation of many of the coral reefs. Supporters of this theory maintain that during the glacial period the level of the sea was three hundred feet or more below that of today; the melting of the ice raised it and obliged the polyps to make their structures higher. But this theory really applies only to the formation of barriers and atolls of relatively recent date. To those of a height of several thousand yards and to the majority of the atolls the lines which Darwin wrote in April 1839 are still applicable:

> The reef-constructing corals have indeed reared and preserved wonderful memorials of the subterranean oscillations of level; we see in each barrier-reef a proof that the land has there subsided, and in each atoll a monument over an island now lost. We may thus, like unto a geologist who had lived his ten thousand years and kept a record of the passing changes, gain some insight into the great system by which the surface of this globe has been broken up, and land and water interchanged.

Not all corals live in tropical waters. There are among the many species some which live in the Mediterranean, on the shores of the British Isles and in the Norwegian fjords. These do not build reefs, but live in widely scattered settlements. As their waving tentacles search for food the coral polyps look more like flowers than animals. What is their prey? This was another question which baffled naturalists for many years, and for a time it was believed that the coral polyps lived on microscopic algae found abundantly in the reefs. In fact, like their relatives the sea-anemones, they are insatiable predators on the zooplankton. With their tentacles they seize and paralyse their prey, but they eat only at night and their digestion is so swift that by dawn their digestive organs are empty. That is why researchers puzzled for so long over the source of their food.

What we first think of when coral is mentioned are the dark red necklaces or the gems of brilliant black to be seen in jewellers' windows. However, the material they use does not come from tropical reefs but from the coral beds of the Mediterranean—red coral, or the Persian Gulf—black coral. For beauty and for colour such specimens are not in the first rank of the coral world. But man is so made that his choice is dictated by his tastes; he has for instance a high regard for the pearl, which is no more than a morbid excrescence developing within certain molluscs.

Unlike the corals, pearl oysters build neither islands nor reefs and have never helped to change the appearance of the submarine landscape. Their single virtue is the discovery of an ingenious way of protecting themselves from hurtful foreign bodies. When a grain of sand inserts itself between their flesh and their shell, or when they are attacked by a parasite, they secrete mother-of-pearl, which seals off the intruder. After from ten to fifty years the pearl attains the size of a pea. In most cases the excrescence forms upon the inner face of the shell and produces a pearl of no commercial value. For every thousand pearls of this type only one perfect pearl develops within the flesh of the oyster and apart from the shell. Fishing for such pearls—which are composed of 92 per cent calcium carbonate, 6 per cent organic matter and 2 per cent water—has a long history and is an adventure still shared by men of every colour. Mesolithic man already fed on oysters and shell-fish and probably lighted one day upon pearls in the fresh-water mussels, *Margaritana margaritifera*, or in oysters of the *Ostrea edulis* variety. The Assyrians, Persians and Indians exploited the beds in the Persian Gulf where the *Meleagrina* species lives. Pearl finery was greatly prized by the Egyptians, and they are mentioned in the Old Testament. After the conquests of Alexander the first pearls reached Europe and the physiologists of classical antiquity wrote of them in philosophical terms; Christians, Muslims and Buddhists have used them to adorn shrines and sacred objects.

The discovery by European mariners of the routes to India and the New World brought explorers in touch with the populations of a large number of islands, coasts and estuaries where the native peoples practised pearl fishing. In the Caribbean, the Gulf of Mexico, along the coastline of California, in the Indian Ocean, amid the islets of Malaysia or the Philippines, in the seas of China and Japan, naked divers everywhere brought up from the sea bed oysters which they opened in the hope of finding a pearly growth.

The *Conquistadores* made a clean sweep of large hoards of pearls collected by the natives at the mouth of the Mississippi and on the coasts of Venezuela and Central America. Later the divers were forced to turn their skill to the profit of Europe. The pearl, 'the tear of God' as it was called in the Middle Ages, has played down to our own day a brilliant but sinister part in the violent and bloody episodes which have punctuated the history of colonization.

The relative scarcity of perfect pearls and the fact that the divers rebelled against their exploitation gave birth to the idea of culturing as a remedy for the risks of fishing. Already in the thirteenth century A.D. the Chinese Ye-Yin-Yang discovered how the *Meleagrina* sets about producing a pellet of pearl. By delicate processes he inserted into the oyster's flesh a minute particle of pearl or porcelain which, a few years later, assumed the form and appearance of a natural pearl. Pearl culture reached its climax in the immense industrial fisheries organized at the beginning of the present century by the Japanese Korichi Mikimoto, and since then it has been hard to distinguish cultured from natural pearls.

As well as obliging oysters to produce pearls, man also exploits for commercial purposes another sea creature—the sponge. The three chief kinds familiar as bath sponges are found mostly in the Mediterranean and the Caribbean, and along with the thousands of other kinds of sponge belong to a very ancient branch of the animal kingdom. Sponges of the Pre-Cambrian might even have been the first multicellular animals, for what we call a bath sponge is the cleaned skeleton of a colony of minute organisms which live by filtering their nourishment from water. Sponge fishers were active in ancient Greece and in America before Columbus, and Stone Age coast dwellers may have eaten sponges as well as mussels and other shell-fish.

Oscar Schmidt was the first zoologist to take up the study of sponges. A convinced evolutionist, he was also a keen dissecter. He observed to his astonishment that fragments of sponges dropped into sea water quickly gave birth to further sponges of perfectly normal appearance. This led to the establishment of sponge hatcheries on the coast of Hvar Island off Dalmatia and in parts of the Mediterranean.

Artificial and cultured pearls have not been able to supplant the natural pearl completely; on the other hand rubber and plastic have become successful rivals of natural sponges. The sponge fishing on

which islanders of the Aegean and the Adriatic, and coast dwellers of
the eastern Mediterranean and the Caribbean depended for centuries
will soon be no more than a memory.

CHAPTER FIVE

THE LANDSCAPE OF THE SEA

AN EARLIER chapter touched upon the way in which, through
the geological eras, water has been shaping and transforming
the relief of the continents. A glance at the map of the world
shows that what is true of the continents is also true of the ocean
floor; there too are pits, basins, mountains, crests and peaks which
reach to or beyond the level of the seas.

For a hundred years oceanologists have been striving to plumb
and classify these submarine landscapes. They have given names to
the valleys and ranges and carefully reproduced their characteristics
upon maps. The troughs of the oceans are not mere deeps with
regular surfaces which separate the land masses; on the contrary,
the sea water is incessantly ebbing and flowing over reefs, fissures,
high plateaux and deep gulfs whose monstrous relief outrivals that
of the Andes or the Himalaya.

Before the great British physicist William Thomson (Lord Kelvin)
invented in 1860 the first practicable depth-finders, little more was
known of the sea bed than the continental shelves, i.e. the projec-
tions of *terra firma* from which rise many off-shore islands such as
the British Isles, the Japanese and Indonesian archipelagos, Newfoundland and New Guinea. Eight per cent of the total ocean
surface covers the continental shelves: if the level of the seas were
a few hundred yards lower the area of the continents would increase
by one fifth.

The continental shelf is the paradise of fish: here, in the comparatively shallow waters penetrated by sunlight, live the majority
of the various species; here gather the deep-sea migrants at the
spawning season. With the regularity of a clock, herring, mackerel,
cod, tunny and haddock assemble, procreate and return by unknown paths to the open waters. Salmon, sturgeon, shad, go farther

still, for they ascend the rivers. To reach the fresh-water spawning-grounds many miles from the sea they overcome the varied obstacles of waterfalls, rapids, rock barriers, barrages and dikes. When their progeny has grown up they set off downstream to reach the edges of the continental shelf and then the deep sea.

Pioneers of free diving with an aqualung, such as the Frenchman Jacques-Yves Cousteau or the Austrian Hans Hass, have become very much at home in the underwater world. They have explored sandbanks, reefs, undersea gardens and seaweed thickets. Countless sea creatures of which little was known have been observed and filmed.

The outer edge of the continental shelf becomes a precipitous scarp known as the continental slope. These continental slopes are the most impressive cliffs one can imagine. In certain places they plunge directly to a depth of thirty thousand feet. Canyons prolong the mouths of present or past rivers. Are all these submarine canyons truly attributable to erosion by the watercourses of the mainland? It is to be doubted, for fresh water is less heavy than salt. Are we to believe that the Congo, the Mississippi and other great rivers hollowed out their courses at a period when the continental shelf was still dry land? It is not very likely, for some canyons of the sea bed are at a depth of 12,000 feet, and not related to any present-day continental features. Shall we then assume that in interglacial periods or as a result of severe earthquakes rivers carried down mud and debris in such quantity and with such a strong current that they scoured deep channels in the sea bed? There are many theories, but these canyons remain one of the secrets of the deep.

At the foot of the cliffs of the continental slope, the real deep-sea world begins, its bed furrowed by mountain chains. The Mid-Atlantic Ridge, for instance, is a chain cut by gorges and interrupted by plateaux or volcanoes and stretches from Iceland to the threshold of the Antarctic; the peaks are as tall as those of the Andes and the highest reaches nearly 25,000 feet. This is the Pico Alto, highest point in the Azores. Submarine mountain ridges similarly arise from the bed of the Indian Ocean, emerging above sea level as the Maldives, the Seychelles and other isolated islands from the latitude of southern India almost to the Antarctic. The Pacific, however, largest of oceans, has a comparatively featureless bed over wide areas.

On the other hand the Pacific has the deepest ocean chasms,

found not at its centre but near its shores, the most extensive following the series of island arcs of the western Pacific from the Philippines and Marianas to the Kamchatka peninsula. The greatest depth recorded has steadily increased with improved techniques and equipment: from 4,475 fathoms (26,850 feet) sounded near the Marianas by H.M.S. *Challenger* with a 200-lb. lead, which took

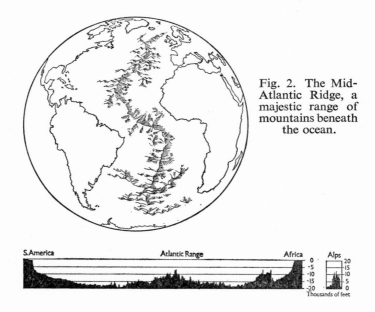

Fig. 2. The Mid-Atlantic Ridge, a majestic range of mountains beneath the ocean.

several hours to reach bottom, in her famous cruise of 1872–76, to 5,940 fathoms sounded by a later H.M.S. *Challenger* in 1951. But this was not the limit. The Russian vessel *Vitiaz* recorded a depth of 6,034 fathoms (36,204 feet), in the Marianas Trench in 1959—over 7 miles down. There are other deep trenches in the Pacific, but the deepest part of the Atlantic, the Porto Rico Trench, is 'only' 4,583 fathoms.

The Phoenicians already used the sounding-line to discover the nature of the depths of the sea, and this method continued until the middle of the nineteenth century. With much toil the sailors immersed many yards of weighted hemp line; when it was no longer taut they concluded that it had touched bottom, but such was not always the case. Soundings undertaken up to a hundred and twenty years ago were thus far from exact and, in some cases, gave depths three times greater than the truth.

We owe a great deal of our knowledge of the seas and of the ocean floors to the enthusiasm of a nineteenth-century American naval officer. Active service for Matthew Fontaine Maury had ended in 1839, when he was 33, with an accident that left him permanently lame. In 1841 he was posted to Washington as Supervisor of the Depot of Charts and Instruments. While still a midshipman Maury had published his successful *New Theoretical Treatise on Navigation* which revealed both a gift for careful, painstaking inquiry and a talent for clear exposition. In his new post he had the opportunity to study old log books, which revealed great differences in the time taken by ships travelling by various routes from one port to another. This discovery gave him the idea of assembling as much information as possible concerning weather, winds, currents, shoals, sandbanks and many other details which might provide evidence of the most convenient sea routes. The masters of merchant ships leaving American ports were requested to complete the special logs which Maury had devised; they took no notice. It was not until officers of naval vessels were ordered to complete Maury's logs that the information he sought began to reach the Depot of Charts and Instruments. Here it was carefully and slowly assessed and transferred to charts, the first of which was published in 1847.

Just as the reluctance of British captains to learn from Yankee mariners and the landsman Benjamin Franklin had continued to delay the mail packets, so the merchant skippers were slow to adopt the Navy's advice. But once the value of those charts was realized, new sailing records were quickly established, and in return for the naval charts merchant skippers completed more logs. Lieutenant Maury's department was expanded and renamed the United States Naval Observatory and Hydrographic Office, and naval vessels were specially equipped for ocean research. The mass of new information provided material for Maury's *Physical Geography of the Sea*, the first book on oceanography, published in 1856. He was already famous; in 1853 he presided over an international conference held in Brussels to discuss co-operation in ocean research. The now elderly Alexander von Humboldt congratulated him on founding a new science and he received many honours. When in 1856 the American financier Cyrus Field suggested the laying of a submarine telegraph cable between Europe and America, it was to Matthew Maury that he turned for advice. Maury joined the Confederate navy in the American Civil War, and afterwards became involved in Emperor Maximilian's scheme for the founding of a Virginian colony in Mexico. When this collapsed he settled in England, but by 1868 conditions permitted his return to his native Virginia, where he died in 1873.

The laying of the trans-Atlantic cable proved a very difficult task, and Professor William Thomson, who had a special interest in the electric telegraph, was called in to advise about the construction of the cable. In was perhaps his work on this cable that led to his improved sounding device, in which the hemp rope formerly used was replaced by fine piano wire run out over reels which automatically recorded the length of wire expended and stopped when the weight reached bottom. The new apparatus was much quicker and easier to use than previous devices, and led to a great increase in the number of soundings and sea-bed samples taken in deep ocean waters all over the world.

In 1916, four years after the *Titanic* disaster, the German physicist Alexander Behm conceived the idea of using sound waves for locating submarine obstacles. With some reluctance the oceanographers came gradually to adopt this new technique. Not until 1925 was the German research ship *Meteor* fitted with echo-sounding equipment, after which the scientists on board recorded 67,000 measurements of depth in three years, crossing and recrossing the Atlantic. This undertaking did much to establish the extent of the Mid-Atlantic Ridge, whose existence had first been suspected during the laying of the trans-Atlantic cable.

Echo-sounding takes place in the following manner. Sound waves are sent out towards the bottom of the sea, and with the knowledge that they move through sea-water at an average speed of 4,800 feet per second, all that need be done in order to discover the depth is to measure the time that the waves take to travel from and return to the receiver on board. A continuous recording is made by a needle passing over a roll of paper. Thus a research ship moving at low speed can make several hundred soundings every hour, depending on the depth, and thus record, without gap or interruption, the outline of the submarine relief beneath its moving keel. In certain conditions echo-sounding is not altogether reliable, and readings are confirmed by a Kelvin-type apparatus. The most modern echo-sounders, however, are accurate to within a foot.

Although the British explorer James Clark Ross had already stated his firm belief in the existence of animal life at 1,000 fathoms and beyond, in the 1840s it was still generally believed that there was no life in very deep waters. The man who took the first steps towards producing firm evidence to the contrary was Edward Forbes, a Manxman of insatiable curiosity and original ideas, interested in all aspects of natural history but especially in sea creatures. In 1841 he sailed as ship's naturalist in H.M.S. *Beacon* on a surveying cruise in the Mediterranean which lasted for eighteen months. Forbes dredged to greater depths than had any naturalist before him, and was astonished to bring up a living shellfish from 230 fathoms and a starfish from 200 fathoms. He nevertheless remained convinced that from what Aristotle had termed *abyssos*, the eternally dark Hades of the deep, all life was excluded beyond a depth of 300 fathoms. Had he lived longer—he died at the age of 39—he might have proved himself wrong; his many published works, which incidentally reveal that he had a great sense of humour, were in any case a substantial contribution to the study of the sea and other branches of natural history.

In 1860 a survey ship brought up a sounding line from over 1,000 fathoms in the Atlantic with starfish clinging to it. Naturalists remained sceptical, but in the same year a telegraphic cable was brought up for repair from a depth of 1,200 fathoms in the Mediterranean: it was covered with a variety of clinging sea creatures. This was a challenge to science.

The challenge was taken up by a Scott, Charles Wyville Thomson, who enlisted the aid of Dr W. B. Carpenter in persuading the Royal Society to recommend the Royal Navy to make a ship available for a scientific expedition. They succeeded, and in the summer of 1868 H.M.S. *Lightning* cruised in the North Atlantic for several weeks, Thomson and Carpenter bringing back proof of abundant animal life at 650 fathoms. Their success resulted in a second expedition the next year, with a better ship, H.M.S. *Porcupine*, and a longer season in which to carry out their investigations. In ooze dredged up from 2,438 fathoms Thomson found many examples of marine life.

The success and prestige won by these brief cruises, and Wyville Thomson's appointment as Professor of Natural History at Edinburgh (a post awarded to Edward Forbes shortly before his death fifteen years earlier), enabled Thomson to propose a much more ambitious expedition, and at the end of 1872 the corvette H.M.S. *Challenger* set sail equipped and with a competent scientific staff for a cruise which was to last three and a half years. From 1872 to 1876 *Challenger* combed the seas, crossing and recrossing the Atlantic, proceeding via Cape Town to the Antarctic Circle, thence by Australia and New Zealand to explore the Pacific, and eventually via Cape Horn back into the South Atlantic and home by the Azores. At frequent intervals throughout this great voyage the ship hove to while scientific observations were made. Depth, water temperature and the nature of the sea bottom were recorded, while drift nets and dredges brought up vast numbers of marine creatures, thousands of which proved to be of new species. From below 2,000 fathoms came weird fish with light-producing organs or delicate touch-sensitive 'antennae'; some denizens of the eternally dark waters had enormous eyes, while others had none at all. The *Challenger* expedition showed conclusively that, while plant life ceased to exist below about 100 fathoms, there is virtually no depth (or pressure) too great for some form of animal life.

Study of the sea bottom was the particular concern of one of the scientists abroad, John Murray, who found that in some areas the ooze consisted mainly of the remains of plant plankton, in others of particular kinds of animal plankton, while in the greatest depths (and we have already seen that 4,475 fathoms was sounded in the Challenger Deep) the bottom sediments were chiefly of a red clay derived from volcanic dust. The report of the *Challenger* expedition took many years and fifty volumes to complete, first under Sir Charles Wyville Thomson—he was knighted after the *Challenger*'s return—and then under (Sir) John Murray. The report is still something of an oceanographer's bible.

International interest in the oceans has scarcely flagged since that time, and many more research vessels have probed the depths of the world's oceans. Marine biological stations have been established in many countries, and scientists have continued to make startling discoveries. Prince Albert of Monaco, for example, brought up from over 3,000 fathoms a predatory fish with a curiously compressed body, dark in colour, which has been named *Grimaldichthys profundissimus*. The Swedish deep-sea expedition led by Hans Pettersson in the ship *Albatross*, in 1948, discovered that in parts

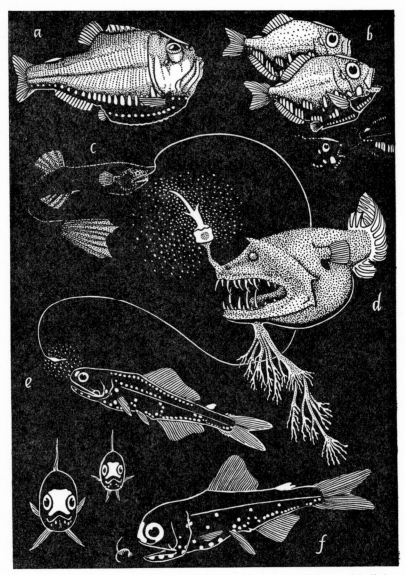

Fig. 3. Light-organs of deep-sea fishes: *a*, *b*, hatchet-fishes, with light-organs along the sides; *c*, *d*, angler or devil fishes, with lights at the ends of their 'fishing lines'; *e*, *f*, lantern-fishes, with lights on the head, the eyes, and along the sides.

of the Atlantic sediments were 12,000 feet thick, a staggering accumulation of the remains of mostly single-celled creatures. Anton F. Bruun, leading a Danish expedition in the ship *Galathea*, on 22 July 1951 brought up from a depth of over 5,500 fathoms near the Philippines seventy-five sea-cucumbers and twenty-five sea-anemones.

The varieties of marine creatures living in the abyssal waters must all have developed, at some period of Earth's history, from types inhabiting the upper waters. Step by step they conquered the deeper layers, adapting themselves to the inhospitable conditions of eternal darkness and immense pressure—as much as 500 atmospheres at about 3,000 fathoms. Unfortunately there are only very few kinds, certain shrimps for example, that can withstand the full range of pressures. Most fish brought up from the deeps are not only dead but also disintegrated by the explosive effect of the abrupt decrease in pressure by the time they reach the surface. This fact stimulated the construction of the bathysphere and other submersibles in which the experts could descend to great depths to observe the abyssal fauna in its natural surroundings. Biologists would prefer to be able to capture deep-sea creatures and examine them in their laboratories. But the manned submersibles have opened up tremendous new areas of exploration.

The first descent in a bathysphere was made by two brave Americans, Dr William Beebe and Otis Barton, in June 1930 off the Bermudas. The bathysphere was a steel sphere, 4 feet 9 inches in diameter with observation windows made of quartz built to withstand a pressure of 100 atmospheres, and provided with a searchlight. It was suspended from a vessel on the surface by a steel cable, and a telephone cable connected the two men inside with those above. On that historic dive they reached 1,426 feet, observing many remarkable creatures at different levels. In 1934 the two men took the bathysphere to 3,000 feet—*Half Mile Down* is the title of Dr Beebe's book describing the descent. Then in 1949 Otis Barton descended in his 'bentoscope', another steel sphere suspended from a cable, to 4,500 feet.

But the undersea researchers wanted a mobile vessel, an observation submarine, in which they could explore the ocean deeps. The Swiss Professor Auguste Piccard, explorer of the stratosphere, decided to design a deep-sea vessel, called a bathyscaphe, on the principles of the balloon: a steel sphere suspended like a gondola under a petrol-filled float. On unmanned trials in 1948 the vessel passed Barton's record, but was damaged by rough seas on the surface. Salvaged by the French Navy and christened *FNRS* 2, this bathyscaphe and one built by the Italians, named *Trieste*, were both ready by the summer of 1953. Piccard and his son Jacques were to man *Trieste*. Lieutenant Georges Huout and First Engineer Pierre Willm of the French Navy manned the *FNRS* 2 and in August reached 6,900 feet; the Piccards on 30 September descended to 10,335 feet in *Trieste*. But records are made to be broken. In 1960 *Trieste*, redesigned and operated by the United States Navy, descended more than seven miles into the Pacific. To the zoologist, however, the observations made by Dr Beebe at a more modest depth have been of far greater value.

Almost half the Earth's surface is covered with cold water to which the sun's rays never penetrate. The 'stars' and 'moon' of the abysses are the luminous organs of fish, shrimps and other creatures. Such points and gleams of light are sufficient to enable deep-sea creatures to see and to be seen. Contrary to widespread opinion the representatives of abyssal fauna are not all blind, though it is true that the eyes of some fish are reduced to almost nothing, or absent altogether. In compensation they have tactile organs which are surprisingly sensitive.

The abyssal depths are just beginning to be known. As in the past there are many problems to be solved, and attempts to explore the great deeps by means of depth-finders, drag-nets, bathyspheres and bathyscaphes seem rather unsophisticated. Man, exerting his skill to explore outer space, too easily forgets that on our own planet the bases of the continents and the great deeps of the ocean are so many blank spaces on the maps.

PART THREE

THE STREAM OF LIFE

He who plunges into a river sees water
come to him, and yet more water.
HERACLITUS

CHAPTER ONE

LEGENDARY STYX

EVERY creature of the land is as dependent upon water as are those of the sea. The movement of water on the surface of the earth may imply plenty for those who live there—or, on the other hand, destruction and death. When water is lacking, life wastes away and is in jeopardy, for vegetals, animals and man suffer more from thirst than from hunger. These are prime truths of which man was aware long before the chemists revealed that water makes up three-fifths of his organism. This is why primeval man had such fear of being without it. Drought, barrenness and the desert are three aspects of an ancestral terror as poignant as that, also associated with water, of which floods, deluges and drowning are the three faces.

The water which holds all land animals in thrall, the water they take into their bodies for the maintenance of life, does not look at first sight as though it sprang from the inexhaustible reservoir of the oceans. For it is fresh: it falls from the sky, gushes from the ground, rises up from artesian wells, collects in brooks, pools, ponds, marshes, rivers; it irrigates and fertilizes a large portion of the land before losing itself in the sea at the end of its long journey. Where does this fresh water come from?

It is a question that perplexed naturalists and philosophers for centuries. Underground streams apparently circulate everywhere below the Earth's crust. Is then the interior of the globe one immense cistern, a fresh-water sea? Or can there be truth in the old notion of the alchemists that air or soil changes mysteriously into water within the bowels of the globe?

The story of the discovery of the sources of fresh water is a long succession of mistakes and follies. From antiquity onwards there were two rival schools of thought: those who claimed that fresh and salt water were different substances, and those who declared on the contrary that it was likely that the ocean was the sole true source of fresh water. With Aristotle, the former maintained that water, the combination of air and earth, formed within the depths of the earth in ice-cold caverns. The others claimed, with Plato, that as the ocean flowed through or around the underworld as the legendary River Styx, the briny water was there filtered and made fresh before regaining the surface.

In support of their opinions both sides elaborated dazzling theories, masterpieces of logic and shrewdness. There were compromises, for example that of Seneca, going as far as to state that there is some truth on both sides and that water really comes—a third solution—from transmuted air or liquefied earth or infiltrated sea-water. Since the authority of the most celebrated figures of antiquity was behind such doctrines, the only man who might have discovered the precise origin of fresh water fifteen years before the beginning of the Christian era was never able to establish his opinion.

This man, Vitruvius, was a military engineer under Caesar and Augustus, and his name appears in the annals of history less because of his practical achievements than on account of his *De Architectura*, a work in ten books in which he assembled a mass of information about building, aqueducts, sundials, military engines and the like. In Book VIII Vitruvius deals with the boring of wells and speculates in this connection upon springs and the provenance of fresh water. Without bothering about the philosophers' theories he states simply that the water lying below ground is the same as that which falls from the clouds or comes from the melting of snow. The water of the rain or the thaw sinks into the ground until the presence of impervious rocks compels it to seek fissures as a means of continuing its downward course. And that is exactly how springs start.

The world of the ancients and of the Middle Ages passed, and no scholar or naturalist paid attention to the theory of Vitruvius. The first hydrologist worthy of the name, the Brussels doctor Jean Baptiste von Helmont, was unaware of it. A spiritual descendant of Paracelsus, he looked upon the world through medical eyes. He had the brilliant and on the whole fairly accurate idea of comparing the circulation of water inside the Earth to that of blood within a living entity. The machinery of the blood's circulation had been discovered shortly before, in 1628, by another doctor, the Englishman William Harvey. These two circuits must, for a disciple of Paracelsus, be brought into harmony: water was for the Earth and the vegetals what blood stood for with man and the animals.

So far this all seems surprisingly modern, but unfortunately the

alchemist in van Helmont awoke. The inside of the globe, he pronounced, was a mixture of sand and water, and mysterious forces
were constantly impelling the water into the sand. Purified by the
latter, it found its way through the Earth's crust, bubbled from the
rocks, flowed to the sea and came back to the bowels of the Earth
whence, re-filtered, it began all over again. It was but one step to
the hypothesis that the Earth, a living organism, drank in and
digested the salt water, exuding it in fresh form; and van Helmont
took it.

The notion of a world drinking up water which it replaced by
means of perspiration met with scepticism from the more realistic
scientists of the period. Nevertheless the old Platonic theory of salt
water being sweetened by means of filtering inside the earth persisted,
and the chief question which bothered men of learning was why the
caves and pits where the filtration supposedly took place were not
full of salt left by the sea water.

To settle this point the Science Academy of Bordeaux in 1740
held a competition. Six years later the prize was awarded to a
certain Professor Kühn, a native of Danzig and author of a learned
paper entitled *Tenable Considerations regarding the Sources of
submarine Water*. Here are some of Kühn's 'tenable considerations',
which were held at the time to be the quintessence of wisdom:

> Sea water is swallowed up by submarine gulfs and flows
> thereafter beneath the *terra firma*. Here, through countless
> channels and branches, it spreads even beneath the mountain
> ranges. As it progresses, and being influenced by the heat of
> the centre of the earth, it vaporizes gradually and imperceptibly
> in the grottoes, caverns and anfractuosities. Through fissures
> the vapours reach the caves of the higher levels of the earth,
> condense and become water, which concentrates gradually in
> sloping beds of gravel and loose stones and forms springs at the
> foot of the mountains. The surplus water collects in under-
> ground basins. Such is the origin of the deeper ground-water.
> The water left behind, partially evaporated, in the bowels of
> the earth is heavier and far more briny than that of the sea. It
> constitutes the mother stream, of great saltness, which returns
> to the ocean through a network of canals and clefts; being
> heavy it falls into the abysses as a gigantic vortex.

But nearly two centuries before the Science Academy of Bordeaux
awarded the prize to this 'apposite' explanation, an amateur
scientist named Bernard Palissy had announced a theory in keeping
with that of Vitruvius: rain and melt-water which have penetrated

into the ground emerge as springs. A potter and enameller by profession and the inventor of new ceramic processes, Palissy adorned the gardens of the Tuileries with terracotta and artificial grottoes and, as has been mentioned, was among the first to offer a correct explanation of the origin of fossils. He was a Protestant at a period of religious intolerance in France, and because he tried to rouse his fellow citizens from their obscurantism by his scientific lectures, he finished his days in the Bastille in 1587. His *Excellent Discourse upon the Nature of Water and Fountains, whether natural or artificial,* lay buried in the archives.

To the credit of science, Palissy was not alone in his opinions. The Dutch scholar Vossius, for instance, considered that a river such as the Nile must inevitably be the product of the diluvial rain of the tropics: while the learned prior of the monastery of St Martin-sous-Beaune, Edmé Mariotte, the first great French physicist, published a treatise about underground water in which he stated firmly: 'The whole of the water contained in the earth comes only from rain.' Julien de la Mettrie, physician and atheist philosopher, expressed the same opinion. But it was not until about 1800 that the true facts began to be accepted by the more enlightened physicists and geologists: the transformation of salt water into fresh does not take place underground; water does not come from the infernal regions, as Plato maintained, but from the sky, and the circuit it follows is infinitely vaster than the philosophers, alchemists and professors of yore could conceive.

The upper layers of the ocean grow warm under the Sun's radiation and enormous quantities of water evaporate, rise up and collect in the form of cloud; then, condensed into rain, they fall upon the land. The quantity of water evaporated from the oceans amounts to billions of tons, to which must be added further millions of tons of fresh water evaporating from the surface of the land. The global volume of precipitation is correspondingly vast.

If the clouds were to release their contents simultaneously upon the land masses all terrestrial living things would be submerged, but fortunately the bulk of the rain is shed above the oceans. Rain falling upon the land works its way in, waters the vegetals, collects in underground systems, flows on and beneath the surface, emerges afresh and returns to the sea in the form of streams and minor and major rivers.

It all sounds very simple, but the circulation of water involves a train of complex phenomena. Further, it is subject to a variety of influences. To the detriment of farmers, meteorologists and hydrologists, the rainfall and the reserves of water are spread unevenly over the surface of the globe: climatic maps are quite explicit as to that. Side by side with those equatorial, tropical and temperate zones which are heavily or at least adequately watered because of winds and currents, and consequently support forests, pasture and crops, there are the deserts that parch for lack of water; animal and plant life exist there as best they can beneath a never clouded sky. Such areas have determined or at least modified the fate of human civilization.

Are we in fact slaves of the water cycle, that concatenation of events which begins with evaporation, continues in the formation of clouds and the falling of rain, snow and dew, and ends, with the help of the subterranean systems and the rivers, in the ocean? May there not be, somewhere in the bowels of the earth, reserves of water untouched by this circuit and to be broached in need? Sixty or more years ago Eduard Süss, an Austrian geologist and social reformer, introduced a new element into the discussion—'juvenile' water. He believed that the water which he so described might come from magma and reach the upper strata as the molten rocks beneath the Earth's crust liberated gases.

Some of the water vapour released by volcanoes is, to use Süss's term, in fact 'juvenile', and the cooling of magma does introduce a quantity of water into the cycle of nature; but this plays a mere secondary part in the water economy of the planet. Hopes centred upon exploiting resources deep within the Earth's mantle are doomed to disappointment; water-hungry man must still look towards the opening of what the Scriptures call 'the windows of heaven'—the clouds.

CHAPTER TWO

'THE CLOUD REARS UP'

IN 1801 the Professor of Zoology at the Jardin du Roi, the Paris Botanic Gardens, sat huddled over a pile of notebooks carefully recording dates, weather forecasts and meteorological observations. None but a few of his colleagues knew what he was about and, to tell the truth, they thought it trivial enough. What had led Jean Baptiste de Lamarck to interest himself in the clouds? He was neither a weather expert nor a physicist; his business was to explain the development and morphology of the invertebrates—a term which he invented. His *Meteorological Yearbooks* were perhaps really no more than the satisfaction of a whim, for Lamarck was not above an occasional eccentricity.

It is strange that no one before Lamarck appears to have thought of studying cloud formations in any detail. To begin with, what was meant by clouds? They consisted of vapour and had curious shapes that changed incessantly; sometimes they were beautifully coloured, sometimes grey and lowering; and from them issued rain, hail or snow according to the season. The knowing had from time immemorial professed to foretell the weather from the shape of the clouds, though this practice suggested the nature magic of primitive peoples. In Lamarck's time there were already several societies for weather enthusiasts, but their prophecies only too often resembled the astrological speculations of a rural almanac.

Lamarck began by endeavouring to bring a little order into the classification of cloud formations. But most of his time was occupied with his work on the natural history of the invertebrates, which (as we have seen) led him to propound an evolutionist theory to account for the diversity of animal life, a view first expressed in 1801 in his book *Système des Animaux sans Vertèbres;* this brought him into opposition to the renowned Georges Cuvier, and consequently into discredit. But while his evolutionist ideas had received by the middle of the century the attention they merited, his studies of clouds were totally neglected until recent times.

Thus the beginnings of nephology, the study of clouds, are generally credited to a British chemist and weather expert, Luke Howard, whose tabulations were praised by Goethe. His system of classification and the terminology he invented to describe cloud formations—cumulus, cirrus, stratus, etc.—were immediately accepted. Lamarck's notebooks show that he too thoroughly understood the different types of clouds and the significance of their appearance; but although he was a more perspicacious observer than Howard he was less apt in his choice of descriptive terms. Lamarck divided the heavens into three zones according to height, and described the clouds characteristic of each zone. Then he dealt with the development of clouds and their changing forms—their life history and evolution. Had not the eleven volumes of his *Meteorological Yearbooks* been so completely ignored he would long ago have been recognized as the doyen of weather scientists.

Today meteorologists have added further names to Howard's terminology, listing four families and ten genera, rather in the way that plants and animals are classified. To the family of high clouds (above about 20,000 feet) belong the cirrus, cirrocumulus and cirro-stratus—delicate and feathery or like a thin veil, almost out of sight. Lower down we have the grey blanket of altostratus, and also the altocumulus which so often produces a 'mackerel sky'; while below about 8,000 feet come the stratocumulus, stratus and nimbo-stratus, which usually bring rain.

In a family by themselves, both to the scientist and to the most casual or poetic observer, are the towering cumulus and cumulo-nimbus clouds. White, majestic, dome-shaped cumulus betokens fine weather; but if it develops into flat-topped threatening cumulo-nimbus, beware of thunder!

'The cloud rears up, dense and splendid,' writes Goethe in one of his poems in praise of Luke Howard. Hundreds of poets have been inspired by the beauty of the clouds, countless painters and other artists have immortalized the fleeting outlines of cloud forma-tions. Like the ever moving billow, the cloud has become the symbol of man's restless roving. How do clouds take shape?

The warmth of the Sun changes water into vapour which rises with the warm air and, as this cools, condenses to form droplets around minute particles of dust and salt always present in the atmosphere. A sizable cloud consists of million of droplets which, if they are carried up into very cold air, become ice crystals. The droplets may form on particles carried into the atmosphere from chimneys, on volcanic dust after a violent eruption, or more sinister still, on radioactive dust from the explosion of an atomic or hydrogen bomb. When the droplets coalesce to form drops, they fall as rain, or, if they have become ice crystals, combine to fall as snowflakes. Raindrops refract and reflect light, and if the necessary conditions are present we see a rainbow, always a wonderful phenomenon.

'I do set my bow in the cloud, and it shall be for a token of a covenant between me and the earth,' says Genesis. And later: 'It shall come to pass, when I bring a cloud over the earth, that the bow shall be seen in the cloud.'

A bridge between heaven and earth, between the pantheon of the gods and the world of men, animals and plants, the rainbow has played a special part in many myths and religions. Even today, when it can be explained scientifically, it remains a natural wonder, like Aurora Borealis.

Lovely as may be these celestial landscapes, aesthetic pleasure is unfortunately not their only gift. Lightning lies hidden within the clouds, rainstorms and hail lurk in their folds; and it is beneath the gorgeous skies of tropical regions that the water-cycle terminates abruptly and often fearsomely. From the ocean come heavy and compact clouds towards the land; clear and blue only a few hours before, the sky is suddenly invaded by dense black clouds. Then 'the rains' begin.

Why are the Tropics in particular liable to periodical and torrential rainfall? One reason is that warm air can absorb more water vapour than can cold air, and a second is that the Sun's rays, striking the surface of land and sea almost vertically in those regions, bring about intense evaporation.

The warm moist air rises rapidly, cools, the water vapour condenses and in the zone of calms about the Equator causes regular heavy afternoon rainfall. Seasonal rain such as that brought by the monsoons to India can be a blessing or a curse. In a normal year the winds blowing from the seas to replace the air rising from the hot land mass of Asia throughout the summer bring welcome, though often torrential, downpours. If the monsoons fail, drought and famine are inevitable; if the clouds bring rain much in excess of the average, flood and devastation follow.

Johann Jakob von Tschudi, a Swiss traveller who explored part of South America a century ago, described a violent tropical storm in Brazil as follows:

> During the afternoon the rain became a cloudburst whose ever mounting violence reached its climax and went on for seven hours without interruption. In my many travels I have often watched diluvial rain, but neither before nor since have I seen anything like this. It was truly terrifying; the water poured over every slope with growing speed and savagery, for the saturated earth could hold no more. The frightened inhabitants of Capellinha feared lest their village should be destroyed. In my house nothing remained dry; the water came in through the roof and ran out by the door. The dark room was lit up by incessant lightning and there were moments when the roll of thunder drowned the crash of the rain. Anxiously

we awaited hour after hour the end of this catastrophe of nature. It was not until midnight that the violence of the tempest was spent. . . .

After such a storm the landscape is unrecognizable. The rivers in spate are discoloured by the soil and debris they carry, and here and there in the swamped countryside are clumps of trees in which representatives of all kinds of animal species have taken refuge. Uprooted tree-trunks whirl in the streams. Then, soon after the floods have subsided, bright funguses invade the debris and a carpet of dark green algae covers the surface of the water. With the speed and exuberance of the Tropics new life is born of chaos and destruction.

The rain forests of these regions are the densest masses of vegetals upon the planet. When he was exploring the virgin forests of the Orinoco and Magdalena Rivers, Alexander von Humboldt recalled a description he had read in *Paul et Virginie*. Writing of the Ile de France, now called Mauritius, Bernardin de St Pierre had said: 'It was like a forest growing on top of another forest.' Humboldt applied this simile to the upper level of the virgin forest of South America, which he too described as a 'forest above the forest'.

To what is the luxuriance of tropical vegetation to be attributed? In Venezuela and the interior of Colombia Humboldt experienced torrential rains, and he measured with a hygrometer the humidity of the air. It often reached ninety per cent, and rose nearly to saturation point in the early hours. The 'curious quality of the air' and the 'mysterious formation of water', as Humboldt writes, explain the rapid and inordinate growth of vegetals. The tropical woodland with its enormous trees, christened 'hylaeum' by Humboldt, is a rain forest.

This is a virtually impenetrable jungle of trees, giant ferns, lianas and parasitic plants piled one upon the other and so interlocked that, as one explorer wrote, 'three-dimensional space seems insufficient to hold them'. Forests of that sort exist in the Tropics wherever rain falls abundantly: in Brazil, on the east coast of Central America, in western and central Africa, in Madagascar, on the west coast of India, in Assam, Malaysia, Indonesia and New Guinea. The average annual rainfall varies from eighty to one hundred and fifty-five inches, twice or four times that of the wettest countries of Europe. In certain parts such as the Khasi Hills of Assam the rainfall reaches over four hundred inches a year.

Deluges in the Tropics, moderate if capricious rainfall in the zones of prevailing westerlies, deserts where the wind blows consistently from across dry land masses—this unequal distribution does not suit man at all. Humanity needs water for its constant tampering with the Earth's surface—neither too little nor too much. And since all civilized lands are short of it, partly because of their own wastefulness, men have hit upon the idea of reaching for the clouds and playing the part of rain-gods. The medicine men of the past have been replaced by the rainmakers of today.

With our present resources we cannot divert rain-bearing clouds from the Tropics to areas of drought. The most the modern rainmaker can do is to 'tap' the clouds in the sky above a dry area. This is done by 'seeding' the clouds with frozen carbon dioxide or fine crystals of silver iodide, in order to set up the drop-forming reaction. In the first experiments the clouds were bombarded by aircraft, but more often particles of silver iodide are now produced in generators on the ground and released into the atmosphere as smoke. This method works, but the amount of rain produced is not very great and is certainly expensive. It also raises a legal point which could become important in the future: does the rain artificially induced to fall in one area belong to people living elsewhere? Have we the right to lay hands on clouds which so nimbly pass over boundaries and frontiers? And could a country demand reparation if its grain crop failed because its neighbours had stolen the rain to which it was entitled?

It remains to be seen how the processes for taming the atmosphere will develop. Pessimists make the point that strategists of the future will be able to capture the clouds, overwhelm an enemy with torrential rain or wipe him out either by freezing him or depriving him of water. For their part the rain-makers are content, for the time being, to confine themselves to providing limited assistance to farmers. Meanwhile the clouds continue to make their ceaseless round, their majesty in no way affected.

CHAPTER THREE

THE HIDDEN FOUNTS

T HE SEARCH for water is as old as man: nomadic hunters, herdsmen, shepherds, farmers, all depend on a supply of fresh water. Where streams and springs are lacking, wells have since early times had great importance. The Old Testament, for example, makes reference to disputed wells; and what better way to outwit a rival tribe than to seize or poison its wells? Mechanical devices to raise water are pictured in ancient Egyptian art, worked by numerous slaves, or oxen, or even dogs, and in thousands of oriental villages today the water-buffalo plods patiently round for the same purpose. Storage of water in cisterns has a long and continuous history in both the Old and the New World, and basins hollowed out of the coralline rock to catch rainwater are still in use on many South Sea islands, which often lack other reliable sources of fresh water.

'The highest form of goodness is like water,' affirmed the Chinese philosopher Lao-tse two and a half thousand years ago. 'For the virtue of water is that it comes to the help of ten thousand people without talk.' All the peoples which depended upon wells revered water, and the well was at the heart of the religious and social life of the community. It was there that men offered the gods wine, oil, flowers, cakes, coins and victims. The survival of 'holy' wells, 'wishing' wells and well-dressing ceremonies in sophisticated modern societies attests their importance even in countries with an abundant rainfall. The most famous of sacrificial wells—in this case a natural water cavern—is perhaps that still to be seen on the site of the former Mayan religious centre of Chichén-Itzá in Mexico. Young girls, ornately dressed, were among offerings cast into the water to appease the god of the depths. In the 1890s the American Edward Herbert Thompson decided to investigate the sacred well and entered the water in a diving suit. Over a period of time he dredged up skeletons, carved jade, gold and copper disks bearing symbolical markings, and many other votive offerings.

It is not surprising that the ability to locate underground water and hence the site for a well was early associated with magical powers, and the dowser's divining rod perhaps harks back to the caduceus (winged wand) of the Greek god Hermes or the staff with which Moses struck water from the rock. In the Middle Ages rhabdomancy, the art of water-divining, achieved almost the status of a science. On St John's Eve, with due rites and ceremonies, a man would cut a forked branch of hazel or mistletoe and, grasping it with both hands so that the point was turned upwards, he paced the ground where water was sought. When the end of the branch turned abruptly downwards, he had found the right place to dig a well. Since many of these rhabdomancers were woodmen or miners they enjoyed much success, for anyone in close contact with nature knows almost by instinct the terrain where underground water is most likely to be found.

Until the middle of the nineteenth century the gifts of the dowsers were scarcely questioned, though scientists rejected the idea of 'magic'. In more recent times metal rods or swinging pendulums have been used instead of twigs by those who claim to be able to locate not only water but even mineral ore and buried objects. The sceptical maintain that when the dowser reaches the position where he expects to find what he seeks, his arm muscles involuntarily contract, making the divining rod jerk. Whatever the truth of the matter, water-diviners have rendered great service by giving villagers and settlers the faith to devote their often slender resources of money and time to digging a new well—an arduous task without modern mechanized equipment.

A dependable source of water is the prerequisite for permanent settlement, and only among settled, thriving communities can the arts of civilization flourish. Ancient Jericho was sited near a perennial spring; the 'cradles' of western civilization in the fertile valleys of great rivers of the Near East and North Africa became so partly because increasing technical ability gave a measure of control over seasonal inundations and allowed skilful use of irrigation beyond the flood plains; away from the river valleys communities could develop not only where a natural spring brought water to the surface but also wherever a well could be dug deep enough to reach underground water. Moreover, the careful tending of wells, springs and oases in regions of low rainfall kept at bay the ever-present menace of the desert.

Some areas that are now desert were not so centuries ago, as is proved by inspection and by written evidence. In many cases man is to blame: deforestation by burning or ring-barking, over-grazing and over-intensive cultivation leave the soil exhausted and a prey to the forces of erosion—procedures by no means unknown today and aggravated by an almost wilful wastefulness which has permanently lowered the water-table and created new 'dustbowls'; yet even now the protests of conservationists go largely unheeded. The disappearance of an ancient civilization, perhaps overwhelmed by a less cultured enemy, often resulted in the abandonment of villages, with their wells and cultivated areas, to the encroaching desert.

Even the Sahara is perhaps in part a man-made desert. Stone Age rock engravings show that large areas of North Africa were once temperate grassland sprinkled with lakes and rivers and supporting abundant game. Most of these pictures are of animals, but one of them shows three men splashing happily in the water. At the time of the former Berber kingdoms, where stretches of stones and sand are all that is now to be seen, there were villages, ornamental tombs, forts and public buildings. Pro-consular Africa of Roman times, which is to say the Libyan desert and Cyrenaica, was the Empire's granary. The boundaries of the fields, the outline of the roads and tracks, and the site of the former olive-groves remain visible from the air.

The decline of formerly productive areas of the Sahara into barren desert is, however, chiefly due to climatic changes. In its progress the desert threatens vast expanses of Africa, 'that dying land', to use the phrase of the French explorer J. A. Ducrot, referring not only to some of the moribund cultures and to the diminishing wild life but also and especially to the steadily decreasing fertility of African soil. In a report to the French Academy of Sciences he said:

> I am dismayed and shocked at the advance of the sand in the north and at the way in which surface water is disappearing in the south. Rivers and streams which flowed regularly fifty years ago are now dry for half the year. The screens of forest and curtains of trees which bordered the great rivers and their tributaries in the Senegal and Niger basins have almost all been cut down.

Africa is but one example among several. Deserts of Mexico, of the Near East and China tell more or less the same story, a story of over-exploitation followed by neglect with the rise and fall of civilizations. The remains of the Assyro-Babylonian culture, the remnants of Ur, of Eridu, of Babylon, of Nineveh have been over-whelmed by the desert. And in Central Asia the Swedish explorer Sven Hedin found among the dunes of the Gobi desert traces of a sizable town with gardens and orchards.

Man's attempts to change the face of the land are not always destructive. The modern state of Israel has shown what can be achieved in restoring fertility to the desert. But in such marginal lands effort can never be relaxed, and often enough the reversion of cultivated soil to arid waste has been due to nature's superior power. Awareness of this thousands of year ago accounts for much of the reverence accorded to springs, wells, and above all the oases, those scattered refuges within the vastness of the desert itself.

Oases usually occur in depressions surrounded by hills; the water feeding them comes either from springs emerging at the foot of the high ground or from a natural underground reservoir of rain-water which has fallen over a wide area and accumulated because of the underlying rock formation. This scanty water is enough to bring forth tamarisks, pistachios, broom, dwarf palm trees and especially date palms, which characterize these water-points. The oases determine the course of the caravan routes: only there can man or beast recruit his strength. The creation of new oases by the boring of deep artesian wells is one of the greatest benefits of which European technology, so destructive in other ways in Africa, can boast.

It was Artois, a pre-revolutionary French province, that gave its name to the artesian well; in the Middle Ages some monks in that region noticed the water rising strongly in wells from time to time, and even overflowing. We know now that this occurs where the ground water lies in a permeable layer of rock with impermeable rock both above and below. If the strata dip to form a basin, the water so trapped will be under pressure from water seeping into the permeable layer from beyond the limits of the upper impermeable rock. In a well bored through the overlying stratum the water will therefore rise to equalize the pressure, the force with which it does so depending on the local geology. Since the Middle Ages countless artesian wells have been bored and still contribute to the require-ments of many industrialized countries.

But artesian wells existed in the drier parts of the world long before the Middle Ages, and indeed some desert oases depend upon artesian water reaching the surface naturally through rock fissures. There is evidence that Thebes as well as other ancient cities were supplied by artesian wells. The Chinese long ago bored wells to a great depth, some of which are still in use.

The immense difference which utilization of deep-lying artesian water can make has been amply demonstrated since 1856, when French engineers first made deep borings on the northern edge of the Sahara. In one area which was then arid desert a hundred and fifty thousand date palms grow; industrial oases using thousands of gallons of water an hour have been established. This is a major contribution which modern technology, by sinking wells to considerable depths, can make towards reclaiming thousands of square miles of unproductive desert. But in spite of the great promise it offers, a warning must be sounded; for if the ground water, at whatever level, is used faster than it is naturally replaced, the consequences may disastrously affect oases and settlements lying far away.

Many problems of making proper use of the reserves of underground water remain to be solved; the solutions must take account of the mistakes man has made for millennia.

CHAPTER FOUR

'THROUGH CAVERNS MEASURELESS TO MAN'

THE TWO men had left their clothes at the foot of the mountain and slipped through a narrow fissure in the rock from which a stream emerged. They had waded, scrambled, crawled, swum underwater, and now, by the meagre light of candles, were examining a cavern deep within the heart of a mountain in the central Pyrenees. Suddenly one of them stopped; before him was a clay statue of a bear. 'I was moved as I have seldom been moved before or since. Here I saw, unchanged by the march of aeons, a piece of sculpture which distinguished scientists . . . have since recognized as the oldest statue in the world.'

It was in the summer of 1923 that the writer of these words, Norbert Casteret,* and his companion Henri Godin entered the

* *Ten Years Under the Earth* (J. M. Dent & Sons, 1939, 1963).

grotto of Montespan which Casteret had discovered, alone, the previous year. Now as they continued the search 'discovery followed discovery. On all sides we found animals, designs, mysterious symbols, all the awe-inspiring and portentous trappings of ages before the dawn of history'. For Norbert Casteret, indeed, 'discovery followed discovery' as year after year that pioneer spelaeologist penetrated fearlessly into numerous subterranean caverns and chasms, often finding in their all but inaccessible depths evidence of the art of Palaeolithic man.

How could this be? How had primitive men reached the inner-most caves which today so often hide sources or courses of rivers? The answer lies in the dry and severely cold climatic conditions in southern Europe at the end of the last Ice Age. Underground water-courses were dry and access to the dark inner caves, though still difficult, must have been easier than it is today. Cromagnon families lived in the outer caves, as archaeological evidence amply proves. The inmost caverns, whose walls were engraved with such remark-able artistic skill, were almost certainly, as Casteret says, 'sacred grottoes where the sorcerers of hunting tribes in the reindeer age performed their magic ceremonies', though we can scarcely guess the nature of those ceremonies.

Underground cave systems are found in limestone massifs all over the world; they have been formed over enormous periods of time by the action of water containing carbon dioxide. First pene-trating from the surface through a fissure, the carbonic acid dis-solves the calcium carbonate of the limestone and hollows out a cavity which it steadily enlarges. Eventually this remorseless process eats out underground watercourses, lakes and networks of galleries and caves, often at considerable depth. Where the water redeposits the carbonate remarkable formations of stalagmites and stalactites develop, drip by drip over thousands of years. The dark underground caverns, never reached by sunlight, are inhabited in many parts of the world by a strange fauna: blind and colourless fish, crabs, insects and spiders which are of such interest to zoologists that in Yugoslavia and the Pyrenees underground laboratories have been established.

When the water has frozen, the underground mazes change into fairy-tale palaces. In 1926 Norbert Casteret discovered at nearly 9,000 feet in the Marboré massif of the Pyrenees the highest ice cave known, an 'indescribably fantastic' scene of frozen waterfalls, stretches of flat ice, a frozen lake, icicles and ice towers. He realized that what he saw bore witness to the fact that in a past geological period of warmer climate a river had here followed its subterranean course; this 'fossil ice' had not melted for countless centuries.

The spell of caves and grottoes has persisted in religious or superstitious beliefs. A deep cave, with its still or flowing waters and its awful darkness, or a grotto from which a spring emerges, became the cradle or dwelling place of gods and demons, the fount of oracles delivered through priestesses and soothsayers; the subterranean labyrinths were the haunt of gnomes, of fairies, of dragons and of heroes returned from the Underworld. Some caves from which hot water springs issued were still regarded in the Middle Ages as gateways to Purgatory. Even today some people of many different religions still have faith in the curative and purifying virtues of springs. Each year a million pilgrims make their way to Lourdes where, a century ago, Bernadette Soubirous had a vision of the Virgin Mary; thousands of sick people have hoped that immersion in the waters of the grotto there will cure their infirmities.

Water reaching the surface of the ground is never pure but laden with mineral matter characteristic of the rocks through which it has passed. This is especially true of warm springs whose waters have first penetrated to considerable depth, rising in temperature the deeper they reach and coming into contact with various kinds of rock, and have then risen under pressure wherever fissures and seams allowed them passage. The mineral content of many springs is remarkable: it has been estimated, for example, that the mineral waters of Karlovy Vary in Czechoslovakia annually bear 600 tons of sodium bicarbonate, 10,000 tons of Glauber salts and $12\frac{1}{2}$ tons of fluorspar.

These details did not escape the eyes of antiquity. There was not a Roman of Imperial times who did not know about the curative properties of mineral waters. In all territories under the Roman aegis there sprang up splendid baths, such as those of Aix la Chapelle, Aix en Provence, Baden-Baden, Badenweiler, Bath, Nîmes and many other places. These 'springs of health and youthfulness', as they were called, survived the collapse of the Empire even though medical learning disappeared after the barbarian invasions. In the Middle Ages alchemists believed that every spring was the lair of a demon charged with bringing to the surface 'the inside life of the world'; yet people continued to visit 'natural' baths which, like the public baths of Roman towns, continued to play their part in social life.

When preachers began to inveigh against those who frequented bathing establishments, the vogue of these places declined; at the end of the fifteenth century it ceased entirely. A new plague had just spread in Europe and was believed to rage most fiercely round the public baths. In December 1494, twenty-one months after the return of Christopher Columbus from his first voyage, syphilis made its appearance among the French soldiers besieging Naples; most of the chroniclers allege that it had been brought by Spanish sailors. There are, it is true, some vague indications that complaints of syphilitic origin had been rampant during classical antiquity. Whether of American origin or not, the epidemic which spread through Europe at the time of the Renaissance might be considered as Heaven's wrath visited upon the cruel invaders and conquerers of the New World; within a few decades the terrible disease was taking its toll of all countries and social classes. Any syphilitic of standing took pains to conceal his 'shameful illness', and he was careful not to cross the threshold of the public baths. Finally, even healthy folk gave up visiting baths and thermal establishments for fear of contagion, not understanding how the infection spread.

It took Europe a couple of centuries to overcome its fears, and when society began again to frequent these places it did so with reserve. Only in the eighteenth century, when enlightened physicians had drawn attention to the curative properties of the waters, did the baths recover some of the popularity they had enjoyed in ancient times.

Belief in holy water and curative water is one of the main threads running through the history of civilization. Even when it did not emerge from mysterious grottoes, was not warm, did not bubble with carbonic acid gas, contained no salts or minerals, water has been treated with respect and has played a part in religious ceremonies. In prehistoric and in historic times water was, for all nations and tribes, a symbol of life and fecundity and a means of purification. In some of the legends of the East, of Europe and of Siberia, the bounteous spring from which have come all the creatures of the earth spouts from the ground at the foot of the tree of life.

We can readily imagine the astonishment of the Viking Ingolfur Arnarson when he landed in Iceland in 874 and, with the Norse colonists and Celtic slaves who accompanied him, found warm

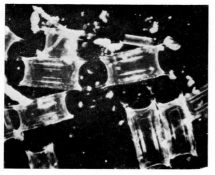 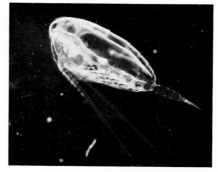

1. PLANKTON. (*Left*) Diatoms, minute plants of the phytoplankton. (*Right*) A copepod, member of the zooplankton (both magnified).

2. The Coelacanth, the fish believed to have been extinct for some sixty million years.

3. An East African ridged frog, a living amphibian.

4. A typical cumulus cloud, growing at the top.

5. A large cumulonimbus cloud which has developed into a threatening 'anvil' shape, with rain falling from the lower part.

6. The volcanic island of Surtsey, which emerged from the ocean off Iceland in 1963, has given naturalists a remarkable opportunity to observe the arrival of life on new territory.

7. The first plant to colonize the shore successfully was the sea rocket.

8. H.M.S. *Beagle*, the brig in which Charles Darwin sailed on a scientific voyage which lasted five years, reaching the Galapagos Islands in 1832.

9. A Galapagoan iguana, a species in danger of becoming extinct.

10 and 11. Water brings life to the parched land. Irrigation allows cultivation in the Negev Desert, Israel, and in the Central Valley, California.

12 and 13. Geothermal power tapped to produce electricity at Wairakei, North Island, New Zealand, and to provide a piped hot water supply in Reykjavik, Iceland.

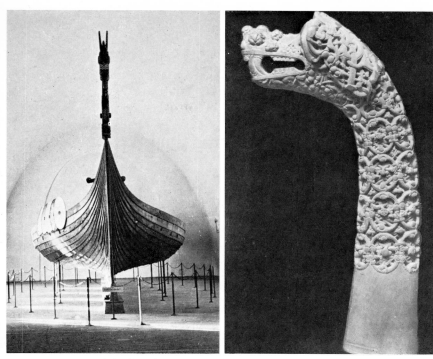

14 and 15. A Viking longship, excavated at Gokstad, near Oslo, and close-up of an elaborately carved figurehead.

16. Sailing outrigger canoes, Fiji.

17. The great days of sail: the clipper *Marco Polo*, which made many fast runs between Liverpool and Australia.

18. The steamship *Clermont* on her first trip up the Hudson from New York to Albany, 1807.

19. Brunel's famous *Great Eastern*.

20 and 21. UNDERWATER EXPLORATION. The bathyscaphe *Trieste II*. An 'aqua-naut' leaves the cylinder which was his sea-bed home during the first United States experiment in underwater living in 1964.

22. Manganese nodules dredged from the sea bed, a potentially rich source of minerals.

23. Oil derricks, Lake Maracaibo, Venezuela.

24. Fur seals in the Pribilof Islands, where they were hunted almost to extinction.

25. A bull sperm whale. Ruthlessly exploited for the valuable sperm oil in the nineteenth century, the sperm whale is now less threatened than the giant whales of the Antarctic.

26. At Versailles the skill of water engineers was employed to unrivalled effect.

27. A model fleet on the Serpentine in Hyde Park in 1814, commemorating the Battle of the Nile.

28. Fresh water from the sea: desalination plant in Kuwait.

29. The Kariba Dam across the Zambezi river, which several times overwhelmed the engineering work before the dam was completed.

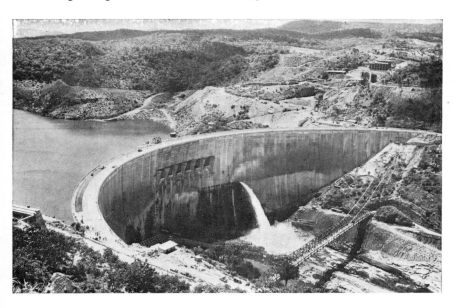

30. Old London Bridge about 1750: begun in 1176 and completed in 1209, it was the first bridge on masonry foundations to be built in a tidal waterway, and stood for over six hundred years.

31. The sweeping lines of Britain's longest suspension bridge, the Forth Road Bridge, with the cantilevers of the railway bridge in the background.

32. Locks on the Panama Canal.

33. A view of the Suez Canal published in 1867, the year of its completion.

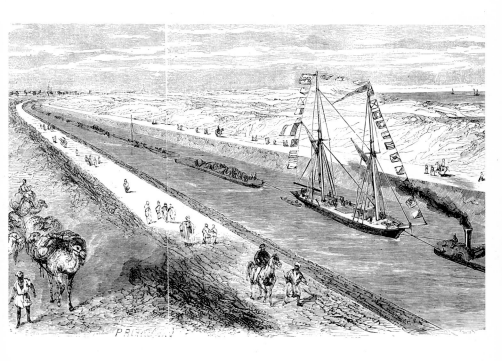

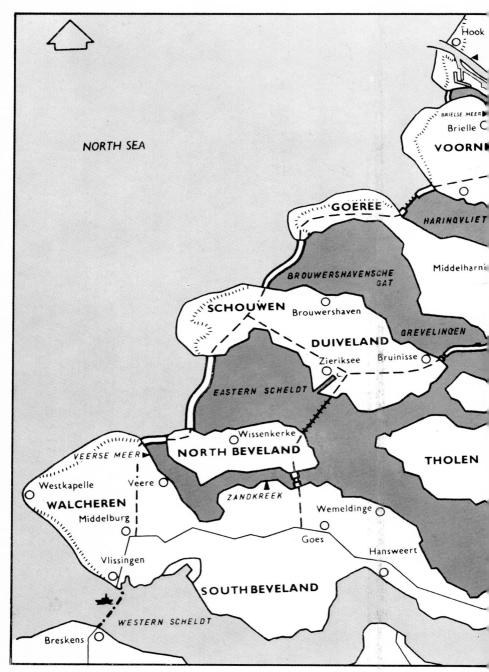

34. The Dutch Delta Project. Between the Western Scheldt and the Nieuwe Waterweg at the Hook the sea inlets will be cut off; the darker areas will be fresh water.

springs from which, at regular intervals, jets of boiling water and steam leapt from the earth to a height of one hundred feet. At that time the Vikings, still worshipping the gods of Valhalla, regarded geysers as the visible sign of the struggle between the giants and the demons of the infernal regions.

Geysers are found in areas of volcanic activity, past or present. It is believed that the intermittent gushing of a geyser is due to pressure built up by superheated steam trapped in irregularities in the geyser's vent, and then more or less violently released. The water itself may have originated as percolating surface water, like that of most springs, or, more rarely, it may be juvenile water of truly volcanic origin. The Great Geyser of Iceland shoots out every twenty-four to thirty hours a jet of steam and water about ten feet in diameter to a height of nearly two hundred feet. Other geysers behave similarly: eruptions are weaker or stronger and the interval between the outbursts varies.

Though Iceland is held to be the home of geysers, they are to be found also in Japan, Mexico, the North Island of New Zealand and elsewhere. But the most spectacular sight is that provided by the Yellowstone National Park in Wyoming; apart from innumerable warm springs and steam vents, there are no fewer than two hundred geysers of various sizes. The mineral-laden waters of springs and geysers build thick deposits where they cool or evaporate at the surface. In Yellowstone Park is a famous series of terraces formed by continuously deposited calcium carbonate.

Whether in the form of an underground river, the column of a well, a spring or a geyser, it is the same water which, following its changeless cycle, falls from the clouds and ultimately returns to them. It may well have played a part in economic, cultural and intellectual life, but such demonstrations have had far less importance in the history of man than the role of the clear and refreshing water which irrigates the cultivable soil and quenches animal thirst. To this water, 'the lifeblood of our planet' as one scholar termed it, we owe the fact that the continents are habitable.

Silent and invisible, this network waters the whole of nature, dividing into millions of threads and filaments which end at the plants, whether great or small. About two thirds of every bundle of hay or wheat or oats, of each potato or beetroot placed in the countryman's barn or store, consists of water and the soluble nutriments it carries. Vegetals need between two hundred and fifty and one thousand grammes of water to produce one gramme of vegetable tissue. It has been calculated that roughly two hundred and fifty million tons of the world's annual crop of grain correspond to an intake and transpiration of a hundred and fifty thousand million tons of water. All terrestrial life depends upon this continuous cycle.

Goethe's definition in *Faust* of blood as a special liquid, a magic elixir in which, according to age-old belief, dwell vigour, health, life and soul, is even more appropriate when applied to the 'life-blood of our planet'. According to folklore, water fends off harm. When drawn at certain times it is believed to banish disease and sorrow, to preserve youth and the beauty of face and body. We drink at the source of knowledge, we try to snatch revelation of the future from the mirror of a fount or lake. Almost all religions prescribe for their adherents baths and ablutions in holy springs or rivers where man is purified of his sins and shortcomings.

Respect for water, the primordial element, has engendered countless rites, customs and symbols, and the emotion aroused by the sight of life-giving water springing from the ground is essentially religious. In a refined form this water symbolism is to be found too in the Christian sacrament of baptism. Once baptized and cleansed of original sin the child is admitted into the bosom of the Church.

CHAPTER FIVE

LITTLE BROOKS MAKE BIG RIVERS

From 1836 to 1839 Helmuth von Moltke, future Prussian Chief of Staff, performed the duties of military adviser and carto-grapher to the Turkish army, which afforded him the oppor-tunity to make several journeys in Mesopotamia and to descend the Euphrates on a raft. In his correspondence are many detailed descriptions of the river which played so great a part in the history of Babylon and in the Old Testament. He writes dramatically of the whirlpools, rapids, outcropping reefs and great rocks which made such a journey so dangerous. In this very Euphrates valley brilliant civilizations had flourished thousands of years earlier; populous towns rose up, terraced with hanging gardens, watered by aqueducts, canals and various hydraulic machines.

Von Moltke pondered the vanished irrigation systems of the Babylonians, at that time known only from ancient texts, and he ended his report with these words:

> One day when an English engineer was asked why God had made the rivers, he replied: 'To feed the canals!' I think he ought to have added: 'And to water the fields.'

The quotation reveals the spirit of nineteenth-century technology, ever mindful of material progress. Man was vigorously setting about the 'correction' of nature. Streams and rivers were no longer to flow as they had done hitherto; they were to be mastered by the regularization of their courses, to be confined between embankments, transformed into drainage ducts; their waters were to be made to supply intricate canal systems. But von Moltke's own stipulation went unheeded: the regularization of river courses has often robbed fields and forests of the water upon which they depend.

When he was in the Near East von Moltke remarked: 'How much natural energy is still unused in these parts!' Since then man has wherever possible tamed and exploited the energy of rivers and torrents. But, necessary though it may have been, such intervention has often proved ill fated. To harness one form of energy is usually to release another; when one danger has been removed a second, often more serious, quickly shows itself. Man, who took pride in imposing his law upon nature, has often paid the price for his presumption.

Today many watercourses illustrate the unfortunate consequences of clumsy or excessive interference. The Rhine is only too good an example of this process. Until 1817 its upper valley was a broad basin with marshy soil, dotted with woods and copses, through which the river meandered sluggishly, enclosing more than two thousand isles and islets. Capricious and unpredictable, the Rhine left its bed at every thaw, overflowed its banks and threatened towns and villages. That might be described as the normal behaviour of a river. All rivers emanating from mountains obey the same laws when they debouch into a plain: they tend to wander as they will and to spread themselves before heading for the sea.

In 1817 there came upon the scene a man commemorated on his monuments as one who had 'subdued the wild Rhine'. Johann

Gottfried Tulla, a native of Karlsruhe, was engineer in charge of the rivers, bridges and roads of the Grand Duchy of Baden, and he determined to set right the vagaries of the Upper Rhine. As early as 1812 he had drawn up a plan for deepening and straightening the river; work began five years later, but its promoter did not see it finished. Tulla died in 1828 and the work continued until 1872. During those fifty years the bed of the Rhine between Basel and Mannheim was shortened by over one third; marshes, forests, copses, obsolete channels disappeared, and in some places the river dug its bed twenty feet lower than before. From that time the waters flowed freely northward, floods were no more than a memory, barges could ascend as far as Basel and the reclaimed ground became fertile fields. In such circumstances it is easy to understand why Tulla was proclaimed, after his death, the greatest hydraulic engineer of modern times.

This enthusiasm lasted until about the end of the century, when the disadvantages of the 'corrected' course of the Rhine began to appear. The embanked waters could no longer vent their spleen upon the meadows, and the now swift current scoured the river bed ever deeper. At the same time the water-table was lowered because underground ducts now trickled into the drainage system into which the Rhine had been transformed; the roots of trees and the reclaimed land were deprived of the moisture they needed. The former swamp between the Black Forest and the Vosges dried out; everywhere wells had to be dug deeper, the climate underwent a gradual change, and the fish formerly abundant in the slowly meandering river disappeared.

Despite such revelations the Rhine was again attacked. Its waters were diverted when the French began in 1932 to cut the great Alsace Canal, which was to produce hydro-electric power. The economic and political reasons behind this undertaking need not concern us: the fate of the Rhine landscape is what interests us here. At present the information to be gleaned from the partial completion of the works is that the opening of this canal has greatly hastened the deterioration inaugurated by the earlier 'improvements' to the Rhine.

Since 1932 the level of the river has sunk by from six to twelve feet according to the locality; after the canal branches off half a dozen miles below Basel the Rhine has become a narrow thread, to be crossed on foot at times of low water. The water-table has suffered a similar dereliction: wells dug by the Romans to a depth of fifty feet are now dry, many orchards have been abandoned, and in long stretches on either side of the river, where there were dense forests a hundred and fifty years ago, even the sallow thorn, one of the less exigent plants, is in jeopardy.

The Rhine is but one example of what is happening almost throughout the world. Man interferes with the watercourses and subterranean reserves: he drains, canalizes, dries up marshes and bogs, isolates streams and tributaries from their natural cycle, transforming some into stagnant backwaters whose polluted water cannot even serve to irrigate the ground and in which, often enough, no life stirs. Where once the drop of water took weeks or months to cover the distance between source and mouth, a day or two suffices in rivers which have been 'improved'.

Water cannot play its part in the economy of nature, as engineers have long known, unless it follows its natural course: the spring becomes a brook and then a river, as a tributary it joins a greater stream which flows into the sea. During its journey from the source to the ocean each drop of water takes on diverse duties. It makes a course in the soil, alters the landscape, brings water to vegetals and aquatic creatures, moistens and fertilizes the valleys; absorbed and then returned by the animals, it must often make its round more than once without quitting nature's cycle.

When man began to organize himself into civilized communities, he was compelled to interfere with the water cycle, just as he had made war upon the forests and the wastes. To exploit the soil for growing crops, to protect his fields and settlements from flooding, to make use of the watercourses for the transport of heavy goods— such were his objects. At a later stage he was obliged to draw off large quantities for drinking water, for the needs of industry and agriculture and to provide himself with fresh sources of power. Hydrology is an essential part of civilization, but the requirements and schemes of the water engineers conflict harshly with water's role in nature.

Will it be possible to reconcile the needs of a rapidly expanding human race with those of the planet on which it lives? It can be done, and several systems of irrigation and barrage construction in the United States, Canada, the Soviet Union and China are there to prove it. The main thing is to slow down as much as possible the journey of the drop of water to the sea. To achieve this, great rivers must be provided with barrages and reservoirs holding back the water of the upper courses, slowing the rate of flow so that they deposit some of their silt; slopes must be afforested and eroded areas replanted; there must be belts of trees to slow down surface evaporation, the volume of floods must be reduced by storing the water and distributing it according to need rather than by carrying it off uselessly to the sea through artificial canals. Have these principles any prospect of world-wide acceptance? This most crucial problem is one that man must settle promptly.

If river water took a smooth straight course downhill it would empty into the sea without having much effect on the land once it had swept away the top-soil. But the bed and banks of any normal river are irregular and offer obstacles which turn the water aside, create rapids, set up whirlpools and cross currents. In a fairly straight, deep, swift-flowing stretch the water along the banks follows the most turbulent course while water at the centre has the strongest current. Rivers continuously change direction and character as the nature of the terrain dictates, suddenly cascading where the land falls abruptly and remorselessly attacking the rocks and soil and deepening or widening their valleys.

Many of the world's highest waterfalls and most spectacular cataracts are today tourist attractions or have been harnessed to provide hydro-electricity. To the explorers of earlier generations they were not only awe-inspiring natural wonders but also hazards and hindrances to be faced as those intrepid men sought, for example, the sources of the Nile or the headwaters of the Zambezi. The origins of numerous waterfalls are attributable to the Pleistocene Ice Ages. Glaciers filling the main valleys of high mountains were joined by those of side valleys; but as the ice retreated the lesser ones were divorced from the shrinking main glacier, which had also probably deepened its own bed, and eventually their courses became the characteristic hanging valleys, over which today in many cases rivers leap dramatically to plunge into the valley below.

In the course of time waterfalls move backwards by eroding the rock behind the fall face, especially where this consists of the exposed ends of more or less horizontal strata of different degrees of hardness; the water eats into the softer stratum, eventually undermining the harder cliff above. This is the case at the Horseshoe Falls of Niagara, which formerly cut back the crest an average of 2 feet 3 inches every year. However, careful regulation of the flow of the Niagara river and agreement between Canada and the United

States about the amount of water taken from it to provide power have ensured the preservation of the Horseshoe and American Falls at Niagara as one of the great scenic splendours of the world.

The erosive power of running water is enormous and has been shaping the Earth's features ever since the planet's first rains. In its natural development a mature river is both destroyer and builder. The spring soon becomes a stream, swollen at times to a torrent by rainwash or melting snow. In this swift-flowing upper course the water, seeking the shortest path downhill, carries with it large and small stones, particles of soil and humus, and shifts and abrades boulders in its bed. When the stream, now grown into a river, emerges from the high land it loses its sense of urgency. The current slows and the waters begin to drop their load: first the larger stones and gravel, then the finer sediments as the river winds through an open valley or across a wide plain to join a greater stream or receive lesser ones as tributaries. In times of flood the river in its lower reaches overtops its banks and spreads a fertilizing ooze across its plain. But not all rivers have extensive flood plains, and when in their lower courses the current is still strong the fertile silt is carried to the sea. Man's intervention can help or hinder the loss of valuable alluvium: if, in seeking to limit the extent of floods, he confines the lower reaches of a meandering river to a course too straight and swift, he hastens the impoverishment of the land; on the other hand he can impede the flow by building barrages and dams and complex irrigation systems.

The fate of vast areas depends upon the activities of big rivers. The first great civilizations arose upon the fertile alluvial lands of the Euphrates, the Tigris, the Nile, and the Indus. The fine particles of mud settle mainly where dense forests edge the river, being held back by the roots of trees. Such mud feeds the virgin forests and great woodlands of the equatorial regions. At Óbidos, in the middle reaches of the Amazon, the river is carrying away each year over 600 million tons of mud. The Mississippi, the Nile, the Hwang-Ho, whose banks are without or almost without trees, carry down masses of sediment greater than those of the Amazon and its tributaries. The Nile, most famous of the mud-laden streams, has one of its sources in the mountains of Ethiopia. During the rains, that is from the end of May until the middle of September, the tributaries of the Blue Nile carry the red earth of Ethiopia across the Sudan to Egypt. Seven thousand years ago Neolithic husbandmen already knew how to use this mud as fertilizer.

Modern Egypt has an area of over 386,000 square miles, but only a small proportion is cultivable land, the Nile Valley being bordered by deserts or semi-deserts. The periodic rises of the Nile have shaped the whole history of the country. In the times of the Pharaohs the day on which the flood water reached the lower Nile was a day of rejoicing. The red alluvium from the mountains of Ethiopia was of such importance that, as Diodorus Siculus records, the ancient Egyptians believed that 'the first men were born of the mud of the Nile'. The amount of taxation was settled by the marks left by the water on the river banks'. The higher the level', Strabo pointed out, 'the greater will be the yield from the fields.' The volume of loess carried by the Hwang-Ho in its journey across northern China is enormous, adding an estimated 2,000 million tons of alluvium to its delta each year. Since 1950 the Chinese have been building barrages and irrigation systems designed to retain the precious mud, but the eroded plateaux of the river's upper reaches defy all man's efforts to re-establish productive soil.

In contrast to natural flooding, barrages have the disadvantage that the water held back drops its load of precious silt, so that the irrigation channels fed by them carry very little to enrich the fields. Such systems confer their greatest benefits only when they form part of large-scale schemes which include conservation of land in a river's upper courses and thus reduction of the amount of top-soil carried down by rainwash. In many parts of the world the terracing of steep slopes has for generations served this end; in others the urgent need for action is due to man's heedless felling of trees and overcropping of land, which accelerate natural processes. Artificial fertilizers can do little to compensate for the millions of tons of fertile soil lost annually by water erosion.

Much engineering work has been done to control the waters of the Mississippi and its tributaries. But so gigantic a system, draining over a third of the area of the United States, is not easily confined, and periodically the 'Father of Waters', as the American Indians call it, bursts through the levees and inundates hundreds of square miles of territory. When this happens the damage to farmland and towns is enormous; but at the same time the great alluvial flood plain which the river has created provides much good arable land.

When a large river carries alluvium to the ocean, or to a lake or inland sea, it often turns architect, building new land out of its sediments if the currents and tides are not too strong and the gradient of the sea bed is slight. The name delta was first given to the mouth of the Nile which, seen from the sea, resembled the fourth letter of the Greek alphabet. There are other kinds: some rivers are producing long narrow deltas by filling in former outlets which have been submerged in past ages; the Mississippi has a remarkable 'bird's-foot' delta, forming embankments above sea level for its main channels and advancing some 200 feet a year into the Gulf of Mexico.

In some cases the increases of land are considerable. The joint delta of the Ganges and the Brahmaputra extends to 16,000 square miles: alluvium is deposited in the Gulf of Bengal over an area as large as France. Every year new and fertile land is emerging, and man hurries to take possession. In Italy, the Po gains up to 200 feet a year upon the sea, a process hastened by the protective embankments which have been built along the river's course through its extensive plain. The ancient port of Adria, to which the Adriatic owes its name, is now fourteen miles from the sea. In the sixth century waves still lapped the walls of Ravenna, which is now six miles inland.

As he did with the sea, man has celebrated and personified rivers, making them the heroes of his myths and legends. Poets and writers have striven not only to extol the beauty and poetry and to recount the perils of the rivers; they have also described life on their shores and in their waters. The Rhine, the Danube, the Rhône, the Loire, the Volga, the Don, the Nile, the Tigris, the Euphrates, the rivers of India and China, all have their place in the literature of the world. The *Mississippi Sketches*, in which Mark Twain described life on the banks of the river and in the boats which plied upon it, are a hymn to the great water artery of America.

Twelve hundred years ago the Chinese poet Li T'ai-po described many a waterside scene:

Butterflies with lilac-dusted wings dip their velvet heads into the flowers. Motionless, the boat is like an island in the pool. The fisherman carefully lets slip his net, shattering the fragile silver mirror.

CHAPTER SIX

UNDER THE FRAGILE SILVER MIRROR

EVER since biology became an organized science biologists have been writing learned papers and arguing whether sea or fresh water has played the more significant part in the history of animals and plants. This controversy is somewhat academic; there is right on both sides. Certainly it was in the sea that life first developed and diversified astoundingly, and the varieties of creatures found in salt water far outnumber those of the fresh-water rivers and lakes. But many forms of plants and animals first evolved in fresh water, some returning thence to the sea, others to conquer the dry land.

The flora and fauna of fresh water have a varied habitat—clear brooks, swift rivers, muddy backwaters, small shallow ponds, large deep lakes, ditches, swamps and bogs. There are glacial streams in whose icy waters plants can scarcely survive, pools with abundant vegetation heated by the tropical sun, and those passing with the seasons from one extreme to the other, some drying up altogether in summer. It is hardly surprising that with such sharply contrasting conditions the flora and fauna of fresh water seem nearly as diverse as those of the oceans.

At a time when it was still believed that life had appeared upon the earth suddenly, some people were nevertheless astonished at the rapidity with which, at certain seasons, pools and ponds began to teem with animals. Frogs seemed to drop from the skies, worms and water-fleas to emerge miraculously from the mud. This was the basis of the doctrine of spontaneous generation. Even later, when the genesis of these creatures was known in detail, some people, both learned and unlearned, maintained that many creatures fell from the clouds or were engendered by slime. A contributor to those fantasies of the eighteenth century was a branchiopod crustacean about an inch and a half long which now bears the name *Triops cancriformis* and looks not unlike the fossils of extinct Trilobites.

This animal is rarely found, and it was not until 1756 that Pastor Schäffer wrote a description of it 'first in Latin, then in German'.

114

One day Goethe was given a *Triops* by a peasant he met during a walk, and was so pleased that he gave him a *thaler* and promised a good reward for further specimens. Urged by this bounty, the man and his neighbours set off to find them, but the crustaceans, which had swarmed in the local ponds a few hours earlier, had mysteriously vanished.

Triops appear in large numbers after summer rains in places where no one has seen them for years, and this oddity explains why they have been thought to fall from the skies with the rain. The most famous 'rain' of *Triops* occurred on 1821, in the outskirts of Vienna. A heavy downpour had soaked the dusty streets of the suburbs, and suddenly thousand of crustaceans began to swarm in the puddles; but scarcely had the sun dried up the water when the *Triops* disappeared as though by magic.

Not until thirty-five years later did zoologists ascertain that the eggs of *Triops cancriformis* (and of other Branchiopods) can resist desiccation for long periods and lie dormant in dried mud until heavy rains produce the right conditions for the eggs to hatch and the creature to develop quickly, lay its own eggs and die.

It is by such means that life has been able to occupy the temporary patches of water which, left behind by floods or rain, lie stagnant in holes and chinks of rock, in hollow tree stumps and even in the funnel-shaped leaves of certain plants. Substances which, once moist, have dried up—soil, foliage, hay, wood, dead organic matter —often conceal dormant life which water will transform into protozoa, algae, sponges, worms and radiolaria. From eggs capable of withstanding drought or frost, water-fleas and other minute crustaceans, as well as *Triops*, emerge. There are even creatures which, buried deep in the mud, await in a kind of catalepsy the end of a dry spell.

The significance of this alternation in fresh water of trance-like slumber and resurrection to the progression of life is almost beyond belief. All over the globe there are stretches of water, large or small, where the presence of life is due to dormant eggs and seeds which develop into the host of plant and animal forms that exist in every pool, runnel or brook as soon as it comes into being. Only because of this do such waters attract other creatures whose existence depends solely upon the presence of micro-organisms.

Pools and watercourses can also receive their population from the air: midges, day-flies, dragon-flies—all kinds of insect lay their eggs in water; the wind and the birds bring seeds or the spores of aquatic plants. In tropical lands it is almost possible to watch the growth of the vegetation which invades the puddles left by heavy rain; the clouds of mosquitoes which gather above stagnant water in such countries are of remarkable density.

He who has not travelled along the great rivers of tropical America [wrote Alexander von Humboldt] cannot understand what it is to be ceaselessly and relentlessly pursued by these insects. They are so numerous that whole districts are uninhabitable because of them. However hardened one may be to pain and whatever may be the object of one's interest, it is not possible to concentrate when the face and hands are covered by mosquitoes; they sting through clothing and crawl into the nose and mouth, causing one to cough or sneeze as soon as an attempt at speech is made. . . . The lower layers of the air, from the ground up to fifteen feet, are invaded by clouds of insects as dense as a fog.

But although man regards mosquitoes as a scourge, other animals enjoy them. Fresh-water fish devour the larvae of insects which reach maturity in still or flowing water; birds and bats skim the surface of lakes and rivers, feeding on midges and ephemeras. In addition, insects which populate the water and the air above it are necessary for the existence of that great and venerable class of animals, the Amphibia.

The Amphibia are more truly children of fresh water than are any other class of animal: there are no sea amphibians, and the few viviparous species which do not spend their youth in fresh water remain in wet areas. The skin of an amphibian would wither if not regularly moistened. Some frogs and toads can, it is true, resist lack of water for several days or even weeks, but a prolonged shortage is fatal.

A cruel experiment demonstrated for the first time the importance of moisture to amphibians. It was carried out at Oxford by the geologist William Buckland, who in November 1825 shut up twelve frogs in containers of impervious sandstone and twelve others in containers of porous limestone, burying them all in a garden at the university. He waited a year before taking them out. Dead several months previously, the frogs from the sandstone vessels were decomposed, whereas those imprisoned in the limestone were almost all alive although deprived of air and food for twelve months. The penetration of the earth's humidity through the limestone had sufficed to keep them alive. Buckland did not stop there; he sacrificed the survivors, shutting them up again. The last frog died eighteen months later.

It was Linnaeus, 'father of botany', who in 1735 first applied the word amphibia (from the Greek *amphibios*, 'both kinds of life') to all the cold-blooded creatures (excluding fish), for he believed that they had a double life: as larvae they lived in water and breathed by means of gills; once adult, they lived on land and breathed with lungs, but returned to water at the time of procreation. In Linnaeus's day the habits and mode of reproduction of many animals were veiled in mystery, and the attendant uncertainty explains why Linnaeus classed among the Amphibia lizards, snakes, turtles and crocodiles—which are reptiles, do not reproduce in water, know nothing of the larval state and hence do not live a 'double life'. Today we realize that there are more differences between frogs and lizards than between lizards and birds.

The transition from amphibian to reptile was a decisive step in the history of vertebrates. For even if they live in trees, in hill forests or on the ground, amphibians are lifelong subjects of the water. Most reptiles, on the other hand, have cut their aquatic ties and lay their eggs on dry land. Although some species, such as the turtle, later became aquatic for a second time, reptiles were the first to leave the water permanently.

We have seen how the Amphibia developed, in the marshes of the Devonian period, from the Crossopterygians with their lust for oxygen. But why did they leave the water to lead a double life? An American biologist, Alfred S. Romer, has attempted to answer this question in his book *Man and the Vertebrates*, published in 1946. The first amphibians could indeed have taken in their supply of oxygen by breathing air at the surface of the water; further, food was more plentiful in the lagoons than on the land; and, finally, they had no enemies in the fresh-water lakes. Romer's theory is that the amphibians took to dry land simply in order to survive in the water. This is a paradox only at first sight, for it was by land routes that the amphibians reached other stretches of water and so could gradually colonize the fresh waters of the planet. Three hundred million years ago, before the existence of reptile or bird or mammal, the ancestors of our frogs and salamanders were annexing to their empire the ponds and lakes and rivers of all the continents.

Every child who has tried to catch tadpoles at the edge of a pool knows something of the life history of amphibians. Tadpoles are to be found everywhere: in lakes, ponds, ditches, and even in the water 'cup' within the rosette of leaves of tropical bromeliad plants. Everywhere, too, there are tadpole-eaters. The carnivores living in and on fresh water hunt the young amphibians relentlessly: water beetles, fish, the larvae of dragonflies consume millions of the young of frogs, toads and salamanders every year. And there are cannibal amphibians as well.

Probably the fresh-water fish began to diversify at a period when there were sufficient larvae and tadpoles to enable small fish to hunt them. Then the big fish ate the small, as had been the case in the ocean. Three hundred and twenty million years ago fish were swimming in the fresh-water lagoons of the Devonian period, but it took a very long time for those species which cannot live in salt water to evolve and adapt themselves to the new *milieu*.

The pattern of rivers and streams is also the network by which many ocean-roving fish return to the heart of the land masses. The perseverance and sense of direction shown by fish in their annual migrations baffled earlier naturalists, and are still not fully understood. Fish have wonderfully keen senses of smell and taste. Fresh water is characterized by the nature of the salts and minerals it contains, by the degree of its acidity, and by the special smells of its mud and the plants which grow there, all of which help the fish to find its way. Thanks to them, salmon and other migrant fish find each year and with the precision of machines the places where they will lay their eggs.

Nowadays many streams, rivers and lakes have been polluted by industrial waste and sewage, and their water, deficient in oxygen, is inimical to all life. Fish, especially sensitive to the chemical properties of water, have died in thousands and the few more robust kinds which survive taste of the noxious substances. In many cases even the smallest protozoa have been eliminated by the contamination.

In spite, however, of public inquiries, conferences, by-laws and prohibitions, selfishness and apathy continue to prevail with regard to this problem of water-pollution. The result is an accumulation at regular intervals above weirs of tons of dead fish, floating belly up, and the fact that lakes whose blue waters look crystal clear have been despoiled of their flora and fauna. An analysis carried out in

1947 by a group of biologists showed that 130,000 organisms and micro-organisms were living in each cubic metre of the lower Elbe; after four years a fresh analysis, made at the same place, revealed the absence of every living creature. Nevertheless, quiet ponds and rural brooks still bear witness to the way in which life teems in waters which have not been abused by man, and fortunately industrial poison has not yet invaded most of the world's fresh water.

As of old the lagoons and great rivers of the tropics, with their branches and side-channels, swarm with fish, some small, others several yards long. They live in muddy or clear water, solitary or in shoals; some are vegetarian, others carnivorous. Films showing African lakes with herds of hippopotamus, colonies of pink flamingo, herons, storks, ibis and waders of every kind, seem to people of highly industrialized countries like pictures of an earthly paradise. In many regions pelicans, turtles, otters, crocodiles and wild geese continue to benefit from the abundance of lake and river prey. But a threat hangs over these too if man is not prepared to learn from his own mistakes. The last beavers go on building their dams, with a skill that any engineer might envy. Biologists may well regret that the engineers did not graduate together with the beavers, for these animals would have taught them how to transform a water landscape and to make use of it without disfiguration and disruption of nature.

CHAPTER SEVEN

DEATH IN THE BOG

MARSH and bog, so hostile to man, are all the more hospitable to other members of the animal kingdom. It is not easy to draw an absolute distinction between them, but while 'marsh' (or 'swamp') conjures up a picture of relatively low-lying ground bordering a sluggish river or a lake, seasonally flooded but always wet, 'bog' denotes soft, spongy ground saturated at all times but not necessarily near open water. Many bogs have formed in ancient lakes. As rivers continuously deposit sediments where they enter a lake they slowly fill it, creating marshy borders with their typical water-loving vegetation of reeds and sedges. As the area of open water grows smaller the marsh plants retreat with it; the muddy edges are littered with decaying vegetation, mosses such as sphagnum take over and eventually perhaps the whole basin of the former lake is filled with waterlogged sour soil supporting typical bog plants. Lowland bog may in the course of time—or aided by man's drainage schemes—dry out and provide good arable land. Bog also forms on mountain slopes where water is trapped by the configuration of the land, and here the poor, usually acid, soil is likely to remain a 'wet desert'. In certain climatic and geological conditions peat forms from the partially decomposed remains of plants, accumulated either under water or on its margins, at sufficient depth to exclude the oxygen required for complete decay.

For many animals, birds and plants for which man has made life impossible in the countryside the marshes provide a refuge, especially for the more timid water birds and waders. The swamps of Louisiana and Florida give shelter to alligators and turtles; the papyrus marshes of the upper Nile are the home of the rare grey shoebill, or 'whale-headed' heron—one of the oddest looking of birds, both majestic and absurd. In tropical swamps lungfish recall the Devonian period, while in 1948 it was discovered that a kind of flightless moorhen called *takahe*, believed to be extinct, still lived on the shores of Lake Te Anau in New Zealand. Upland bogs support less varied and more specialized flora and fauna.

Since Mesolithic times man had made his home, seasonally or permanently, by lakes which, besides fresh water, provided fish and waterfowl for food and reeds for thatching. Permanent villages of huts built on piles driven into the shallows were established, and their remains have been found by the edges of lakes or former lakes in northern Italy, southern Germany, Switzerland and elsewhere. But the quaking ground of marshes and bogs must always have been feared and avoided. The eeriness of such an environment can still be felt: the croaking of frogs and the calls of unidentifiable creatures, drifting patches of mist, and especially at night the elusive and mysterious lights of will o' the wisp (now generally attributed to the rise and combustion of marsh gas from the decomposition of organic matter) and the phosphorescent glow of certain fungi. Hence, and not surprisingly, the long-standing belief in ghosts, lost spirits, 'burning souls' and other preternatural beings haunting the dreaded ground and giving rise to many legends.

In A.D. 98 the historian Tacitus made a study of the various European races living beyond the frontiers of the Roman Empire. To this work, *De origine, situ, moribus ac populis Germanorum*, better known as *De Germania*, we turn as our earliest source for the history of northern and eastern Europe. Its information, however, is not always reliable. Tacitus, for whom the Empire from Augustus to Domitian represented all that is most degraded and degrading in human life, sketched a picture intended to provide his contemporaries less with a faithful image of Germania and its people than with a pattern of moral virtue and simplicity. In the eyes of Tacitus the ancient Germans were free, healthy and straightforward men living close to nature, the embodiment of virtues whose absence he regretted in his fellow-countrymen.

De Germania is nevertheless of first importance for the study of the protohistory of Europe; it contains much information about the way of life and beliefs of people of Celtic Iron Age culture, upon which few details are to be found elsewhere. Tacitus is the first historian to have described the part played by marshes in the religion and the jurisprudence of Germania.

According to Tacitus, every year the tribes living in what are now Denmark and north Germany made sacrifices of servants or slaves to Nerthus, goddess of spring and fertility; after cleaning the statue and chariot of the divinity the fettered victims were plunged into the waters of a marsh or lake. In other contexts Germanic law laid down two kinds of capital punishment: hanging for traitors and deserters, and drowning for those guilty of cowardice, rape or unnatural practices. Corpses found lately in bogs of northern and central Europe seem to confirm these particulars.

It is likely that similar discoveries have been made for centuries by those working the peat bogs. Not knowing the period at which death had occurred they would notify the priest or pastor, who would give Christian burial to the bodies. In 1835 human remains exhumed from the peat caught the attention of the prehistorians for the first time; it was realized that these remains had been preserved because the presence of tannic acid and exclusion of oxygen had prevented putrefaction.

Up to the present about one hundred and fifty corpses have been taken from the peat bogs of what was once Germania and from areas formerly populated by Celts and Balts. These anonymous victims had all met a violent end; most are naked, shackled and wearing a sort of garotte round the neck; sometimes the throat has been cut or the skull broken with some blunt weapon. A girl of about fourteen found in a bog in Schleswig-Holstein was wearing a bandage over her eyes and the left side of the head had been shaven; not far off lay a man, strangled with a twig of hazel. The most complete body was that of a man found in 1950 in the Tollund peat bog in Denmark; a leather noose was round his neck and he wore a leather cap and belt. His head has been carefully preserved, and examination of the body revealed the last meal of this Iron Age man to have been entirely vegetarian.

Specialists have long puzzled over these primitive killings, but no satisfactory explanation has yet been provided. Probably they are, as Tacitus reports, of executed criminals or victims sacrificed to the goddess Nerthus. Among other female bodies is that of a clothed woman fixed to the bottom with stakes; she was taken from a bog in Jutland.

It may readily be imagined that these places of execution filled later generations with terror, and it was only a few centuries ago that man began, very timidly at first, to turn marshes and bogs to account, to drain and clear and plant them. Such cultivation brought the settlers no more than momentary rewards. In various times and countries marshes have had a dubious reputation; vagabonds, delinquents, prisoners and others whom authority wished to segregate were sent there to hard labour.

In 1765 an edict of Frederick the Great declared the marshes of East Frisia a Prussian possession. Special commissioners installed there in the following decades twenty thousand paupers and 'social misfits'. These raw colonists were supposed to burn the vegetation, dig the ground and plant cereals. The experiment ended in fiasco. We know today that such a result was inevitable and that the practice of clearing land by burning brings with it the destruction of the soil. The wretched colonists entrusted with the clearance of the East Frisian marshes were forced, in order to survive, to become brigands and beggars. Only at the beginning of the nineteenth century was an end put to this disastrous situation.

At all periods sphagnum moss has been dried and used as fuel in areas devoid of timber, but it was not until the thirteenth and fourteenth centuries that a small country, poor in wood but rich in bog, marsh and lake, revealed to the world a large-scale technique of peat-cutting and its possible results. The Netherlands, formed very largely of river deltas, has much low-lying land and from remote times the coastal areas have been constantly threatened by the sea. From the twelfth to the fifteenth century the Dutch lost in this way one fifth of their territory. At all times the Dutch have been forced to struggle obstinately in order to conquer and then to hold their fields. Thus they achieved a rare mastery of agriculture, horticulture and the regeneration of waterlogged ground. They defended themselves by building dikes and embankments and by digging canals to facilitate the outflow of salt or brackish water, so injurious to cultivation. The water was raised by pumps worked by hand and then, from the seventeenth century, by the windmills whose outlines have become a part of the landscape. The Dutch took advantage also of their 'amphibian' situation, and became a nation of fishermen, sailors and traders. And as the resources of their country were limited, despite such efforts, they sought in the East and West Indies the riches which Holland could not provide.

But those measures did not suffice to replace the agricultural land lost to the sea, and so the peasants looked toward the moors. They cut the turf and sold it to the townsfolk for fuel, thereby increasing the danger; for the trenches and pits filled and created new stretches of standing water which could not drain away.

In the north-east they grappled with the problem differently. The floods of 1287 had claimed 50,000 victims in the area between the mouth of the Ems and the Zuider Zee; those of 1421 twice as many. So two centuries before Dutch overseas trade and colonization reached their zenith the people of Groningen 'occupied' their neighbouring wastelands. They excavated canals allowing ships access to the peat bogs, and as they had no desire to create new lakes and ponds but wanted, on the contrary, agricultural land, they linked together the extraction of the peat, land drainage and the growing of crops. First they made an intricate canal system, after which they could take up the peat without causing the trenches to fill with water. Then, when the layer of peat had been removed, the ground was divided among the settlers—with the obligation to develop it. The rules were strict: nothing might be burned, and it was compulsory to till and manure the soil, to keep the canals and runnels clean, and to plant hedges and trees as wind-breaks. The general adoption of such methods gradually changed the face of Holland.

The example of Groningen was copied by other districts with

peat bogs to exploit. Villages grew up in the newly fertile areas. Sale of the turf provided the settlers with the capital needed for increasing the network of canals; ships plied upon the watercourses, fetching manures and taking away the dried peat and the produce of the harvests. The success stimulated similar undertakings in other districts.

The achievements of Dutch engineers in reclaiming their inundated coastal areas need no emphasis. But it is easy to forget that many of the prosperous, clean, attractive Dutch towns and villages, the green pasture lands with their cattle, the fields of tulips, the bright parks, have been largely won back from the former marshes. Rehabilitation of the waterlogged soil made the fortune of this little country which has fought so valiantly and successfully against the encroachment of river and sea.

PART FOUR

WATER MAKES HISTORY

Look! Here is water,
The liquid of life:
May water and life be
           your portion!
           Prayer of the Polynesians of Hawaii

CHAPTER ONE

SHELL MOUNDS AND SEAFARERS

HOWEVER systematically archaeological digs are conducted, many of the prehistorians' discoveries have been made by chance. Since it is not possible to ransack the face of the whole world to find stone implements, burial places or other relics, it is to be hoped that when someone turns up something unusual he will be intelligent enough to inform the specialists.

Such a man was one Olsen, owner of Meilgaard Farm in north-east Jutland. In 1849, having decided to cut a road through his property, he told the workmen to dig into a mound near the seashore, covered with trees and brushwood. He believed it to contain gravel, but instead of gravel the labourers found beneath the top-soil a bed of shells over seven feet thick. Olsen was not disheartened; suitably pounded and crushed the shells would help to form a solid roadway. The fact of their being heaped was in no way surprising: piles of empty shells lay scattered all along the northern coasts of Denmark. But Olsen rubbed his eyes when the workmen brought out of this layer of shells flint implements, animals' bones and a four-toothed comb of bone, finely worked and pierced. Olsen sent the comb to the National Museum in Copenhagen.

It was a fortunate decision, for the packet was opened by Jens Jacob Asmussen Worsaae, a pioneer of prehistoric research. His interest roused, he began to wonder whether the sporadic heaps of shells along the Danish coasts might not be the work of primitive man. He immediately sent out a working party with instructions to make an inventory of the contents of several well known shell mounds. He himself went to Meilgaard Farm, to talk to Olsen, and had the good luck to discover in the mound several finds of the greatest interest.

He found that the oyster and mussel shells had been deliberately opened by people intending to eat the contents. Flint tools, polished and pointed antlers, bones from which the marrow had been scraped out, potsherds and cinders were brought out one after the other. All the evidence tallied: the piles of shells were the remains of meals left in heaps by men who fed upon molluscs collected at low tide. To what period should they be assigned? In his report Worsaae wrote cautiously: 'It seems permissible to suppose that this spot was one at which the local inhabitants of a very early period were wont to meet and have their meals.'

He was to be proved right. In the course of the next few years, especially in the 1890s, Danish prehistorians studied the problem of the shell mounds and concluded that they dated beyond all doubt from the Middle Stone Age. In addition to the shells of oysters, mussels and cockles the mounds included those of crustaceans and snails, the bones of fish, ducks and other birds, particularly sea birds, and those of seals, dolphins, deer, wild pig, lynxes, wolves and smaller mammals. Some had apparently been gnawed by dogs, from which Johannes Steenstrup deduced that the inhabitants of the period had owned domesticated canines. The implements were of stone, horn or antler; none of the sites contained either metal objects or any indication of the contemporary existence of agriculture or pastoral life.

The most recent dating gives the Danish *kjøkkenmøddingen* ('kitchen middens') an antiquity of seven thousand years, a period when the North Sea was encroaching on the land and Denmark was finally separated from Sweden. Nor are those piles unique; the *concheros* of Spain and Portugal, the *sambaquis* of Brazil, the monticules along the coasts of South Africa, Australia and Japan all show that the inhabitants of the land masses settled everywhere by the sea and fed upon the creatures of the beaches. It is clear that the people of the shell mounds did not live entirely upon molluscs; they fished, gathered fruit and berries too, and, like their forbears, hunted in the coastal forests. The new fact is that they scarcely left the littoral; squatting there they built shelters and huts, and thus from generation to generation refuse—shells, bones—piled up close by the settlements. Some of the mounds were raised over a period of a thousand years.

Archaeology has revealed also that men who fished and hunted reached the coast of northern Scandinavia and settled along the shoreline when the sea level was several hundred feet above its present level—perhaps as early as 7000 B.C. The remains of this Komsa culture (which lasted several thousand years) so far discovered are confined to stone tools and implements, but these include arrowheads and axes. Where did these people come from?

Many theories have been put forward, assigning them origins in central Russia, Siberia or the north European plain, and postulating a variety of routes by which tribes trekked through forests or down rivers to reach the Arctic coast. Professor Anders Hagen,* however, summarizing the evidence with proper caution, infers that 'these tribes of Finnmark were the most northerly of all the known groups of the Early Stone Age', and that they may more plausibly be associated with the contemporary or earlier coastal settlements of the hunting-fishing Fosna culture numerous around the fjords north and south of Trondheim. Hence, a coastwise route up the length of Norway to the Arctic seems the most probable.

It is reasonable to conclude that, as the ice withdrew, men of the post-glacial period followed the herds of wild animals as these slowly moved north with the shifting belts of vegetation. People who had lived by hunting the creatures of the tundra, such as reindeer, would not readily adapt to forest living, and in any case there was no sudden change in conditions. Did these Old Stone Age people already have boats? It is tempting to think so. Among the rock carvings of Scandinavia, generally ascribed to an unspecified period in the Stone Age, is a group at Tysfjord, south of Narvik, showing reindeer and other animals and the unmistakable outline of a whale, about twenty-five feet long. The question arises: was man capable of hunting the whale in the Early Stone Age?

Such hunting cannot, of course, be thought of apart from boats. Rock engravings have been found in which figure small primitive craft, whales, dolphins and seals. In shape these boats are suggestive of the *umiaks*, or skin boats, manned by Eskimo women. The first, or at least early, colonists of the Norwegian and Arctic coasts could have made them from reindeer skins stretched over a framework of wood. If, in such fragile boats, they ventured into the ocean and harpooned the mammals of the sea, the first stage of the conquest by man of the ocean, so fraught with consequences, may date back beyond the Mesolithic shell-mound period.

The next maritime civilization of northern Europe belongs to the Bronze Age, by which time man had long risked himself upon the sea. It is appropriate to mention that culture here, for it too has endured through rock engravings. In southern Scandinavia there are rock slabs, polished by the friction of ice, which carry drawings of scenes from the daily life of a population practising agriculture

* *Norway*. Thames and Hudson, 1967.

and fishery at the same time: there are husbandmen, hunters, domestic animals, two-wheeled carts, sledges and, above all, rowing or sailing ships singly or in groups. When these drawings were discovered is uncertain, for the local peasants have known them all their lives. Even so, prudish passers-by used to avert their gaze, scandalized at the attributes given to the male figures. Prehistorians assign these drawings to the Early Bronze Age, making them three to four thousand years old.

With their curved keels, their bows and sterns high above the water, and their decorated prows, some of the ships are deceptively like those of the Vikings. They are, it is true, without masts or sails; on the other hand some appear to be decked, and there are indications that those vessels were provided with benches for the oarsmen. A prominently placed 'solar wheel', or disk, figures in nearly every picture, a sign that the farmers and sailors of the early Bronze Age worshipped the sun, which they regarded as the emblem of life.

The artists of the ship and sun-disk engravings were most likely direct ancestors of the Vikings, those first great navigators of Europe who, in the ninth century A.D., made an abrupt appearance upon almost all the coasts of Europe before flinging themselves upon northern Africa, the Middle East, the shores of the White Sea and, later, Greenland and North America. As far as it can be placed historically, the heyday of the Vikings began about A.D. 800. Now the rock engravings found in southern Scandinavia reveal that this area was already inhabited, several thousands of years ago, by tribes and communities who owned high-sea ships propelled by oars. Certain details in the drawings suggest also that those sun-worshippers may have already known the British Isles, the Iberian peninsula and the shores of the Mediterranean. If this is so the rise of the Vikings was no beginning, but the glorious epilogue to countless voyages of discovery.

We know what the Viking long-ships looked like, because the Vikings buried their kings and chiefs—and queens—in the hull of the ship they had used during their lifetime: arms, clothing, jewels, horses, dogs and provisions accompanied the dead into the after-world. Some thirty ship burials have so far been identified and excavated. As La Varende writes in his *Navigation sentimentale*, the long-ships brought to light 'are among the most perfect achievements that ever left shipwrights' hands'. Measuring up to eighty feet in length the long-ships were decked, had central mast and square sail, and their raised stem and sternposts were elaborately carved, often with 'dragons' or other frightening figures.

It was in this kind of ship that Erik the Red and seamen from Iceland sailed in 982 to Greenland. There they established several settlements which maintained regular relations with Iceland and Norway until the fifteenth century, when with a deterioration of the climate they fell victims to scurvy and other diseases and gradually disappeared. From Greenland the Vikings pushed on to the west and south-west and reached, nearly five hundred years before Christopher Columbus, the coasts of the New World. Bjarni Herjulfson was probably the first European to sight the American shores (c. 985); first to set foot on the beaches of 'Vinland' (c. 1000, probably in the neighbourhood of Cape Cod) was Leif Eriksson, son of Erik the Red. The first colonies founded by the Vikings on the coast of the New World held their own for some time. The archives of the Vatican contain documents supporting the theory that the Scandinavian settlements—or perhaps seasonal lumber camps—in Vinland were, in the fourteenth century, sending timber to the colonies of treeless Greenland and paying their dues to Rome.

Arctic rock engravings and Mesolithic shell mounds, Bronze Age pictures with sun-god insignia and voyages of exploration by the Vikings are all typical staging-points in the long evolution which brought the human race to impose its law upon the seas. Some six thousand years elapsed between the piling of shells upon the beach at Meilgaard by hunter-fishers and the 'discovery' of America by Leif Eriksson. During those six millennia other shores, those of the Mediterranean, of the Persian Gulf, the northern coast of the Indian Ocean, of south-east and eastern Asia, witnessed a similar development. Aboard rafts of tree-trunks, reeds or inflated skins, in dug-outs, skiffs, kayaks and sailing-boats man ventured forth upon the ocean; he pushed back the frontiers of his living space and reached isles and coasts where he settled and bred. Then, with rowing or sailing boats, he gradually enlarged the sphere of his investigation until, when he had learned to build vessels for the high seas, he dared to go out and conquer distant lands.

CHAPTER TWO

THE LAKE DWELLERS

AT A TIME when the ocean shores were mostly unpopulated, man had already taken possession of the inland waters. The nomad hunters of the Old Stone Age very often found their way barred by rivers large and small. They could halt upon the banks, fishing and pursuing the aquatic birds, but they wanted to cross the water in order to see what lay upon the other side. From Early Palaeolithic times onward, therefore, pioneers used tree trunks or bundles of branches for crossing rivers.

By the Neolithic period man had command of cutting tools and of fire, and he used them to hollow out the trunks of trees. Thus was born the canoe, that almost unsinkable vessel, ideal for river navigation and still used by millions in all the continents. It extended the range of settlement sites, for the man who owns and can paddle a canoe is able not only to go where he will upon most waterways but also, in case of need, to make his domicile on the islands and shores of lakes and rivers.

In 1853 the peasants owning fields alongside the lakes of Switzerland congratulated themselves upon an exceptionally dry winter; everywhere the low level of the water made it possible to encroach upon the lakes and increase the area of cultivated ground. Indeed an immemorial custom required them in such circumstances to dam the dried-up inlets and fill them with mud taken from the lake. In the spring of 1854 they set about their task, but in many places their work was impeded by strange obstacles, clusters of stakes driven into the lake bottom and forming a sort of palisade two or three hundred yards from the shore. The stakes were stout and from six to a dozen feet in length. To remove them would have taken time and required heavy toil. So they confined themselves to removing the mud between the stakes, which they wisely left alone.

They went down with their buckets, cursing the Romans for having stupidly barricaded 'their' lake. At first no one noticed that the mud contained implements of stone, wood and bone, and all were astonished when one of the workmen brought back in his pail things that looked like ornaments of bronze. Knowing that schoolmasters and museum officials were interested in Roman relics, the Swiss peasants informed them. Thus it came about, in March and April 1854, that the schools and municipal offices in the townships by the lakes of Zürich, Pfäffikon, Biel, Neuchâtel and others were invaded by peasants who brought with them their miscellaneous collections.

Although Switzerland had no professional archaeologists at that time, some of the amateurs were quick to realize that these objects were not Roman. As Johannes Aeppli, schoolmaster at Obermeilen on Lake Zürich, declared, 'They must come from the most ancient inhabitants of our country.' Inspired by curiosity, Aeppli the schoolmaster, Ferdinand Keller, teacher of English, Friedrich Schwab, a town councillor of Biel, the notary Emanuel Müller-Haller and several other local notabilities came to inspect the newly discovered palisades. They engaged workmen to rake the bed of the lake with shovels, dredges, tongs and cramps; each clod of mud was broken to pieces. At the end of some weeks the harvest was impressive: stone and bronze axes, graving-tools, knives, daggers of hardened wood, spoons, needles, awls of horn and bone, potsherds, vestiges of cloth, of nets, of baskets and mats, the bones of wild and of domestic animals, piles of grain, nuts and apples. This was proof that the stakes driven into the mud were the supports of platforms upon which prehistoric men had built their dwellings.

The discovery caused a stir, for its magnitude exceeded that of any other collection of prehistoric finds. The Swiss lakes had provided the prehistorian with tools, arms, household utensils, skulls, bones, and had enabled the world for the first time to envisage the homes and daily life of a community in the distant past. Keller and Schwab—after the discoveries in Lake Zürich and Lake Neuchâtel they had resigned their posts in order to devote themselves to prehistory—recalled that there were villages on piles in Indonesia, New Guinea and some parts of central Africa. To protect themselves, their families and their property against wild beasts and attack by enemies, the inhabitants erected platforms over water or marsh. Everything showed that the construction of the lakeside villages of Switzerland had been dictated by similar requirements.

A selection of objects taken from the Swiss lakes was placed on view in Paris during the Universal Exhibition of 1867. It gave the general public an opportunity to acquaint itself with the relics of the lakeside dwellers, as well as with flint implements, sculptures and incised drawings of the Old Stone Age, newly found in France. All Europe was agog for prehistory. True, the precise antiquity of the lakeside villages was not known, but fresh discoveries followed —remains on the shores of Lake Constance, of the Bavarian lakes, of the marshes of Swabia, in eastern France, northern Italy and Austria. By the close of the exhibition the number of recorded lakeside settlements was exactly two hundred.

Thanks to the devoted labours of the Swiss prehistorians and museum officials, scale models of these villages on piles were soon available, showing how the huts, with walls of wattle and daub or split timbers, clay floors and thatched roofs, had been erected on platforms and how the occupants had lived and worked—grinding corn, making tools and pottery, spinning, weaving, preparing animal hides, cooking. Subsequent years of drought revealed the remains of more lake villages, and in 1927 one was even reconstructed on its original site at Unteruhldingen on the German side of Lake Constance. Narrow gangways or dikes linked the settlements to the shore and its stretch of fields won from the forest, in which the lake villagers had used stone axes for cutting down the trees. They grew barley, beans, flax and wheat, and kept oxen, pigs, goats and sheep. The discovery of traces of roomy cattle pens may indicate that the livestock spent the night in the safety of the village.

The accuracy of the reconstruction has been disputed; and not all the experts agree that the dwellings were built over water, contending rather that the piles and platforms supported the huts over spits of marshy ground. Undeniably, however, the people chose a watery environment for the settlements, many of which were continuously occupied for a long period.

The culture of the lake dwellers differed essentially from that of the food-gathering hunters. The inhabitants of the lakeside villages certainly continued to hunt, and they fished in the pools and gathered wild fruits; but they were first and foremost tillers of the soil and pastoralists. They lived, not in small family groups or clans, but in large village communities; it has been estimated that there were five thousand people in the one discovered on the shores of Lake Neuchâtel. Their agricultural skills enabled them to produce and store enough grain to last from one harvest to the next; their cereals and some of their domesticated animals were not native to Europe. Nor would it have been possible to build those pile-dwellings without stable, steerable boats from which to drive the stakes into the mud and in which to transport the stones used for anchoring them. And when the hunting grounds close to the settlement had no more game, a flotilla of canoes could set out for the opposite shore.

Whence did these people come? At what period did they live? A few decades after the discovery of the Swiss lake villages it became possible to answer the second question: the oldest of them dated from Neolithic times, about 3000 B.C. But those lakeside settlements met so well the requirements of a farming population surrounded by forest-dwelling hunters that many of the sites were occupied into the Bronze Age and a few into Roman times. There is evidence of successive conflagrations, whether accidental or the result of attack by hostile neighbours, and of successive rebuilding. The way of life of the lake dwellers did not alter greatly, but later generations had horses, cultivated vines and fermented the pressed grapes in terracotta vessels.

The arrival of these alien immigrants around the bigger lakes of Europe is part of the larger story of the 'Neolithic Revolution' which prehistorians and archaeologists have patiently pieced together. While the scattered populations of Europe were still at Palaeolithic or Mesolithic stages of development, in the Near East a new way of life had developed from about 7000 B.C.: farming communities living in permanent villages. Their superior stone implements, especially axes, enabled them to clear and cultivate land for growing a variety of good crops and herding domesticated animals; their improved weapons made the hunting of game more rewarding. A supply of food in excess of immediate needs furthered the development of crafts and specialist craftsmen. These farmers flourished and, seeking new territories, penetrated slowly into south-east Europe with their Neolithic culture, some by way of the Danube Valley.

Although they could hardly have offered organized resistance, the indigenous people were probably hostile to the immigrants who settled in their hunting and fishing grounds; perhaps the natives regarded domesticated cattle as 'fair game', and raided the new settlements even if they did not often openly attack. But a village built out over marsh or water would give the farmers the twofold advantage of a good defensive site and no loss of hard-won cultivable land.

In time the older peoples were displaced or absorbed as the Neolithic culture spread across the whole of Europe. In time also, by similar stages, were introduced the use of metals, the wheel, sailing ships and many other new techniques originating in the Bronze Age river-valley civilizations of Mesopotamia and Egypt.

CHAPTER THREE

'MAKE THEE AN ARK OF GOPHER WOOD'

IN THE THIRTIES of the last century an impecunious young man learning to become a solicitor in his uncle's London office was finding it difficult to keep his mind on dry legal texts. He was restless and longed to travel, above all to see the lands described in *The Thousand and One Nights*, which had stimulated his imagination since he was a boy. In 1839 he set out to travel overland to Ceylon, but he did not reach the Far East. Austen Henry Layard, soon to achieve fame as an archaeologist and later to become Member of Parliament, Minister of the Crown and ambassador, spent most of the next ten years excavating the mounds of the ancient cities of Nineveh and Calah (Nimrud). What he found there belonged to a period far older than that of the caliphs.

Most important perhaps were the thousands of tablets, inscribed with cuneiform characters, which he uncovered in the library of King Assurbanipal at Nineveh and which, more than anything else, have enabled scholars to build up our present knowledge of the Assyrian and Babylonian world. Hormuzd Rassam, Layard's former assistant who from 1852 carried on the excavations at Nineveh, found among those tablets a version of the Flood older than the biblical narrative, the beginning of which runs as follows:

Make thee an ark of gopher wood; rooms shalt thou make in the ark, and shalt pitch it within and without with pitch. And this is the fashion which thou shalt make it of: The length of the ark shall be three hundred cubits, the breadth of it fifty cubits, and the height of it thirty cubits. A window shalt thou make to the ark, and in a cubit shalt thou finish it above; and the door of the ark shalt thou set in the side thereof; with lower, second, and third stories shalt thou make it. And, behold, I, even I, do bring a flood of waters upon the earth, to destroy all flesh. . . . But with thee will I establish my covenant; and thou shalt come into the ark. . . .

To judge from this account in Genesis, Noah's ark was a floating home planned with much thought and large enough to receive a numerous clan, its livestock and the necessary provisions, rather than a complete zoological collection. Had such ships really existed in prehistoric times? And what lay behind this diluvial legend? The excavations at Nineveh allowed a corner of the curtain to be lifted for the first time and helped to clear up some of the mystery in which the Flood was wrapped. Some of the tablets, which were sent to the British Museum, contained extracts from the earliest known great epic poem of humanity, the story of the tyrant, hero and demi-god Gilgamesh, and narrated episodes of a catastrophic deluge in much more detail than is given in Genesis.

Many years were needed for the deciphering of the cuneiform script. It was George Smith of the British Museum who in 1872 unravelled the Gilgamesh epic—with growing wonder, for the correspondence with Genesis was amazing. But the texts were not complete, and Smith himself went out to Nineveh in 1873 and again in 1874 to seek the missing portions in the ruins of the King's library. He was successful, but died on his way home in 1876 at the early age of 36. With the deciphering of the Gilgamesh epic the world learned, to the confusion of some and the joy of others, of the existence of a story of the Creation earlier than that of the Bible and bearing a striking resemblance to the account in Genesis. The Hebrew authors of the Old Testament had apparently dipped into a source of legends common to both texts.

Noah's counterpart in the epic of Gilgamesh, Utnapishtim, advised by the god Ea also builds a ship which he covers with pitch inside and out; and 'all I possessed I laded aboard her . . . into the ship I embarked all my kindred and family . . . cattle and beasts of the field. . . .' For six days and nights hurricane, deluge and tempest swept the land; when the seventh day came, 'assuaged was the deluge, so did I look on the day . . . all human back to its clay was returned, and fen was level with roof-tree . . . into the distance I gazed, to the furthest bounds of the ocean, land was upreared at twelve points, and the Ark on the Mountain of Nisir grounded.' * Then Utnapishtim releases one after the other a dove,

---

* From the translation by R. Campbell Thompson, 1928.

a swallow and a raven. The raven discovers that the waters have abated, and finds food to eat. Utnapishtim leaves the Ark and makes a sacrifice to the gods.

The epic of Gilgamesh, which dates from the Sumerians, was taken up and copied by the Babylonians, the Assyrians, the Hittites and the other nations of the Near East, who completed it and touched it up. Most of it refers to the multi-millenary struggle between the people of northern and southern Mesopotamia. In the course of the centuries the legends centred upon kings; gods and heroes were woven in. Then, at a time which the most recent research places in the second millennium before Christ, the legend of the Flood was incorporated in the epic of Gilgamesh: it had been known five thousand years ago to the river people of the lower Euphrates.

Now Genesis specifies that Abraham, progenitor of the Hebrew people, was born at Ur, a Sumerian town situated on the lower Euphrates, and it seems reasonable to infer that it was he who introduced the legend of the Flood into the future Promised Land. Later, when the Hebrews began to write the history of their nation, they included with other traditions of foreign provenance this one relating to a disastrous flood, quite inconceivable in a dry country such as Palestine. It meant something entirely different in an area as subject to inundation as the Euphrates valley.

Almost all peoples living close to the banks of large rivers have flood legends. The Edda of Scandinavia, the Vedas of India, the myths of Persia and China, of the Eskimos and Polynesians, all tell of deluges which drowned mankind; lesser risings of the water figure in the myths of the Incas, the Mayas and the Aborigines of Australia. As Alexander von Humboldt reported, the Indians of the Orinoco spoke of legendary ancestors who 'at the time of the great waters' were said to have reached mountain peaks in their canoes. The natives of Fiji—much as in the epic of Gilgasmesh or in the Old Testament—attribute the mythological flood to divine punishment. On the other hand nations which have virtually no contact with the water, such as the inhabitants of Central Asia or the Berbers of Africa, have no knowledge of this sort of legend.

Certain parallels among the flood traditions of the various peoples supported for a time the belief of orthodox theologians in one universal and extirpating flood. Setting the theological and geological data side by side, some scientists dally with the possibility of a flood at the end of the Ice Age, brought about by the melting of the ice and by excessive rainfall, the recollection of which, perpetuated in human memory, might have taken shape in the religious myths.

Nobody believes any longer in a universal deluge. Most experts consider that the diluvial legends grew up independently of one another, based upon high waters rising locally at different periods. The parallels are more apparent than real. Nothing is more human than to accord to each disastrous flood the dimensions of a cataclysm, to see in it divine punishment and thereafter to glorify the forbears who, with the aid of arks or boats or rafts, escaped destruction.

Nearly eighty years after the first tablets recording the epic of Gilgamesh were brought to light another British archaeologist, Sir Leonard Woolley, was excavating the town of Ur, birthplace of Abraham and more than five thousand years old. Forty feet down he found a layer of alluvium nearly eight feet thick, plain evidence of an exceptional flood. Woolley compared this fact with the details given in the Old Testament and the epic of Gilgamesh, as well as with the tables of the kings of Sumeria which mentioned ten kings 'before the flood' and named those who had lived 'after the flood'. From these he concluded that the high waters which had laid waste the valleys of the Tigris and the Euphrates and annihilated the civilization of Sumeria were those referred to in Genesis.

Most historians and archaeologists have since adopted Woolley's views. Some of the countless floods which have ravaged Mesopotamia were probably so sudden that only the Sumerians, who had boats, survived. After the fall of the waters those who had escaped, the forerunners of Utnapishtim-Noah, settled again in the valley of the Tigris or Euphrates, founding fresh dynasties and taking literally the injunction of God to his people to be fruitful and multiply. But, more particularly, they saw to it that towns and villages were protected from further floods and obliged their subjects to build protective dikes.

Mesopotamia, the land of the flood, became also the cradle of a great civilization. Within the flood plains, under the double incentive of controlling winter inundation and conserving water for use in summer drought, the Sumerians transformed the branches of the rivers into canals. They built their cities upon mounds, put up embankments and made fields or grazing land on the fertile soil. Their successors, the Babylonians and Assyrians, dug canals several hundred miles long, made hanging gardens and invented several types of boat: rafts of inflated skins, vessels coated with pitch, ships of trade or war propelled by oars. It was from Mesopotamia that the wheel, the chariot, bronze, agriculture, cattle-breeding, hydraulics and navigation spread into the Near East.

Civilizations based on water throve also upon the banks of two other great rivers, the Indus and the Nile. There is much still to be learned about the culture of the Indus Valley, the remains of which were first excavated at Harappa in 1922 and at Mohenjo-Daro in 1924 by the British archaeologist Sir John Marshall, but the existence of close ties between it and the Sumerian civilization is by no means ruled out. The digs made at Mohenjo-Daro and Harappa show that some five thousand years ago the towns of the Indus valley were provided with locks, wells, cisterns and baths. The conquerors of the future, Persians, Aryans, Arabs and Mongols, were to construct all over India canals, aqueducts, dams and dikes of which many would be built upon sites dating from the dawn of history. India's water network was dismembered three hundred years ago after the disorders leading to the collapse of the Mogul Empire.

In the same way much Egyptian engineering work was carried out in order to conserve the waters of the Nile. Besides the dikes and locks, the Pharaohs had built four thousand years ago one of the largest reservoirs in history by embanking Lake Moeris in the Fayum depression. It has been calculated that it was then some two hundred and fifty square miles in area, and it stored a volume of water permitting the irrigation for a whole year of all the cultivated areas in the Nile delta. The Egyptians also dug canals connecting the river with the Red Sea. The unfinished canal dug about 600 B.C. in the reign of the Pharaoh Necho II cost, according to Herodotus, the lives of about one hundred and twenty thousand slaves.

Peoples able to control great rivers would not come to a halt at the coast for long, and the prospect of mastering the sea would surely have appealed to them. It is not known for certain whether there was regular contact by sea between the Indus and Sumeria (the Sumerian cities were nearer to the open sea than are their mounds today; in the intervening millennia the Tigris and Euphrates have extended their deposits of silt, shortening the head of the Persian Gulf considerably), but it is certainly possible, and there are also some indications of sea traffic between India and East Africa in very ancient times.

But setting aside such conjectures, the first voyages of discovery are to be attributed to Egyptian seafarers. In the reign of the Fifth-Dynasty Pharaoh Sahu-Re, oared ships with square sails passed along the coasts of the Red Sea and tied up in the 'Land of Punt', which might have been the present-day Eritrea or much farther south along the coast of East Africa. In the fifteenth century B.C., by order of the Eighteenth-Dynasty Queen Hatshepsut, a fleet of large ships, which passed from the Nile by canal into the Red Sea, was sent on a very successful commercial expedition to the Land of Punt.

Soon the slim, swifter ships of the Phoenicians, the supreme traders of antiquity, had command of the commercial traffic of the Mediterranean. Their cedar-wood vessels ventured much farther than had those of their trading predecessors of the Eastern Mediterranean, the Cretans. These were the 'ships of Tarshish' (Tartessus) and their bold captains could navigate out of sight of land. The Phoenicians established colonies on the shores and islands of the Mediterranean such as Carthage, Rhodes, Cyprus, Cadiz, Cagliari, and depots on the perimeter of the Indian Ocean; they sent out expeditions to West Africa, the Cassiterides or 'Tin Islands' (Scillies?) and the Canary archipelago as well as organizing overland trade with the Orient. Phoenician ships were chartered by the Pharaoh Necho II about 600 B.C. to make the first circumnavigation of Africa, a feat which (according to Herodotus) they successfully accomplished in three years.

It is likely that a mere fragment of the achievements of Phoenician and Carthaginian navigators is known to us today. The Phoenicians left almost no documents regarding their sailors' voyages; on the other hand they had the pleasant habit of circulating in the ancient world terrifying reports of the wildness of the distant seas, populated by monsters, thus discouraging potential competitors. Nearly all that is known of the maritime exploits of Phoenicia and Carthage comes from Egyptian inscriptions, the Old Testament, Greek chronicles and Latin texts. Thus it may well be that those sailors knew the North Sea and had seen the kinds of ship used by those living in the Bronze Age of Scandinavia; nor is it impossible that Pytheas of Massilia, the first to describe the northern regions, travelled in a Phoenician ship. Some scholars even suggest that, fifteen hundred or two thousand years before Leif Eriksson, Phoenician seamen had discovered the route to the New World.

We are rather better informed about the expedition organized jointly in 945 B.C. by Hiram I, King of Tyre, and King Solomon, in which Phoenician ships, built at and sailing from a Red Sea port in the territory of the Hebrew monarch, set out for 'Ophir' and brought back 'four hundred and fifty talents of gold' to embellish the temple at Jerusalem. The famous Ophir is one of those fabulous places which have perplexed generations of historians. It has been identified with southern Arabia, with Persia, India, Malaysia, South Africa and even with the continent of America. But most of the clues suggest that biblical Ophir is no other than the 'Land of Punt' of the Egyptians, a region of East Africa.

About a century after the first Phoenician circumnavigation of Africa, the Carthaginian admiral Hanno fitted out a fleet of sixty galleys, each propelled by fifty oarsmen, to encircle Africa in the opposite direction. He took thirty thousand colonists as passengers; probably he planned to establish bases on carefully chosen sites and by this means to establish, as far as it could be done, Punic hegemony in the Dark Continent.

Hanno's narrative, found by the historian Polybius in the archives of the temple of Baal after the destruction of Carthage, is among the most thrilling documents devoted to Africa. For even though they were obliged to turn back after reaching the latitudes of the Cameroons or Gabon, the Carthaginian sailors observed far more than all their European successors down to the age of the great discoveries. Hanno describes impressively the virgin forests, the camp fires, the language of the drums, the torrid heat, an eruption of the Cameroon volcano, the black warriors and the human-looking gorillas. Confronted by mysterious Africa he seems to have felt the respectful awe of the nineteenth-century explorers.

Thus from the mythical ark of Noah had sprung solid and sturdy sea-going ships, and the progress in navigation and naval construction opened to humanity, two thousand years or so before Columbus, the gates of a wider world. From now on man was no longer confined to coastal waters: he was able to plough the seas and become familiar with other parts of the globe. Many of the coastal peoples turned the new possibilities to account. With their triremes and their cargo boats the Etruscans, the Cretans and the Greeks travelled into every corner of the Mediterranean; ships made use of the monsoon winds to sail to India and back. With their long-ships the Scandinavians dominated the North Atlantic from America to the White Sea. Finally the Arabs, the greatest seafarers of the Middle Ages, raised navigation to the level of an art, making general the use of the compass and the astrolabe and the taking of bearings. Their feluccas, galleys, frigates and brigantines set off for Africa, India and China.

The man who seeks to discover archipelagos or distant coasts has no need of a boat of great tonnage. Before the time of the Incas the Indians of Peru, aboard rafts of balsa wood, reached Chile, the Galapagos Islands and perhaps even more distant areas of the Pacific. In the East Indies and Malaysia the natives still use bamboo rafts which are said to be unsinkable, and it was perhaps in vessels of this kind that mariners from south-east Asia first sailed to the discovery of the Indian and Pacific Oceans. The voyages of the *Kon-Tiki* and the *Tahiti Nui* have drawn attention to the possibilities of the raft, stable and manœuvrable even in heavy weather if provided with a centre-board.

Thor Heyerdahl, the Norwegian ethnologist, was convinced that the islands of Polynesia had been settled by people from South America. In 1947 he built *Kon-Tiki*, a raft of the type formerly used by the Indians of those coasts; it was made of balsa trunks, and in it he sailed four thousand three hundred miles westward from Peru in order to prove the accuracy of his theory. Ten years later the Frenchman Eric de Bisschop covered an even greater distance but, unlike Heyerdahl, he was endeavouring to show that the southern Pacific could be crossed in the opposite direction and that South Sea islanders could just as easily have reached South America. Sailing a bamboo raft, the *Tahiti Nui*, from Tahiti, de Bisschop entrusted himself to the prevailing westerly winds and currents of the South Pacific. But as he neared the shores of Chile his craft was caught in a storm and severely damaged, and de Bisschop had to radio for help. Apart from this incident the two experiments proved that, provided full use is made of winds and currents, a determined crew in a simple but stout vessel is capable of crossing an ocean such as the Pacific from east to west or vice versa.

Heyerdahl's and de Bisschop's voyages are an excellent introduction to a description of migrations across the Pacific. A thousand or more years before Magellan's circumnavigation of the world the forbears of the very islanders in whom Heyerdahl and de Bisschop were interested had sailed its waters in every direction. They deserve the nickname 'children of the sea', for they have provided some of the world's greatest seafarers. Here, in the labyrinth of the Polynesian archipelagos, early navigation reached its zenith.

CHAPTER FOUR

THE CHILDREN OF THE SEA

NO PART of the world in which man has settled bears the impress of the sea more clearly or is more dependent upon seamanship than what geographers have aptly named Oceania. It is a vast area of the Pacific comprising about an eighth of the surface of the globe; but the land is no more than two per cent, and it is parcelled out in a seemingly endless scatter of islands and islets.

The men who first discovered and colonized the more easterly islands, Polynesia, must already have been practised seafarers; for a rare familiarity with the ways of the ocean, with the winds and currents, was required of those who ventured into the unknown. In the course of a thousand years or more the Polynesian explorers achieved many feats comparable, in their courage and their endurance, to that of Columbus's crossing of the Atlantic.

For the majority of European historians and naval chroniclers Christopher Columbus, son of a Genoese weaver, was the first who had the courage to abandon coastal waters and to head for the uncharted sea. This way of presenting the matter is unrealistic but flatters the European sense of superiority. Columbus accomplished something unique not because he ventured upon what none had dared before, but because he gave a fresh lead.

Fifteen hundred or two thousand years before Columbus—it is not possible to be more precise—seafaring people with light brown skins and straight black hair, living somewhere on the western shores of the Pacific, set out boldly eastwards into the ocean far from sight of any land to guide them. This colonizing enterprise was as far-reaching as that of the Conquistadores who followed in the wake of Columbus. But the opening up of Polynesia had no momentous consequences and the West has shown only belated interest in the history of this area on the other side of the globe. Hence the Polynesian voyages of discovery are generally accorded only a marginal reference in the story of world exploration.

Nevertheless the colonization of Polynesia forms one of the most pleasing chapters in the story of colonial expansion and, in contrast to what took place everywhere else, few blots have marred its pages. The newcomers shed no blood; there was no civilization to be destroyed or people to be subjugated, for the isles on which they landed were unpopulated. Later, after the arrival of fresh streams of immigrants, the inhabitants of the various islands quarrelled, and that was how the first occupants of New Zealand, the Moriois, were virtually exterminated by the Maori invaders. Cannibalism also took its toll. But such stains upon the history of Polynesia are trifling when compared with the slave trading, massacres and *autos-da-fé* attributable to other conquerors.

From the sixteenth century, or in other words from the time when ships conveying Europeans made their way into the vastness of the Pacific, the origins of the Polynesians and the nature of the various island civilizations have never ceased to arouse interest. Since they knew nothing of metal, the natives, as seen through western glasses, were living like men of the New Stone Age. Yet they dwelt in villages, reared cattle, grew vegetables, made artefacts, had shrines and temples and, in some of the islands, even raised gigantic statues; moreover they could move about in their outrigger-canoes with a swiftness incredible to European ship-builders until the nineteenth century. And finally they amounted to a cultural, ethnic and linguistic entity. From Tonga to Easter Island, from Hawaii to New Zealand, the Polynesians had the same appearance, the same religion, the same customs, the same grammar.

Could their culture have sprung from these isles and atolls, separated by hundreds and even thousands of miles? It seemed more likely that their progenitors had brought it from their native land, a mysterious country called in the native legends 'Hawaiki'. What country lies hidden behind this word? Hundreds of books have been devoted to the problem: the first Polynesians have been traced to Indonesia, the Philippines, Asia (Major and Minor), China, Japan, the Middle East and, since the exploit of *Kon-Tiki*, to South America.

The Polynesians are of a distinct physical type; their language has affinities with those of South-east Asia, especially Indonesia. Moreover their way of life and, above all, their maritime technique reveal an origin in South-east Asia. Thus, despite the arguments provided by Heyerdahl and others, authorities are almost unanimous in placing the fabulous 'Hawaiki' in the Malay peninsula or East Indian archipelago. This does not mean—for ethnologists are cautious people—that the ancestors of the Polynesians were cousins of the Malays; from a strictly racial point of view, they are closer to the Indo-Europeans. Nevertheless there is every indication that they lived a long time in southern Asia and that their language, their mode of life and skill as sailors developed there long before they ventured into the waters of the Pacific for reasons unknown.

Furthermore, the East Indian archipelago is the birthplace of that unusual craft, the sailing outrigger canoe, without which the conquest of the Polynesian mosaic would have been unthinkable. No galley or barque or raft of balsa or bamboo would have made it possible to reach and link together the thousands of islets, atolls and archipelagos with anything like the speed of these fragile craft which skim over the water at the slightest puff of wind. The canoe itself need be no more than an improved dug-out—a hollowed tree-trunk with wash-strakes added, shaped and decorated fore and aft—or it may be plank-built. It is the outrigger that makes the canoe a racing boat. A plank or shaped timber held parallel to the canoe by booms, the outrigger gives the craft stability and prevents it from capsizing. Thanks to it, a thirty-foot canoe of very narrow beam can carry a considerable area of sail, and before the wind, with the outrigger rising clear of the water, such a boat can achieve 15 to 20 knots. Since the outrigger must be kept to windward, the canoe is double-ended and sail and rigging must be similarly reversible, so that great skill is called for in handling and manœuvring the craft. The Pacific Islanders have developed a variety of styles and hull shapes on the same general principle, including single-ended canoes with a balancing pole or platform on the opposite side to the outrigger to act as counterpoise. A platform may be built over the booms connecting outrigger to canoe, or right across canoe and counterpoise as well, and a shelter or deck-house is often built on the platform. The greater the ballast the greater the area of sail that can be carried.

An alternative way to obtain stability is to lash two hulls together, thus producing a double canoe. Abel Tasman saw Maori double canoes in 1642, and Cook on his second voyage witnessed a remarkable assembly of war and transport double canoes at Tahiti: in three hundred and thirty vessels there were over seven thousand seven hundred men. Clearly, such craft could carry a considerable number of people over long distances from island to island.

Where trees of sufficient girth are available to provide timber for a broad-beamed canoe the outrigger is unnecessary to provide stability. Of such a type were some of the great war canoes of the Maoris drawn by the artist Sydney Parkinson who sailed on Cook's first voyage. Elaborately carved, they had a high sternpost and projecting figurehead at the prow, and carried up to a hundred warriors. Such craft survive today only for ceremonial purposes; but, since a canoe of whatever size is a valuable possession, the ancient Polynesian taboos and rites associated with choosing the timber and building and embellishing a canoe have by no means died out, and the names of vessels which made historic voyages have been preserved in legend.

It need scarcely be said that the builders of these canoes were (and are) good swimmers and most dexterous with the paddle, able to bring their craft safely through the surf pounding the reefs which surround so many of the islands. The Polynesians, and the Melanesians also, made charts with bamboo stems, fibres and shells which, together with celestial navigation, enabled them to make repeated return journeys between widely separated islands.

A glance at a map of South-east Asia explains why man developed and perfected the art of navigation in that part of the world. The land-bridge linking Asia with New Guinea and Australia collapsed in the Mesozoic and broke up into countless islands. Tribes and peoples which, in the course of thousands of years, made their way to the Sunda Islands, the Moluccas, the Philippines, Australia and Melanesia, were in need of boats. If it is correct that Australia was populated as early as seventy thousand years ago by dark-skinned, wavy-haired men, it was because those immigrants were already using boats and rafts. Otherwise the Australoid ancestors of the Australian and Tasmanian Aborigines would not have been able to cross the Timor Sea or the Torres Strait, even though these would have been much narrower than they are today.

The Negritos of the Philippines, the Papuans of New Guinea and of Melanesia, and the peoples who came after them, can also have spread into the islands only by sea; the Melanesians are in every respect excellent seamen and have no reason to envy their Polynesian neighbours. Thus it may well be that outrigger canoes coursed the sea several thousand years ago in the area bounded by Formosa, Timor, Sumatra and Micronesia. It is certain that sailors of Malayan stock played a decisive part in Asia and the Indian Ocean during the first years of the Christian era, and shortly afterwards Malay colonists with their wives and children crossed this ocean and settled in Madagascar, bringing with them weapons, implements and seed.

The voyages which brought Malayan people west to Madagascar may be compared to those which took the Polynesians to the islands and archipelagos of the Pacific, and they were on a vaster scale than the maritime achievements of the contemporary peoples of Europe and the Near East. Unfortunately almost nothing is known of them, although documents of Arab and Malay provenance suggest that, between the first and sixteenth centuries of our era, these seafarers made for Madagascar in four invading waves. Their ships must have been of considerable size, since they carried for four thousand miles animals which do not belong to the fauna of the island. The light-skinned Malagasies of today are their descendants.

Probably the Polynesians too, starting from 'Hawaiki' in their outrigger canoes, spread into the eastern Pacific in a series of expeditions. The Austrian ethnologist Robert von Heine Geldern estimates that the initial immigration took place in the first century B.C. The second outward expansion of about A.D. 400 carried them to the Society Islands, which became their centre and from which they reached Hawaii about fifty years later; then, between the seventh and the tenth century, the Polynesians took possession of the most important of the Pacific islands, which received a third Polynesian wave in the eleventh or twelfth century. The fourth migration occurred in the fourteenth century: setting out from the now over-populated islands of Polynesia a great fleet of canoes came round towards the south-west. The colonization of New Zealand by the Maoris, with their good organization and discipline, dates from this time. Many Maoris today trace their descent from these colonists and know the names of the vessels in which they sailed.

It is scarcely possible to appreciate the nautical prowess of the

Polynesians without some idea of the enormous distances they had to cover in their canoes. The Hawaiian islands, for instance, were discovered and settled by Polynesians from the Society Islands, over two thousand miles away. Almost the same distance separates New Zealand from Raiatea, one of the Society Islands and homeland of the Maoris. Easter Island was populated in the fourteenth century by Polynesians from the Marquesas Islands and Mangareva, over two thousand miles away across waters where land is extremely rare. The longest known voyage of modern times credited to an outrigger canoe was that made by natives of Mangareva who reached the atoll of Sikaiana, in the Solomon Islands, three thousand seven hundred and fifty miles to the west.

For fifteen hundred years at least, with or against the wind, the 'children of the sea' have ploughed the waters of the Pacific, setting their course by the winds and currents and the stars. During long crossings they fed on fish, dried fish, breadfruit, coconuts; their drinking water they stored in gourds.

This colonization of Oceania by men who knew neither metals nor the compass is truly a great epic, excelling the maritime feats of Phoenicians, Greeks and Romans. Only the colonial enterprises of the European powers have reached greater dimensions. And by 1492, the year marking the start of the great voyages of discovery, the navigators of Europe had behind them mathematical, nautical, technical and geographic traditions which had been maturing for hundreds of years. But the Polynesians remained primitives of latent tradition. As the historian Kurt von Boeckmann writes: 'Their achievement is unique and will remain so until the end of time.'

CHAPTER FIVE

ALL GREAT NEPTUNE'S OCEAN

'HE WHO dominates the sea holds the keys of trade. He who holds the keys of trade owns the riches of the world and is its master.' The seafaring nations knew this to be true long before Sir Walter Raleigh spoke the words; all of them took it to heart and strove to dominate as wide as possible an expanse of ocean as a prelude to their conquest of the globe. On the eve of the Renaissance man discovered 'space' and was dazzled; from then on he felt the need to push back the horizon ever further.

This need had manifested itself in Europe in the fifteenth century with the impetuosity of a landslide. The half-century of voyages and discoveries which followed that break with the past saw the birth also of new longings: a hunger to learn more and more, a thirst for exploration and unlimited possessions. The age of imperialism opened upon the waters.

What had the situation been just before the great discoveries? In the Arctic the Eskimos in their kayaks fished and hunted seals and whales; dug-out canoes skimmed the blue water of the Caribbean; the outrigger canoes of the Polynesians mastered the Pacific; making skilful use of the monsoon winds and the currents the Arabs scoured the coastlines of the Indian Ocean. The waters were the scene of much suffering at that time; the oars of the Muslim galleys were pulled by Christian prisoners, while Muslim or heathen galley-slaves, chained to their benches, rowed in the galliasses of Genoa and Venice.

Man dreamed of distant lands yielding such wonders as Marco Polo had beheld. But he knew not yet how to attain those riches, or indeed how to keep them if he should ever make them his own. Suitable ships were lacking, so were nautical instruments and qualified captains. Above all he had no idea of the sea's immensity.

Want of nautical skills was particularly marked among the Chinese, who, if their admirers are to be believed, excelled the peoples of the West in their knowledge both of water and of ships. On the labyrinths of inland waterways and along the coast millions of Chinese spent their entire lives in houseboats or junks; and hundreds, if not thousands, of years ago the Chinese invented watertight bulkheads, which were not adopted by the naval shipyards of Europe until the nineteenth century. The sails of Chinese junks were divided into strips stiffened by horizontal bamboo laths, resembling a Venetian blind, and could be handled very easily. Like so many sea birds, embodiment of those painted so daintily upon rice-paper by Chinese artists, the junks manœuvred gracefully upon the waters of the Yellow and the East and South China Seas.

Yet the Chinese, with their vast territory and their turbulent frontiers to the north and east, never established an overseas empire. They lived, travelled, transported cargoes in their sampans and junks, celebrated festivals aboard them or turned to piracy; but, except in the first quarter of the fifteenth century when the last great emperor of the Ming dynasty dispatched his fleets to dominate the Indian Ocean and Arabian Sea, Chinese maritime power was chiefly confined to home waters.

The West behaved very differently when, at the end of the fifteenth century, the gateways of the world began to open. The voyages of the Spanish and Portuguese were like the bursting of a dam; the seafarers of Europe spread into all the oceans of the globe. The first Conquistadores sailed in ships no better than those of the Arabs or Chinese, and their feats of navigation were no greater than those of the Vikings or Polynesians. As for the motives which spurred them on, these were no more noble or disinterested than those of the seafaring nations who followed them. Columbus admitted frankly: 'Gold, the wonder of wonders! It is with gold that fortunes are made; he who has gold gains what he will in this world and can even bring comfort to the souls in purgatory.'

The liberation of the mind and the rediscovery of science, which we call the Renaissance, encouraged Europe to look outwards beyond her coastal limits. Inspired by Henry the Navigator and emulating the Phoenicians, the Portuguese first explored the west coast of Africa, seeking the empire of Prester John and the land of spices. Then Columbus, with the *Santa Maria* of a hundred tons and two smaller caravels, crossed the Atlantic in the hope of discovering the legendary kingdom of Xipangu (Japan), and a westward route to Cathay and the Indies, and arrived in the New World. Vasco da Gama landed in India, thus breaking through the Arab blockade which had hindered European trade expansion for five hundred years. Sword in hand, Cortes and Pizarro broke like demons into the hitherto secluded Central and South American civilizations. Balboa was the first to see the Pacific; Magellan, circumnavigating the globe, proved what Galileo had so tirelessly affirmed—that the world is round. The quest for a north-west passage drew Barents, Frobisher, Baffin and others into northern waters. Europe perceived that it could impose its hegemony upon the other continents.

Alexander von Humboldt was justified in writing that Columbus was an exceptional man, a Titan who by his strength of character 'exerted without wishing it an important influence upon the destiny of man'. The same could be said of other explorers. But the age of the European voyages of discovery was one of bloodshed. Flourishing civilizations were crushed beneath the jackboots of European adventurers. Within a century of the discovery of the New World Montaigne was already lamenting the evils of colonial settlement:

> We have taken advantage of the ignorance and inexperience of the natives to bend them more readily to the treachery, vice, avarice and every kind of inhumanity and cruelty of which our own lives are the model and the pattern. Whoever rates the pursuit of trade and commerce at such a price? We see all these razed towns, these exterminated nations, so many put to the sword, and the richest quarter of the globe rushing helter-skelter to bargain for pearls and pepper: these are tradesmen's triumphs! Never have ambition and national strife brought men opposing each other to such horrible forms of warfare or to such sordid disasters.

In the following centuries European ships transported an estimated thirty million Negroes, the infamous 'black ivory', to different parts of the New World; a whole race was abased to the level of beasts of burden. Charles Darwin on his voyage in the *Beagle* encountered 'heart-sickening atrocities' perpetrated upon slaves in the New World.

> And these deeds [he wrote] are done and palliated by men, who profess to love their neighbours as themselves, who believe in God, and pray that His Will be done on earth! It makes one's blood boil, yet heart tremble, to think that we Englishmen and our American descendants, with their boastful cry of liberty, have been and are so guilty. . . .

To begin with the European maritime powers took little notice of the protests and warnings of humaner spirits, for they were too busy squabbling over the treasures of the world. The Caribbean Sea became the happy hunting ground of pirates and filibusters, and a good number of the explorers divided their time between piracy and discovery.

In the course of these voyages of exploration and conquest the mystery of many great rivers was cleared up. The hero of one of the wildest adventures in the conquest of South America was the Spanish nobleman Francisco de Orellana, who deserted one of Pizarro's expeditions and, crossing the Andes from Ecuador, in 1541 explored the Amazon from source to mouth. The Sieur de La

Salle, *voyageur* and fur trader, in 1682 descended the Mississippi to its delta and made French claim to the surrounding territory, naming it 'Louisiana' for his king. Similar exploits took place later in other parts of the world; one by one blanks upon the map disappeared. In 1862 John Hanning Speke and J. A. Grant solved the riddle of the source of the White Nile; and fifteen years later, with a fierce energy worthy of the Conquistadores, Henry Morton Stanley travelled the entire course of the River Congo downstream.

The age of discovery produced geniuses, heroes, utopians, fools, idealists and madcaps, treasure seekers such as Coronado, romancers like Amerigo Vespucci, kindly explorers like Captain Cook, despots such as Cecil Rhodes. The map of the world was radically altered; world economy drastically changed; money-grubbing prospered; hordes of emigrants poured into the two Americas, South Africa, Australia and even into the islands of the Pacific. More than any other, this age hastened the development of shipping.

CHAPTER SIX

WIND, STEAM AND NUCLEAR ENERGY

THE SAILING ships of the fifteenth and sixteenth centuries were broad-beamed, cumbrous vessels. Charts were still somewhat crude and navigation depended upon compass, astrolabe, cross-staff and sand-glass. The mariners' compass had developed from a magnetic needle floating on a piece of wood in a container to a pivoted needle mounted over a card marked in degrees. Lack of an accurate timekeeper, however, meant that measurement of longitude was less than approximate, and not until after the invention of the sextant and the chronometer in 1731 and 1735 did navigation become an exact science.

Upon the more accurate, detailed charts which came into use charmingly imaginative scenes of ships, terrifying marine monsters and idyllic views of palm-fringed shores were replaced by the real outlines of coasts and islands and the location of reefs and shoals. The publication of Matthew Maury's charts of winds and currents in the mid nineteenth century shortened some ocean crossings by days or even weeks, and marine cartography became an accepted science.

By this period the heyday of the sailing ship was already approaching its close. Nevertheless some of the fastest and finest sailing ships ever known were built in the middle years of the nineteenth century: the clippers. In the 1830s and '40s these splendid American-built ships, with their beautiful lines and great spread of canvas, could overhaul any other type of vessel then afloat, including steamships. Shipbuilding in Britain had been in decline since the end of the Napoleonic Wars, and British shipowners, in order to compete, sought Yankee clippers from the yards of Baltimore and Boston, so completely did those vessels dominate the traffic in valuable and perishable cargoes. Under that stimulus British ship-building revived, and from 1850 British-built clippers came off the slipways in increasing numbers. For several years rivalry was intense, and during that period the American and British mercantile fleets together eclipsed those of all other nations. The outbreak of the American Civil War left the sea routes open to British ships, and rivalry henceforth was between clipper and clipper. One of the most notable 'races' took place in 1866 when the Clyde-built *Ariel* was just first to dock in London at the end of a voyage of over 14,000 miles, which three of the clippers bringing the China tea crop from Fuchow completed in ninety-one days.

The opening of the Suez Canal in 1869 put an end to the great days of the tea clippers. For some twenty years more many of them shared the Australian run with the wool clippers which, with a bulkier return cargo, were generally of greater tonnage than the average 800 tons of the tea clippers. Ships of over 2,000 tons—twenty times the tonnage of Columbus's *Santa Maria*—had long since been built by the major maritime nations for both war and trade. The largest wooden sailing vessel of all was the four-masted *Great Republic*, 4,555 registered tonnage, built by Donald McKay of Boston in 1853 for the Australian trade. But by the end of the century the building of ocean-going sailing ships was almost at an end; sail had given place to steam.

In September 1707 the emigré French physicist Denis Papin and his family climbed aboard his hand-cranked paddle boat, intending to travel from Kassel down river and then cross to England, where he hoped to find the means to build a steam engine for propelling ships by power-driven paddles. Having, with difficulty, obtained permission from the authorities for his strange boat to pass from the River Fulda to the Weser, he reached Münden; here his vessel 'was seized by the boatmen of the river, and barbarously destroyed'. Ideas for other 'floating tea-kettles', as they were mockingly called, were put forward in Britain, France and America in the early eighteenth century and some steam-powered vessels were built; generally they excited both scorn and fear. Steam power for ships was not a practical proposition until James Watt's inventions had improved the steam engine.

In 1787 John Fitch, a clockmaker and ingenious craftsman of Windsor, Connecticut, fitted a boat with a steam engine to drive paddles dipped and raised in the manner of hand paddles; later he built a small vessel, the *Perseverance*, with a steam-driven screw propeller. But he could obtain no support even from such men as Benjamin Franklin, and took his ideas to revolutionary France. Frustrated there too, he returned to America where in despair he committed suicide in 1798.

Meanwhile a variety of steam-powered craft with paddle wheels had appeared. In 1788 a Scot, Patrick Miller, built a twin-hulled boat with paddle wheels amidships between the two halves of the vessel; in America Samuel Morey tried a paddle wheel at the bow; in 1801 William Symington, another Scottish engineer, produced the successful stern-wheeler *Charlotte Dundas*. This craft, of advanced design, was studied by the American Robert Fulton, artist turned engineer, who proposed to apply steam power 'to working boats up our long rivers in America'. Back in New York and with the financial backing of the American government, Fulton designed a true steamship of 180 tons, 130 feet long with paddles at either side powered by a Watt engine. Named the *Clermont*—and also known as 'Fulton's Folly'—in August 1807 she steamed up the Hudson River 150 miles to Albany in thirty-two hours, and back in thirty, amid scenes of great excitement and astonishment. The New York–Albany run became a regular service which the *Clermont* provided for many years.

In 1804 another American, John Stevens, had returned to John Fitch's idea of steam-powered screw propulsion and successfully fitted a small boat with twin screws. But he abandoned this line of development and built the paddle steamer *Phoenix*, which in 1809 was the first steamship to make a sea voyage—from the Hudson River to the Delaware. In 1812 Henry Bell's *Comet* introduced steam navigation to the Clyde; in 1814 the first steam vessels appeared on the Thames, in 1816 on the Rhine; while the Irish Sea was crossed in 1818. But the real portent of things to come was the crossing of the Atlantic by the *Savannah*, a sailing ship with auxiliary steam engine and paddle wheels, from Savannah, Georgia, to Liverpool in 1819. Her engine ran for only eighty hours on the voyage but her port to port time of twenty-seven days fifteen hours was a record, for sailing ships ordinarily took from thirty to forty days on the west to east crossing. Eight years later the first all-steam crossing was made by the Dutch paddle steamer *Curaçao*, which took a month east to west from Rotterdam to the West Indies; but the first all-steam west to east trans-Atlantic voyage was not made until 1833, when the Canadian-built *Royal William* carried passengers in twenty-five days from Quebec to Liverpool.

Paddle steamers had their heroic age on the Mississippi. By about 1850 over a thousand steamboats, of a quarter of a million tons burthen, plied the 'father of rivers'. On the one hand they carried the food and equipment needed by the new settlers in the Middle West, on the other they conveyed to the towns and ports the cotton and sugar from the plantations of the South. This river fleet was as important as any navy; newspapers were even printed on some of the Mississippi steamers. There were opera boats, museum boats, show boats. Contesting paddle steamers sometimes burst their boilers. For a time there were even river pirates who held the passengers to ransom. The leadsman in the prow would sing out: 'By the mark, twain. Mark twain!', which gave Samuel Langhorne Clemens, himself apprenticed as a river pilot, the idea for his pseudonym.

The combination of steam power and iron hull found its most remarkable expression in the middle years of the nineteenth century in a ship built by Isambard Kingdom Brunel, the great railway engineer. Named *Leviathan* at her launching in 1857, she was always known as the *Great Eastern*. She was designed to carry 3,600 passengers—and enough coal to voyage to Australia and back without refuelling, as well as her own small steamboats for landing and taking on passengers, since no port in the world could accommodate her 674-foot length. Two sets of steam engines powered a 24-foot propeller and two 58-foot paddle wheels, while her six masts could carry over 6,000 square yards of sail in case of need. But Brunel's ideas were far ahead of the technological capacity of the time, and the troubled history of the *Great Eastern*'s building, launching and fitting out caused the early death of her creator just as she started on her first ocean voyage in 1859.

In the end it was the combination of screw or bladed propellers and steel hulls that gave steam mastery over sail. Thus the technical and industrial revolutions of the eighteenth and nineteenth centuries extended to the oceans of the globe. By the end of that period liners of over 20,000 tons were averaging over 20 knots on the trans-Atlantic 'ferry'. Sailing packet, steam packet and liner had between them carried millions of emigrants from Europe to the New World. The opening of the Suez Canal gave steam the advantage on the route to the East; finally, increased engine and bunker capacity, cutting down the need for refuelling, enabled steamships to oust sail from its last long-haul route, to Australia.

In 1897 Charles Parsons startled the Royal Navy by racing his steam-turbine-powered *Turbinia* through the ships assembled for the Diamond Jubilee review. Capable of 35 knots, *Turbinia* easily outpaced the vessels sent to catch her. The Admiralty were forced to concede the superiority of Parsons's invention, and the steam turbine was rapidly adopted for naval and large mercantile ships. With the general introduction, after the First World War, of oil fuel in place of coal, and of Diesel and semi-Diesel engines for motor vessels, the hot, malodorous boiler rooms and the strenuous job of stoking have largely disappeared, together with the dirty task of coal-bunkering. Neat fuel-oil tanks and more compact boilers and engines allow precious space in both cargo and passenger vessels to be used for other purposes. Heavy oil is now the lifeblood of shipping, but another source of energy is waiting to take its turn —that of the atom.

Today there are over forty thousand medium sized and large ships in the world's mercantile fleets with a total gross tonnage of over a hundred and sixty million. The network of shipping lines remains, despite the competition of aircraft, the lifeline of the world. But how many wrecks lie at the bottom of the sea! It is not possible to ascertain their number. In the last quarter of the nineteenth century alone fifty or more disasters—none of which was as grave as that of the *Titanic* later on—caused the death of ten thousand people. Even in our own time, the age of radar, stringent safety regulations and defined shipping lanes, great ships still fall victim occasionally to the sea. The loss of the Italian trans-Atlantic liner

Andrea Doria on 25th July 1956 after a collision with the Swedish cargo vessel *Stockholm* is one example.

Yet sailors' cutlasses, fire-ships, artillery and other weapons have claimed many more victims than have accidents or the calamities of nature. From antiquity onwards coast-dwelling peoples have fought their battles upon the sea. In the fifth century B.C. a thousand Greek and Persian ships carrying two hundred thousand sailors and soldiers did battle in the roadsteads of Salamis. From then onward naval clashes and conflicts have succeeded each other almost without pause.

In 1571, when an allied Christian fleet confronted the Turkish galleys off Lepanto, at the entrance to the Gulf of Corinth, some thirty thousand men perished. One of those who took part, losing his left hand in the fray, was Miguel Cervantes, who later wrote *Don Quixote*. Seventeen years after Lepanto two great maritime powers of the age of exploration, Spain with its 'invincible Armada' and England, a rising maritime nation, encountered each other in the English Channel. At the end of a running fight which lasted ten days half the Spanish ships lay upon the bed of the sea and two thirds of the men aboard were dead.

At the battle of Trafalgar, in 1805, Nelson robbed Napoleon of the hope of maritime supremacy. During the American Civil War 'iron-clad' steamships met each other in battle for the first time, and henceforth armoured vessels, initiated by the French a few years earlier, were built by all the naval powers. Successive naval battles—Manila, Santiago de Cuba, Tsushima, Jutland and engagements of the Second World War—demonstrated the increasing weight of armour and firepower of fighting ships, and brought death to thousands of men.

Submarine navigation is a subject which exercised inventive minds hundreds of years before man had the technical ability to put the idea into practice. Leonardo da Vinci outlined an underwater vessel but, with a foreboding that such craft would be used for other tasks than submarine exploration, did not give details 'because the wicked nature of men might tempt them to bore holes into the bottoms of other vessels, thus sinking them with their crews'. The future was to prove him right, although to their credit governments and naval men for years showed less enthusiasm for such 'abominable weapons' than did their inventors. A Dutchman, Cornelius van Drebbel, demonstrated a diving-boat in the Thames about

1624; unsuccessful attempts were made to use a submarine built by David Bushnell to blow up British ships during the American War of Independence; and it was only after his submarine *Nautilus*, built in 1801, had been rejected first by the French and then by the British as 'inhumane' that Robert Fulton returned to America and the development of steam boats for river navigation. But inventors persevered, and throughout the nineteenth century a number of underwater vessels of great variety of shape appeared, intended both for peaceful exploration and for war. The invention of the Diesel engine in 1892 made the naval submarine, armed with torpedoes, a practical proposition, and in both world wars they sank millions of tons of merchant shipping as well as warships.

The first nuclear-powered vessel, the U.S. submarine *Nautilus*, was launched in 1954. In 1958, with her sister ship *Skate*, she travelled from the Pacific to the Atlantic under the Polar ice, and in 1960 the larger *Triton* encircled the globe without surfacing. But while the prospect of fleets of nuclear-powered submarines armed with missiles is an alarming one, the development of nuclear power for ships is not entirely sinister. In 1959 the Russians brought into service the ice-breaker *Lenin*, which can operate throughout the winter months without refuelling; in 1961 the first nuclear cargo and passenger ship, the experimental American *Savannah*, was commissioned; and the development of large nuclear-powered mercantile submarines may do much to improve safety at sea.

The great trans-ocean migrations which began with the voyages of Columbus, Vasco da Gama and Magellan are over, the colonial epoch is finished, and the heroic era of navigation when man dreamed of treasure and of remote paradises, of epic struggles against elemental forces, has given way to a less romantic age.

Yet seafaring has not altogether lost its element of adventure: the riches that man may still harvest from the sea are by no means exhausted. But they no longer lure him to distant shores; he must search for them on the ocean floor and in the water itself. It may happen that the exhaustion of mineral resources and the shortage of food will make the development of the wealth of the sea a vital necessity. The potential value and importance of that wealth far exceed those of the riches which colonial possessions have brought to the conquering nations over the centuries.

CHAPTER SEVEN

THE GOLD OF THE BILLOWS

W HEN in 1870 Jules Verne invited his readers to accompany him on a voyage of twenty thousand leagues under the sea, his flights of fancy showed them how they might one day make the treasures of the deep their own. He described the abyssal waters as though they were meadows, gardens and plantations where stocks of fish fed upon submarine plants, waiting for man to catch them in order to allay his hunger. The wealth of the ocean seemed inexhaustible.

Technical development has outstripped many of the ideas hatched by that utopian genius. Yet man has scarcely begun to exploit the riches of the sea, although the dreams of chemists and biologists of the present day go far beyond the prophecies of Jules Verne. If the number of the inhabitants of our planet continues to double every seventy years the despoiled land will, sooner or later, be unable to feed them or to provide the raw materials without which life cannot be sustained. Unless man has learned by that time to make many essentials synthetically he will have to look for them in the sea.

Sea water contains not only an abundance of mineral salts and elements but also, in plant and animal plankton, the basic food substances required by man: carbohydrates, fats, proteins, vitamins and trace elements. Directly or indirectly plankton supports all the animal life of the seas and offers a vast source of nourishment for man if he can but devise ways to make use of it. Theoretically the total sources of nourishment, including large and small fish and mammals, of the Atlantic alone could, if numbers remained constant, feed the human race for a period six times as long as that of man's past history.

Jules Verne's submarine plantations are less fanciful than some of the schemes which have been put forward in recent years. There have been plans to construct apparatus to filter and distil all useful constituents from sea water, or 'factories' where phyto-plankton and fresh-water algae grown in plastic containers would provide a daily crop. One of the most fantastic yet determined efforts to wrest riches from the sea was made by the German chemist Fritz Haber who, in 1918, had been awarded the Nobel prize for inventing a method of producing ammonia synthetically. Haber conceived the idea of extracting gold from sea water in sufficient quantity to pay Germany's war debts; and one of the chief tasks of the German South Atlantic expedition of 1924–28 in the research ship *Meteor* was to test the feasibility of his plan. *Meteor* was well equipped with a laboratory and filtration plant, and she established that the amount of gold in sea water is worth millions of pounds. But the cost of extracting it would be some five times greater than its value.

The fauna of the sea include many creatures which are far more efficient chemists than man. The molluscs *Murex trunculus* and *Purpura lapillum* absorb bromine and produce a deep red fluid which, extracted from their crushed bodies, provided the famous Tyrian purple dye, much sought after in antiquity. Lobsters extract copper and cobalt; many kinds of mollusc assimilate nickel. Chemists became aware of the existence of certain elements in sea water only because these were discovered in the bodies of marine creatures.

From the remotest times coastal peoples have evaporated sea water in order to extract salt. Seaweed was formerly the sole source of iodine for commercial purposes, until it was found in nitrate deposits in South America. In many districts lacking limestone the crushed shells of mussels and other shellfish provide the calcium necessary for mortar and cement. Most magnesium, that light metal without which the aircraft factories would close down, is now chemically extracted from sea water—which also yields potassium in commercial quantities. The water of the Dead Sea, a lake over twelve hundred feet below the level of the Mediterranean and subject to a high rate of evaporation which equals the volume of water brought into it by the Jordan and other rivers, has a salinity of about 22 per cent—far above the average 3·5 per cent for sea water. No plant or animal can live in it, but the salts are a valuable source of minerals for both Jordan and Israel. The vanished seas of earlier ages have provided the extensive beds of salt mined in many parts of the world.

Oil too is a gift from ancient seas. It was formed by the decomposition of countless marine organisms on the sea bed, which were subsequently covered by sediments and subjected to enormous pressure. The earliest formation of oilfields is considered by geologists to have taken place as far back as the Silurian period—three hundred to four hundred million years ago—with more recent formations in Tertiary times. Pressure and changes in the Earth's crust caused the oil to seep through the sedimentary layers until trapped by impervious rocks. Traces of oil at the surface must have been known to man for thousands of years, especially in the Middle East, but the exploitation of what was stored below had to wait for the technology of modern times.

Geologists are far from having discovered all the possible oil fields beneath dry land, but already man is finding it economic to drill through the sea bed to tap new reserves; forests of derricks offshore in regions of the Caribbean and the Gulf of Mexico are nothing new, while both gas and oil have been found beneath the North Sea. In spite of the difficulties and dangers of drilling the sea bed, especially in northern waters, the value of this vital fuel on the doorstep of industrialized western Europe makes the enterprise worth while.

Among the sediments dredged up by scientists on board the *Challenger* on her world-wide cruise in the 1870s were some curious nodules, but they were disregarded until the International Geophysical Year of 1957–58, when they were found to consists of about 30 per cent manganese, together with other metals. Since the United States has to import all the manganese it needs in industry, American scientists consider that it might be worth while to exploit this source, even though dredging economic quantities from about 13,000 feet would require elaborate equipment. But access to the floor of the ocean is still less costly and hazardous than landing upon the Moon.

CHAPTER EIGHT

ALL THE FISHES OF THE SEA

'THE BLESSINGS OF THE SEA' is a phrase generally used less to describe salt, petroleum, iodine, bromine and magnesium than the harvest netted by trawlers and fishing-boats of all sizes. We read in Genesis, in the context of the Flood: '. . . all the fishes of the sea . . . into your hands are they delivered.' And there is no coast-dwelling people which has not profited from this gift made by God to Noah.

There are four great fishing grounds frequented regularly by the high-sea fleets: the European, i.e. the North Sea, the Barents Sea, the Bay of Biscay, the Mediterranean, the waters west of Norway and around Iceland; the Newfoundland, which the Breton cod-fishers perhaps knew before Columbus discovered America and where fishing rights set England and France at loggerheads for centuries; the Japanese, perhaps the richest ground of all; and the West Canadian, stretching from the Bering Strait to Vancouver Island.

Other fishing grounds, not yet fully exploited, lie in zones swept by the Humboldt current, the Falkland and Agulhas currents, and in the Antarctic. Peru lands an enormous catch from the rich grounds of the Humboldt, but a large proportion is of small fish used to make meal. In all these areas fishing will have to be further developed to help to feed the world, for the numbers of fish are declining in the four classical areas. The ancient craft is degenerating more and more into an industrial exploitation.

Until the nineteenth century fishing was chiefly confined to coastal waters, and the majority of shore-dwelling people depended almost entirely upon their catches for sustenance. There is even a tradition in India and Ceylon that fish-hooks were the first form of currency. In the Middle Ages the herring took first place in providing fast-day and Lenten fare in western Christendom. Fishermen of the North Sea and Baltic must have become familiar at an early date with the regular migration routes and breeding grounds of the herring shoals, and Dutch and Baltic ports in particular owed their prosperity to their herring fleets. The failure of the Baltic herring fisheries in about 1500 sounded the death knell of the Hanseatic League, and the demand for fish both as a general supplement to diet and for fast days brought increasing rivalry notably between the Dutch (who invented a more palatable way of curing herrings than preserving them in brine and thus commanded the inland markets of Europe) and the English. New fishing grounds must be discovered.

In 1497 the Genoese merchant John Cabot, who had settled in Bristol, set sail westwards in hope of exploiting the new territory so recently discovered by Columbus or of finding a western route to Cathay. He landed at Cape Breton Island and has thus been credited with the 'discovery' of North America. The following year, with the backing of the English King Henry VII, Cabot, and probably his son Sebastian, led another expedition across the North Atlantic.

Whether it was on either of these voyages that the Cabots made the first attempts to find a North-West passage has been disputed; but it is certain that in 1498 John Cabot saw 'the sea swarming with fish' in the region of the Grand Banks off Newfoundland. The fish were cod and so numerous that in succeeding centuries European fishing boats found it worth while to cross the Atlantic for their catch.

The Cabots must have reached the Grand Banks at spawning time, for the cod is a deep sea wanderer during most of the year but, like the herring, assembles in great numbers at its regular breeding grounds. In northern European seas, off the Lofoten Islands especially, the cod begin to congregate early in the year, seeking the warmer waters of the Gulf Stream in which to spawn before returning to their Arctic feeding grounds. Thus these rather barren islands, north of the Arctic Circle, produce year after year a very valuable 'crop'—a harvest of the sea reaped in the short winter days. Long ago, even before brine was in general use, the Norwegians devised a method of preserving cod by air-drying. The heads are cut off and the gutted fish are hung in pairs on wooden racks, either in the open air or in sheds, until they become *törrfisk*, or stockfish. Norway had an export market in Europe for stockfish in the twelfth century, and today supplies dried, salted and canned fish to South America as well as southern Europe, and also produces cod liver oil and fertilizers from the heads and offal: nothing is wasted.

The world's fishing industry depends very much on the cod and herring families. After these come other round fish such as haddock, whiting, hake, salmon, tunny, mackerel; the flat fish such as plaice, halibut, sole and turbot; and shellfish. Fishing methods depend partly on the type of fish and partly on the means available to the fisherman—drift nets for herrings, trawls for fish which live on or near the sea bed; seine nets for inshore fishing, and long lines with baited hooks; even a means of electrical fishing has been tried. All the world's best fishing grounds lie on or above the continental shelves, but since the nineteenth century the fishing fleets of Europe have had to seek their catches farther and farther beyond the national 'three-mile limit'. As sail gave way to steam and then to the Diesel engine, and as refrigeration became increasingly efficient, so the size and number of distant-water trawlers have grown. Such vessels are equipped with echo-sounding gear to locate shoals, and since they stay away from port for weeks at a time they usually return with well filled holds. Quick-freezing with crushed ice containing an antibiotic, and processing and deep-freezing carried out at sea on board big stern trawlers or special depot ships are more recent developments which have helped to make it economic to bring distant-water catches to continental markets, and thus have contributed to the tremendous increase in the tonnage of the world's catch in the last fifty years.

Nevertheless the industry is not conducted scientifically and it has been realized, perhaps rather late, that the harvest of the sea is not inexhaustible. Some kinds of fish are no longer to be caught in the traditional grounds; others are steadily decreasing in size as well as in numbers. Experiments carried out in the last decade, however, show that it should be possible to maintain stocks by hatching fish eggs, rearing them in sea tanks and then releasing the young fish into the ocean at an age and size when they are less likely to fall prey to inedible predators. But clearly 'fish farming' is a subject which demands close international co-operation. What nation, as things stand today, will go to the trouble and expense of rearing fish and then releasing them into waters quartered by rival fleets?

Shellfish as part of the basic diet are relatively unimportant to Europeans; but in the Far East these, and other sea creatures which Europeans generally regard as inedible, are essential food. Varieties of sea-slug or sea-cucumber, also known as *bêche de mer* or by the Malay name *trepang*, are popular and regarded by the Chinese especially as a great delicacy; to Alfred Russel Wallace, however, the trepang looked 'like a sausage which had been rolled in mud and then pulled through a sooty chimney'. The German naturalist and South Seas traveller Karl Semper described a hundred years ago the elaborate method of drying and curing the *trepang* in the Palau Islands. But for all the careful preparation he found it, when served in a kind of soup, 'as insipid as the edible birds' nests; it consists of gluey whitish pellets, appreciated by Europeans for their digestibility and by the Chinese for their aphrodisiac properties'.

Also in the Pacific, on the sea bed around Samoa, Fiji and Tonga, lives a marine worm, *Eunice viridis* (*palolo* to the islanders). It comes to the surface to spawn only once a year, at the October full moon—to the worm presumably the time of a particular tide. There is a preliminary rising, eagerly watched for, and then the following night, shortly before sunrise, the sea is suddenly teeming with the pale green, transparent worms. To the islanders this is a great festive occasion as, in innumerable canoes and all kinds of craft, they scoop the 'delicacy' out of the sea. One European traveller has described the *palolo*, eaten raw or cooked, as like 'rather fishy spinach'.

Far more perilous than the gathering of *trepang* is the hunting of marine mammals, which Neolithic man already practised. Herman Melville, in *Moby Dick*, quoted from Obed Macy's *History of Nantucket:* 'In the year 1690 some persons were on a high hill observing the whales spouting and sporting with each other, when one observed; there—pointing to the sea—is a green pasture where our children's grandchildren will go for bread.' And again, from Thomas Fuller: 'The mighty whales which swim in a sea of water, and have a sea of oil swimming in them.' It is this oil that man has sought to wrest from them.

CHAPTER NINE

THE END OF MOBY DICK?

THE HUNTING of whales and other marine mammals has left an indelible mark upon the history of discovery, for it was the tracking of those beasts that led the Eskimos to settle on one after another of the northern isles and coasts of the American continent. In the ninth century the Norwegians, in the thirteenth and fourteenth the Basques, took the lead in such hunts. The English, Dutch, Danish, Russian and American searches for the North-West and North-East Passages were not only prompted by urgent geographical, political or economic requirements: they were also attempts to find new seal colonies and whaling grounds. Among the most renowned whalers were the Scoresbys, father and son, who explored the eastern coast of Greenland and the ice-floes between Spitsbergen and Novaya Zemlya. William Scoresby the younger published an account of his adventures in 1823 under the title *Voyage to the Northern Whale Fishery*.

Anyone looking at the sea from an angle different from that of the hunter, the trader or the business man must be depressed by what has been happening for centuries to the whales and seals. Herman Melville and other authors have certainly extolled the great moments of whale hunting and exalted unforgettably the struggle between man and beast. Hundreds of harpooners must have shown the same courage as that of Captain Ahab and his crew in Melville's masterpiece *Moby Dick*. But this cloak of romanticism cannot hide the fact that hunting seals and whales is also a grim illustration of man's greed, expressed in horrible slaughter.

As early as 890 the Norse sea captain Ottar boasted of being 'one of the six who, in two days, killed sixty whales'. Possibly this refers not to the Atlantic or Greenland whales but to pilot whales, large dolphins which move in schools and can be caught by being driven ashore; if so, Ottar and his companions showed moderation, for it is recorded that on one occasion in 1845 hunters slaughtered 1,540 pilot whales in two *hours* off the Shetland Islands.

Early northern seafarers also hunted seals and walruses. These latter, the most inoffensive creatures of Arctic waters, were valued for their tusks as well as for their oil and hides. Then and later men landed on the ice or, particularly, on the rocky shores where seals assembled in their 'rookeries' at the breeding season, clubbed large numbers to death, flayed and eviscerated them on the spot and loaded the spoil into their ships.

It was Vitus Bering who, in 1741, introduced European hunters to the paradise of marine mammals among the Aleutian and Kuril Islands. Members of his expedition who survived shipwreck and a winter on a North Pacific island, and eventually returned to the Siberian coast, brought back pelts of the sea otter, an animal which had proved a plentiful source of food during the months of their isolation. The value of the beautiful fur was quickly recognized, and very soon Russian ships were returning with huge cargoes of skins from the shores of Alaska and the Aleutians. Numbers inevitably declined, and the scarcity of the sea otter was among the reasons which in 1867 prompted Russia to sell her Alaskan territory to the United States for a modest sum. Steller's sea-cow, a large relative of the manatee and dugong, had already been totally exterminated, since it was an easily caught source of food for the sealing crews.

In 1786 Pribilof discovered, on the islands which now bear his name, the breeding grounds of the fur seal, a creature which until then had been taken from the sea in comparatively small numbers. The slaughter which followed was enormous and indiscriminate, and within twenty years the millions observed by Pribilof had been so reduced that the Russians called a temporary halt to sealing. Time after time the hunters massacred more seals than they required. Thus in 1803 on Unalaska Island, when eight hundred thousand fur seals had been slaughtered in one season, three quarters of the skins were burned or thrown into the water and only the best specimens, commanding a high price, were retained.

Resumption of sealing again brought the fur seal under threat of extermination in the 1830s, but the Russians had by this time devised a method of preserving both the seals and the fur trade. They stipulated that only adult male seals were to be hunted, leaving the females to breed and the young to develop. This policy allowed the fur seals to re-establish their colonies, and by the 1860s their numbers were estimated to be over two million. For a few years the transfer of Alaska and the Aleutians to America, ending Russian control of the Bering Sea, brought an increase in sealing and the hunting of the sea otter, whose rarity now gave its pelt additional value. Fortunately for the seals the policy of selective killing was retained, and in 1870 the United States confined the right to hunt seals in its territories, which now included the Pribilof Islands, to the Alaska Company on a quota system. This wise move was almost nullified by the development of shooting seals in the sea, a particularly wasteful method since male and female could not be easily distinguished and the bodies of many of them sank before they could be hauled into the boats. It was chiefly British and Canadian sealers, excluded from a profitable trade by the Alaska Company's monopoly, who were guilty of this slaughter, and a tense international situation arose which was not settled until a treaty between America, Russia, Japan and Britain in 1911 regulated the hunting of all marine creatures in the Bering Sea. The treaty also forbade the killing of the sea otter, although it was generally believed that this animal had in any case met the same fate as the northern sea-cow. Almost incredibly, this was not so, and in the 1930s a small colony of sea otters was observed on one of the Aleutian Islands and given prompt protection by the United States Fish and Wildlife Service.

The fur seals, elephant seals and leopard seals of the southern hemisphere were almost as ruthlessly exploited as those of the north, and international control came only just in time to save some species from extermination. But in spite of protective measures, some species both of true seals and of sea lions (the fur seals belong to the sea lion family), such as those formerly abundant on the Galapagos Islands or the Mexican island of Guadalupe, are either greatly reduced in numbers or already extinct. Following a scientifically conducted survey Victor Scheffer, an American biologist, concluded in his book *Seals, Sea Lions and Walruses* * that the northern fur seals, the most numerous single species of the sea lion family, numbered fewer than two million, at the most optimistic estimate; that Pacific and Atlantic walruses together totalled at best ninety thousand; and, he says, 'Reports from zoologists in northeastern Canada and Alaska suggest that the future of the walrus is insecure'.

Whales provide man with even more valuable products than do other marine mammals, so that, in spite of agreement between the whaling nations to limit catches, the most commercially useful species are perhaps under a graver threat of extermination than the fur seals. Edible oils from the blubber are now by far the most important product; until displaced by paraffin in the middle of the nineteenth century whale oil was used principally for lamps and in the manufacture of candles. The flesh of dolphin and porpoise was eaten in the Middle Ages, the tongue being considered a delicacy. Whale meat, however, has not proved acceptable for human consumption: while some of the crews of Antarctic whalers declare the meat of rorquals very good, others will not touch it. But nothing need be wasted; flesh and bones are processed to provide animal food and fertilizers, and there are additional by-products such as vitamin A from the liver. Whalebone (baleen) has lost its former importance as a stiffener for corsets, however.

The greatest of all cetaceans, the blue whale of the Antarctic, is estimated to reach a length of up to 100 feet. One, carefully weighed and measured, was 89 feet long and weighed over 136 tons: the flesh over 40 tons, the liver 1 ton, the heart 1,000 pounds, although the amount of oil obtained from the blubber, over 22 tons, was somewhat below average. The other great rorqual, the fin-whale which now provides the greater part of the Antarctic catch, reaches a maximum of 80 feet, while the humpback, at about 50 feet, is 'middle-sized' (the average elephant weighs a mere five tons).

* Stanford University Press and Oxford University Press, 1958.

The sperm whale, of about 55 feet, is a dangerous toothed whale which feeds on octopus and squid and can dive to great depths. It is hunted chiefly in tropical waters and is remarkable for the production of spermaceti. This 'sperm oil' (strictly speaking a wax) was for a century or more of special value for the manufacture of the best candles and as a lubricant for delicate machinery. The spermaceti is produced in cavities in the creature's head—up to 11,000 pounds of it in a full-grown specimen—but its biological function is still unknown. The sperm whale was probably saved from total extermination by the introduction of mineral oils. Even more valuable is ambergris, a substance formed in the sperm whale's intestines and sometimes found floating in greyish lumps on the surface of the sea. In classical times ambergris was worth its weight in gold: a handful cast upon the fire released fragrant vapours believed to assuage cramp. It is still a substance in demand by the perfume industry for 'fixing' scents.

The sperm whale, hero of *Moby Dick*, aroused greater fear and respect than other species then hunted. As Melville wrote:

> Not even at the present day has the original prestige of the Sperm Whale, as fearfully distinguished from all other species of the leviathan, died out of the minds of the whalemen as a body. There are those this day among them, who, though intelligent and courageous enough in offering battle to the Greenland or Right Whale, would perhaps—either from professional inexperience, or incompetency, or timidity—decline a contest with the Sperm Whale. . . . Nor is the pre-eminent tremendousness of the great Sperm Whale anywhere more feelingly comprehended, than on board of those prows which stem them.

Appreciation of the potential value of whales perhaps arose from the discovery of stranded specimens. The Basques are credited with the earliest organized whale hunting, and by the fourteenth century the Atlantic right whale had disappeared from the Bay of Biscay. Hunted in more distant waters, the right whale was perhaps only saved from extermination by the discovery of the Greenland whale in the Arctic Ocean in the sixteenth century, when the whaling industry was centred on Spitsbergen. The Greenland whale is now so rare that hunting it is totally forbidden, though Eskimos may still take an occasional catch on the Pacific side of the Arctic Ocean. The Japanese had a well-organized whaling industry in the seventeenth century, and the American whaling fleets based on Nantucket,

New Bedford and San Francisco became so important in the eighteenth century that the value of their catches in both Pacific and Atlantic, of the sperm whale in particular, counted for a great deal in the economy of the young United States after the War of Independence.

All these whalers worked with hand harpoons from open boats, very dangerous work which nevertheless accounted over the centuries for large numbers of cetaceans; today this way of hunting whales is practised only in the Azores. Modern whaling began with the invention of the harpoon gun by Svend Foyn, a Norwegian seal hunter, in 1864, and from his first successful whaling cruise four years later dates Norwegian predominance in whaling. By the end of the century the harpoon gun, together with the introduction of steam (and subsequently motor) vessels, had resulted in a tremendous increase in the numbers killed of all species.

In 1905 the Norwegian Captain Karl Larsen pioneered whaling in the Antarctic, and within a few years the big rorquals were subject to indiscriminate slaughter from vessels working around South Georgia and the South Shetlands. The introduction in 1925 of a stern ramp on the factory ships, up which the carcase could be hauled for cutting up on deck, instead of being dissected while made fast to the side of the ship, increased the speed with which the catch could be handled and hence the profitability of whaling. In the 1931 season the world catch reached a staggering figure of over 43,000 whales—which, fortunately, led to overproduction and a drop in the price of oil. Commercial interests began to realize the need for control and in the 1930s attempts were made to reach international agreement on the numbers and species killed. These met with only modest success, some nations and some companies disregarding all limits, so that after fluctuating the figure rose again to a record of 54,835 in the 1938 season—46,039 of these taken from the Antarctic.

The war years brought a respite, and in 1946 there was established the International Whaling Commission whose work both in controlling catches and in promoting research into the natural history of the cetaceans averted a probable disaster. For the introduction first of aircraft and then of helicopters to locate the whales and guide the catchers to them, suggestions even of bombing them, and the use of echo-finders to trace the route of a submerged whale, could have brought excessive exploitation within a few years. But there is still waste—for example, the practice of using whales as fenders between factory ship and tanker when refuelling: the carcase is so damaged that it is virtually useless.

Various methods of killing whales have been used over the centuries. The Norwegians, for example, used to close the entrance to a narrow fjord with nets if a whale strayed in, and then fire poisoned arrows into it which set up septicaemia, killing the whale in a few days. Fortunately, since edible oils are the most important product of modern whaling, the use of poisons is now strictly forbidden. The introduction of the harpoon gun with a charge in the head of the harpoon which explodes inside the body of the whale has shortened the length of time it take the animal to die, compared with the effects of the hand weapon. But even this mechanical device does not kill instantly, and man has no means of knowing the agony suffered by its victim. One modern development, therefore, is greatly to be welcomed: the electric harpoon capable of electrocuting a whale in a matter of seconds. Its general introduction would eliminate the gross cruelty which has always characterized whaling.

Today enforcement of the regulations proposed by the Whaling Commission is not an insoluble problem, although they are still evaded all too often; the real question is whether the regulations are based on sufficient knowledge to prevent the continuing decline of certain species of what Francis Bacon, in his translation of the Psalms, called 'the great Leviathan that maketh the seas to seethe like a boiling pan'.

PART FIVE

THE TAMING OF THE WATER

Bid the broad Arch the dang'rous flood contain,
The Mole projected, break the roaring main;
Back to his bounds their subject sea command,
And roll obedient rivers through the land.
ALEXANDER POPE, *Moral Essays*

CHAPTER ONE

A CHALLENGE TO MAN

T HROUGHOUT the prehistoric period and then through history itself man has been familiar with the element and elemental force of water. He has sought it out, striven with it, worshipped it, and, with the aid of technology, tamed it. This struggle against water and with water, bulking so large in the story of all peoples and all lands, has reached its climax in the building of audacious works.

For thousands of millions of years water has been shaping the face of the earth, and for more than one thousand million it has sustained plant and animal life. Man, most recent of living beings, since his appearance dates back less than a million years, has achieved a ·breathtaking ascendancy in a moment of geological time. He has succeeded in imposing a measure of control upon the elemental forces, altering permanently the face of the globe. His great hydraulic undertakings are symbols of all the cyclopean structures made by the technocrats of all the ages. Just like the Tower of Babel, the Pyramids, the Chinese Wall, the temples and cathedrals and palaces of the different civilizations, his barrages and dikes are the most recent expression of a very ancient dream of humanity: to achieve the everlasting.

The legendary Emperor Yü, whose reign is assigned by the Chinese chronicles to as early as 4,300 years ago, said: 'Nine rivers have I led unto the ocean and I have brought all the ditches to these rivers.' It is significant that the Chinese should have made Yü, the most important of their early rulers, a water engineer, a man who, if the chronicle is to be trusted, vanquished the Hwang-Ho, that destroyer and scourge of China. The dikes built under Yü held firm until the seventh century A.D., when the Hwang-Ho abruptly changed its course.

It has been said of the Chinese that they can move mountains with wheelbarrows, and it is a fact that over two thousand years ago, by mobilizing hundreds of thousands of men and without the use of machinery, they succeeded in building reservoirs and an extensive network of canals and ditches. Their methods were scarcely different from those employed in recent years to subdue the rivers. At times there have been ten million men and women, often provided only with barrows and baskets, working at the enormous barrages and embankments which have been rising since 1950 in many parts of the great river valleys. The Great Wall is no longer the most representative monument of China: primacy must now be given to the hydraulic system of the Yangtze-kiang. By bringing its watercourse under control China expects to increase her electric power tenfold, to multiply by seven the extent of her arable land, and thus to save the lives of millions who would otherwise fall victim to famine or flood, as has often happened in the history of that country.

When describing the seven wonders of the world in 250 B.C. Philo of Byzantium included among them the hanging gardens of Semiramis at Babylon. But when compared with the hanging gardens and terraced plots of the Indians of Central and South America the gardens of Semiramis begin to lose their glamour. The Indian civilizations prior to the time of Columbus created irrigation systems of superlative scope and perfection. In the twelfth century, according to the Spanish chronicler Sarmiento de Gambóa, writing in 1572:

> Pachacuti Inca Yupanqui, considering the small extent of land round Cuzco suited for cultivation, supplied by art what was wanting in nature. Along the skirts of the hills near villages, and also in other parts, he constructed very long terraces of 200 paces more or less, and 20 to 30 wide, faced with masonry, and filled with earth, much of it brought from a distance. . . . He ordered that they should be sown, and in this way he made a vast increase in the cultivated land, and in provision for sustaining the companies and garrisons.*

It is clear that the Incas were already familiar with such techniques and with artificial means of irrigation, for Sarmiento also says that the eleventh-century Inca Rocca

> . . . discovered the waters of Hurin-chacan and those of Hanan-chacan, which is as much as to say the upper and lower waters of Cuzco, and led them in conduits; so that to this day they irrigate fields; and his sons and descendants have benefited by them to this day.

Possibly the terraces and irrigation schemes of the Andes originated

* *History of the Incas*, translated by Sir Clements Markham, 1908.

even before the days of the Incas; certainly the pre-Columbian Indians were well aware of the importance and sacred nature of water and arable land.

Sir Clements Markham, who was among the first to rediscover the civilization of the Incas, in 1852–53 travelled extensively in Peru. He wrote of the Nasca Valley:

The whole of this space is covered with rich and fertile *haciendas*, yielding large crops . . . ; yet, all that nature has provided for the irrigation of this lovely valley, is a small watercourse, which is dry for eleven months out of the twelve.

But, in former days, before the arrival of the destroying Spaniards, the engineering skill of the Incas had contended with the arid obstacles of nature, and, by executing a work almost unequalled in the history of irrigation, the wilderness of Nasca was converted into a smiling paradise.

This was effected by cutting deep trenches along the whole length of the valley, and so far up into the mountains, that to this day the inhabitants know not to what distances they are carried.

High up the valley are the main trenches, called, in the language of the Incas, *puquios*. They are some four feet in height, with the sides and roof lined with stones. As they descend, they separate into smaller *puquios*, which ramify in every direction over the valley, supplying each estate with the most delicious water, and feeding the little streams that irrigate and fertilize the soil.

The main trenches are many feet below the surface, and at intervals of about two hundred yards there are *ojos*, or small holes, by which workmen may go down into the vault and clear away any obstruction. The *puquios* diverge in every direction, some of them crossing over others, and, before they reach the termination of cultivation towards the south, all the water has been exhausted on the various estates. There are fifteen vine and cotton estates watered by this means in the vale of Nasca.*

The European educated in the classical tradition is apt to look down upon the ancient civilizations of the Americas, but from there have come about a hundred cultivated plants, of which many, such as potatoes, maize, tomatoes, cocoa and rubber, now form part of his staple diet or serve to make objects of everyday use. So thoroughly, however, did the Spaniards destroy the irrigation systems and terraced fields where these plants were first cultivated that they have never been rebuilt.

* Sir Clements Markham, *Cuzco and Lima*, 1856.

In Europe in prehistoric times people living on the North Sea coasts learned to build primitive dikes against the encroachments of the sea and to erect their dwellings on artificial mounds reinforced with stakes. The Romans, with their more advanced engineering skills, developed a system of dikes to protect the Netherlands and improved many waterways to aid the rapid transport of troops to the Empire's frontiers.

In the Notebooks of Leonardo da Vinci, that universal genius, are several hundred references to water, and sound advice which has not always been followed by later engineers:

> The straighter the course of a river, the swifter its current and the greater the erosion of its banks. To prevent this, the beds of such rivers should be widened, or their waters must be made to follow a winding course or be divided into branches. But if a river with many meanders becomes sluggish and marshy, its course should be straightened to an extent which gives its waters sufficient movement but does not lead to the undermining of the embankments.

Of Leonardo's many plans for the building of canals, the diversion of rivers and the draining of marshes, few were realized in his own time.

As we have already seen, however, in water engineering the palm must go to the Netherlands. From the Middle Ages, wherever a scheme for land drainage and reclamation or the building of dikes and embankments was proposed, Dutch engineers were in demand.

One of them was Cornelius Vermuyden, who arrived in England in 1621 to carry out work on the Thames embankments and at Windsor. Next he undertook to reclaim drowned land in Royal Hatfield Chase in Yorkshire. Part of his scheme was unsuccessful and resulted in the flooding of an area to the north-west of Hatfield Chase, which in turn gave rise to riots by the local population and attacks on the Dutch and Flemish workmen he had engaged. Nevertheless, Vermuyden retained the confidence of Charles I, who knighted him in 1629.

Accordingly in that same year, when proposals were made for large-scale reclamation of land in the Great Level of the Fens, an area of about 700,000 acres, in spite of a general outcry against the further employment of foreigners it was soon discovered that the only man capable of planning this enterprise was Vermuyden. Haphazard and piecemeal drainage of England's fenlands had been attempted for hundreds of years; but since the Reformation the older ditches and embankments formerly maintained by monastic establishments had been neglected, and the new landowners commanded neither the resources nor the skill to carry out more than local improvements. The new works put in hand soon encountered active opposition from the fenmen who, although they led a miserable existence in their watery environment, living on fish and wild fowl, could see in its conversion to farmland nothing but a loss of their rights of common for the benefit of foreigners and intruders.

When the King took a personal interest in forwarding the scheme alarm spread to the towns bordering the fenlands, such as Cambridge and Huntingdon, which had long since been strongholds of Puritanism and where the King's motives were suspect. The opposition, fundamentally political, crystallized before long in the person of Oliver Cromwell, whose energetic resistance brought the project to a halt. Vermuyden was undaunted, however, and even during the years of civil war he continued to put forward his plans. In 1649 Parliament authorized a renewal of operations and in 1653 his perseverance was rewarded when the drainage works of the Great Level were declared complete. But Vermuyden had ruined himself financially and he passed into impoverished obscurity; neither the place nor the date of his death is known. Although in subsequent years much more work had to be done, especially in improving the outfalls of the rivers, England owes the reclamation of a substantial acreage of her most fertile land to this single-minded Dutchman.

In the seventeenth century the elector of Brandenburg and then the Prussian kings, Frederick William I and Frederick the Great, set about the rehabilitation of the heaths, bogs and flooded areas of Brandenburg and East Prussia. The work was carried out by the Frisian Count Leonhard van Haarlem, who was familiar with Dutch methods. He encountered the same difficulties as had Vermuyden: fever, sickness, the hostility of the ferrymen and fishermen who feared to lose their livelihood. In East Prussia a number of the new settlers forsook the land won from the bogs, and Frederick William had to threaten with death those who left their farms. As in England, despite setbacks, incidents and difficulties of all kinds, Prussia won, in Frederick the Great's phrase, 'a principality without a war'.

In the baroque period waterworks took a more frivolous turn. Basins, fountains, cascades and grottoes enlivened any suggestion of formality in the gardens: hosts surprised their guests with hydraulic organs imitating various sounds, or sprays of water which besprinkled unwary strollers. In the princely courts of that period engineers used their knowledge and skill to create settings, deceptions and whimwhams which today seem childish. Sea battles were re-enacted and spectacular entertainments mounted upon floating stages; water invaded the theatres, with storm and shipwreck becoming for a time an essential part of drama and even of opera. The single object of such diversions was to please the senses and the imagination; none the less they helped to perfect water techniques. By the end of the rococo period a new age was starting, that of the natural sciences and industrialization.

New ways to harness the power of water were now sought. Since prehistoric times man had known how to make modest use of the energy of flowing water. In the workshops of the Middle Ages water had of course long been playing the part to be taken by steam in the factories of the nineteenth century; without it many flour mills, saw mills, powder mills, paper manufactories, foundries and grinding shops so important in medieval economy would never have come to life, while without pumps mining would have been almost impossible.

A water turbine was invented as early as 1750 by Dr Johann von Segner of Göttingen. This was a 'reaction turbine' and consisted of a cylindrical vessel with two nozzles inserted at the sides of the base. When the cylinder was filled with water the thrust of the water leaving the nozzles made the cylinder revolve about its own axis. But Segner himself regarded this 'turbine' as little more than a toy, and three quarters of a century passed before the principle was applied successfully to a practical water-powered prime-mover.

In 1826 the Paris Société d'Encouragement offered a prize of six thousand francs for the construction of an economical turbine with high performance. Many inventors set to work, encouraged by industrialists. The prize-winner was Benoît Fourneyron, a brilliant young French engineer, who built a radial turbine. Shortly afterwards hundreds of patents were taken out in the United States for as many sorts of turbine, some of steel, some of cast-iron. In the twentieth century, giant water turbines came into use in all parts of the world, converting the energy of falling water into electricity.

The great barrages and their associated hydro-electric installations are the most impressive technological achievements of our own time, and they have had a large part in changing the appearance of the landscape. They convert streams into lakes, seal up gorges and defiles, hold back enormous rivers, and thus permit the watering of parched valleys and of deserts. Description of them seems to demand superlatives. The enthusiast for technical achievement will certainly regard the high walls of smooth concrete and their graceful lines as a pleasing combination of the functional and the aesthetic. For a few years the 932-foot high Grand Dixence Dam in Switzerland, completed in 1961, had the distinction of being the world's tallest, but for the time being at least the record goes to Ingurskaya Dam in the U.S.S.R. with a height of 988 feet. The barrage across the Mahanadi River in India, combination of concrete and earth dams, has a total length of over fifteen miles. The Owen Falls dam across the White Nile where it leaves Lake Victoria Nyanza makes the lake in effect a reservoir with an area of nearly 27,000 square miles.

The advantages of such awe-inspiring engineering feats are not always obvious, however, to those who are displaced as the waters rise and submerge their former homelands. The building of the Kariba Dam, for example, created a man-made lake which will eventually cover an area of two thousand square miles. Nor was the Zambezi lightly conquered even by the massive resources of an international engineering consortium: more than once the river in unprecedented flood devastated the work being carried out in the Kariba Gorge. With the building of the High Dam at Sadd el-Aali on the Nile, a few miles above the older Aswan Dam, the valley above it is being turned into a lake three hundred miles long. Beneath its waters will disappear not only temples, tombs and many pre-historic sites of great interest, but also villages, good agricultural land and the Sudanese town of Wadi Halfa. Nevertheless, to Egypt as a whole the value of this immense reservoir and of the hydro-electricity produced by the scheme outweighs other considerations.

We shall turn later to some other large-scale plans for altering the face of the earth. But that scheme known by the name of Atlantropa, conceived by the German engineer Hermann Soergel in 1928, deserves a mention here.

Soergel's plan was to build dams across the Dardanelles and the Straits of Gibraltar, with large locks to allow the passage of ships, so that the Mediterranean would be steadily reduced in area because water lost by evaporation would not be replaced (as it is at present) by inflow from the Atlantic and Black Sea. He calculated that in a hundred years the Mediterranean would have fallen 330 feet, and that then the building of two more dams, one across the Straits of Messina and one from Sicily to Tunis, would divide the Mediterranean into two basins whose water level could be controlled. All the countries bordering those sea basins would gain an enormous acreage of fertile land, and in addition the dams would supply hydro-electricity. Europe and Africa would be so much closer that they would become one continent, to be called Atlantropa.

This was not the only bold scheme put forward by Hermann Soergel. In 1935 he proposed that the River Congo should be dammed and its waters turned northwards to create an enormous lake in the swampy Congo Basin, at the heart of the continent. The main outlet from this lake would be northwards into Lake Chad, which is considered by geologists to be very much smaller than it was some ten thousand years ago and today has no outlet to the sea. Restored to the size of an inland sea, Lake Chad would provide irrigation for the Sahara Desert. It would have an outlet to the eastern Mediterranean basin and thus also provide a new navigable waterway longer than the Nile.

These projects belong, fortunately perhaps, to the domain of Utopia. Geology, climate, economics and politics stand in the way; man too recoils against the realization of such titanic schemes. If the dams of Soergel's plan were to be bombarded and destroyed during hostilities, a wave a thousand feet high would rush from one end of the Mediterranean to the other, drowning millions of the people living on its shores. Nor is it possible to foresee all the results of interference with the ocean currents, for example, on this scale. But perhaps other and more practicable projects will replace Soergel's Atlantropa.

CHAPTER TWO

LINKS ACROSS THE WATER

THE ADVANCE of a band of Old Stone Age people is stopped by a deep and swift river. It would be risky to allow the women and children to go into the stream. Exploring the bank they notice, on the other side, a tree fallen half way across the river but still held by its roots. The men set to work to cut down another tree, put it in the water and lodge it against the first, thus making a bridge which can be crossed.

All primitive people made bridges of a kind wherever a watercourse barred their way and could safely be crossed with the help of floating logs. They used tree trunks or flat stones for narrow streams, or swung across on long creepers, or built frail bamboo footbridges for crossing steep-sided gorges. In other words, bridges are the oldest architectural works applied to water, one of the earliest challenges to man's technical skill.

A long evolutionary process leads from simple improvised river crossings to massive masonry bridges and modern giants built of concrete or steel. As he passed from one extreme to the other man gathered experience and knowledge of different methods of providing permanent links across broad streams and the heads of estuaries. He thought of building ramps extending from either bank to shorten the span to be bridged; of using boats to serve as pontoons; of filling boats with stones and sinking them to provide foundations for piers to carry a timber deck; and then of building piers of stone or timber into the river bed. Pointed arch construction probably originated with the Sumerians, while the Romans perfected the round stone arch and used it in their many bridges and aqueducts, which are among antiquity's most notable technical achievements.

With the wane of classical civilization the art of bridge building vanished from the West, and Europe knew nothing of the Chinese invention, about the first century A.D., of the suspension bridge. Under Charlemagne Europe's roads and bridges were partly restored, but by the twelfth century, when the continent was ready for an economic revival, inland communications were very poor, and there is a tradition—or, as some contend, a legend—that a 'Brotherhood of Bridge-builders' arose either in Italy (the *Fratres Pontifices*) or in southern France (the *Frères Pontiffes*) who pledged themselves to care for travellers and to build and maintain bridges, and whose communities spread throughout Christian Europe. Whether this was so or not, there was a revival of the building of substantial stone bridges: work began on Old London Bridge in 1176 and on the Pont d'Avignon a year later. In the succeeding centuries were built such famous bridges as the Ponte Vecchio (1360–67) and Ponte Santa Trinità (1566–69) in Florence; the Rialto (1588–91) in Venice; the Pont Neuf (1578–1604) and Pont Royal (1685–89) in Paris; the Neuilly Bridge (1768–74) over the Seine.

Then was introduced a revolutionary new material for bridge-building: iron. In 1775–79 a cast-iron arch of 100 foot span was built over the Severn at Coalbrookdale; others of greater span quickly followed. Iron-founding techniques improved rapidly, and Thomas Telford used wrought-iron links for the chains of his great suspension bridge carrying the Holyhead road over the Menai Straits, which was opened in 1826. When the building of the railway from Chester to Holyhead called for very strong, rigid structures to carry the line over the Conway estuary and the Menai Straits without interfering with the passage of shipping Robert Stephenson designed tubular spans of wrought iron inside which the tracks were laid. The longer, the Britannia Bridge, consists of two tubular beams each 1,511 feet long and weighing 4,680 tons, supported on masonry piers, 230 feet above the Menai Straits; both bridges have carried the increasingly heavy rail traffic since the opening of the line in 1850 to the present day.

It is not surprising that the railway engineers, the men of the iron road, turned to iron as the material for the bridges needed to carry their thrusting new lines over water obstacles. Confidence and ambition grew, and in the 1870s plans were made for bridging the wide and often stormy Firths of Tay and Forth, to provide a direct rail link from Edinburgh to Dundee and eliminate the uncomfortable ferry crossings. There were sceptics and scoffers, but in 1878 the two-mile-long bridge over the Firth of Tay, designed by Thomas Bouch, was opened and acclaimed as an engineering masterpiece. The wrought-iron spans, supported more than eighty feet above the water on cast-iron columns founded in brick and concrete piers in the river bed, for eighteen months carried the trains of the North British Railway, to the great satisfaction of the erstwhile ferry passengers. Then, on a wild night in December 1879, people in Dundee watching the bridge for the arrival of the Edinburgh train saw a flash of sparks and a trail of light sweep down to the stormy waters: all thirteen high spans across the navigable part of the firth—more than half a mile of the bridge—had been blown down, carrying with them the train, its crew, and about seventy passengers.

The reason for this disaster was never established, but it is more likely to have been due to a weakness of design than to a failure of material—a lack of understanding of the stresses imposed on the superstructure of a high bridge exposed to gale-force winds. A new Tay Bridge (which is still one of the world's longest over water), in which much of the ironwork of the original was re-used, was built in 1882–87 alongside the line of the first one, the stumps of whose piers can still be seen by today's railway travellers.

Before the catastrophe Sir Thomas Bouch had designed a suspension bridge to cross the Firth of Forth in two spans of 1,600 feet, and the central pier was already rising on an island in the middle of the firth. With the loss of the Tay Bridge and the subsequent public outcry this plan was abandoned; Sir Thomas died, his health broken, in 1880.

Meanwhile there had been important developments both in Europe and in the United States. In 1867 the German engineer Gottfried Heinrich Gerber built across the River Main the first modern cantilever bridge, with a central span of 425 feet. In 1874, after seven years' work, the St Louis Bridge over the turbulent waters and shifting bed of the Mississippi was finished. Designed by James B. Eads, the bridge has three arches, all over 500-foot span, in which for the first time extensive use was made of steel for the structural work.

Thus when in 1881 the task of bridging the Forth was placed in the hands of John Fowler and Benjamin Baker, technology had already provided the means to confound the pessimists, and the two engineers thought along entirely new lines. For the next eight years the local people observed with interest, wonder and pride the growth of three massive steel cantilever towers 1,710 feet apart —one on either bank and one on the island—the outward extension of their tubular steel arms and, finally, the erection of the 350-foot suspended spans closing the gaps between them 150 feet above the waterway. The Forth Bridge was and remains a masterpiece; it has defied William Morris's description 'supremest specimen of all ugliness' and become the very symbol of the age of steam and steel, appropriate to its setting.

Steel, wire cables of unprecedented strength, reinforced and prestressed concrete; girder or cantilever, arch and suspended span— the engineers have the means to take increasingly great leaps over river, estuary and sea inlet and to set up new records for longest single span or total length. The longest arch span, 1,652 feet, belongs to the Bayonne Bridge; but the waterway it crosses, the Kill van Kull river between Staten Island and Jersey City, cannot compare with the setting of the Sydney Harbour Bridge, a mere two feet shorter. The opening in 1965 of the Verrazano Narrows bridge across the entrance to New York Harbour, with a record span of 4,260 feet, ousted San Francisco's Golden Gate from first place among suspension bridges, a position it had held for nearly thirty years. Since 1962 a multi-span bridge $5\frac{1}{2}$ miles long has crossed the Maracaibo Lagoon in Venezuela, linking the oilfields to the rest of the country and to the Pan-American Highway; while in the following year a combination of bridges and tunnels provided a $17\frac{1}{2}$-mile link across Chesapeake Bay on the eastern seaboard of the United States.

Tunnels by their very nature cannot appeal to the imagination as bridges do, but driving a tunnel to carry modern rail or road traffic can present formidable engineering problems even with the most up-to-date technological aids. The Romans built a number of tunnels for water supply and drainage, but it was the growth of canal networks in the eighteenth century that spurred engineers to devise new tunnelling methods—in this case to carry waterways through land obstacles. The first substantial river tunnel was the Thames Tunnel, which was proposed as early as 1798, started, and abandoned in the early years of the nineteenth century. In 1818 Marc Isambard Brunel patented his 'tunnelling shield', and in 1825 he was appointed engineer for the Thames Tunnel, to run from Rotherhithe to Wapping; his son Isambard in the early years acted as superintendent engineer. The task proved extremely difficult and costly in both lives and money, and the tunnel was not completed until 1843; today it carries one of the lines of London's Underground beneath the river.

Before the end of the century such important underwater links as the rail tunnel under the Mersey, the four-mile Severn Tunnel and London's Blackwall Tunnel were in use; 1908 saw the completion of Rotherhithe Tunnel, at that time the largest of its kind, and of the first Hudson River Tunnel in New York, which had a history as long and troubled as that of Brunel's Thames Tunnel.

The development of underground railways, especially in London and New York, and the rapid increase in motor traffic called for numerous underwater connections. The Mersey Road Tunnel, for example, was opened in 1934; because of the nature of the river bed, it had to be driven at a depth of 170 feet below high water mark, whereas the 1963 addition to the Thames road tunnels, from Dartford to Purfleet, is at a maximum depth of only 100 feet.

But the most ambitious underwater project is undoubtedly that for a tunnel under the English Channel, which may be fulfilled before the end of the twentieth century. Schemes for linking Britain to the Continent in this way go back at least to the days of Napoleon, and later in the nineteenth century work actually began on both sides, but was abandoned. Boring through the chalky sea bed should offer few problems, but the ventilation of a tunnel about thirty miles long is not an easy matter; the latest proposals therefore are that the Channel Tunnel should be for electric trains capable of carrying motor vehicles as well as passengers.

Underwater links of quite another kind connect country to country and continent to continent: the submarine cables. Samuel Morse, who with his code made the electric telegraph a really practical means of communication, demonstrated in New York in 1842 that underwater telegraphy worked in principle. In 1850 a thin cable insulated with gutta percha was laid under the English Channel, but this was soon broken—reputedly by fishermen who accidentally hauled it up and thought they had caught a monstrous eel. An improved cable laid the following year was successful and the London papers soon carried columns of continental news headed 'By Electric Telegraph'; submarine cables were laid between Denmark and Sweden, England and Holland and through the Mediterranean.

It is not known who first had the idea of connecting Europe and America by submarine cable. In 1850 the Roman Catholic bishop of Newfoundland, John Mullock, complained in print that 'in every plan for transatlantic communication Halifax is always mentioned and the natural capabilities of Newfoundland entirely overlooked'. He described a route for a cable to connect St John's to the mainland which, by enabling news brought by trans-Atlantic steamers to the port to be telegraphed to the rest of the continent, would 'bring America two days nearer to Europe . . . should the telegraphic communication between England and Ireland be realized', and he concluded with the hope that 'the day is not far distant when St John's will be the first link in the electric chain which will unite the Old World to the New'.

The bishop's words made sense. Matthew Fontaine Maury, the pioneer of oceanography, already had an inkling that between Newfoundland and Ireland the ocean bed was generally level with no great submarine chasms, and soundings carried out between 1849 and 1853 under his direction confirmed that opinion. Early in 1854, in a letter to the Secretary of the United States Navy, he wrote: 'The bottom of the sea between the two places is a plateau which seems to have been placed there especially for the purpose of holding the wires of the submarine telegraph. . . .' Meanwhile work had begun in 1853 on a cable across Newfoundland, but the company undertaking it failed; this brought the engineer responsible, Frederick Gisborne, to New York where (also early in 1854) he turned to Cyrus Field for help.

Cyrus Field was a man of considerable business ability and great determination. He had already, by sheer hard work, paid off in full the debts incurred by a company in which he had been a junior partner and was now, at the age of 34, a very wealthy man. The laying of the trans-Atlantic cable was to make heavy demands upon both his tenacity (in furthering the project he crossed the Atlantic forty times) and his fortune. Field was immediately interested in what Frederick Gisborne had to say and quickly saw the advantages of a link not merely across Newfoundland and the water separating the island from the continent, but across the ocean itself. He consulted Maury and Morse, convinced others of the feasibility of the scheme, and the 'New York, Newfoundland, and London Telegraph Company' came into being. In 1856 the cable linking St John's to the telegraph system of the United States was completed: Cyrus Field left for England.

In London his drive and enthusiasm impressed those whose help he enlisted, including members of the government, and at the end of the year the Atlantic Telegraph Company was organized with the declared aim 'to continue the existing line of the New York, Newfoundland, and London Telegraph Company to Ireland by making . . . a submarine telegraph for the Atlantic'. One of the directors was a young university professor whose skill in overcoming technical difficulties with the first submarine cables had already proved invaluable—William Thomson, afterwards Lord Kelvin. Orders for the cable were placed before Cyrus Field returned to Washington, where he was at once involved in obtaining government support.

By the beginning of August 1857 the miles of cable had been designed, manufactured and coiled in the holds of two ships—the U.S.S. *Niagara* and H.M.S. *Agamemnon*. The shore end of the cable having been secured, the *Niagara*, with Cyrus Field aboard, steamed westwards from Valentia Harbour, Ireland, paying out the cable behind her over a system of revolving drums. H.M.S. *Agamemnon* was to meet her in mid Atlantic, splice the cable and sail on to Newfoundland with the other half. But when over three hundred miles of cable had been laid it snapped as the braking drum was applied too suddenly. The cable end was lost and the ships returned to port.

Cyrus Field refused to give up, and the directors supported him. With new equipment, *Niagara* and *Agamemnon* set out in June 1858 for an Atlantic rendezvous; this time they were to lay the cable from mid ocean to either shore. Having ridden out a violent storm, the ships met, spliced the cable and set sail in opposite directions. When they were forty miles apart the cable broke, but they were able to make a fresh start; then once more, when there was a distance of about 150 miles between them, the cable parted, and it could not be recovered. Still undaunted, Cyrus Field and his associates swiftly organized another attempt, and this time *Niagara* steamed safely into Trinity Bay, Newfoundland, with her end of the cable, while *Agamemnon* brought the other end into Valentia Harbour, on 5 August 1858. The first message sent under the ocean began: 'Europe and America are united by telegraphic communication. . . .'

The union was short-lived, however. The cable was unable to withstand the stresses and by October no more messages were passing through it. Cyrus Field was still not prepared to admit defeat, but he was unable to raise more capital before the Civil War intervened. Then in 1864, thanks to his 'valuable and successful exertions', the Atlantic Telegraph Company came to life again. It was proposed that the cable should be laid by a single vessel, eliminating the need for splicing in mid-ocean. There was only one ship capable of coiling in her holds the miles of cable needed to cross the Atlantic from side to side: Brunel's *Great Eastern*. Unsuccessful as a passenger liner, the great iron ship now came into her own, although even her first attempt, in July 1865, ended with a broken cable lost after twelve hundred miles had been laid. Cyrus Field determined to try again; the company was re-organized as the Anglo-American Telegraph Company. With an entirely new cable and Cyrus Field on board, on 13 July 1866 *Great Eastern* once more steamed westward from Valentia and two weeks later reached Heart's Content, Trinity Bay, more than 2,000 miles of cable safely laid in her wake. It was an occasion of great rejoicing.

Moreover, *Great Eastern* successfully grappled for the cable lost the previous year, spliced it and completed a second underwater link between two continents.

In the century which has passed since Cyrus Field's faith in the trans-Atlantic cable was finally vindicated many ships have spun a web of telegraph and telephone cables around the world, crisscrossing the great oceans. In this one respect, if in no other, the continents may truly be said to be united.

CHAPTER THREE

THE VICTORY OF SUEZ

IN 1567 His Most Catholic Majesty King Philip II of Spain issued a proclamation stating that any subject making so bold as to separate two continents would be liable to the death penalty, and citing the authority of the Church he declared that if God had intended that there should be a waterway between them it would have existed naturally. This warning was addressed to certain Spaniards, enthusiasts for progress, who contemplated digging a canal across the isthmus of Darien and bringing the Pacific and the Atlantic in touch in order to hasten the transport of the gold and riches of Peru to Europe.

It seems likely that Philip II was in fact thinking of the English: if such a canal were built they would have made every effort to gain control of it. The Caribbean Sea was indeed infested with English pirates. But political considerations apart, it was the contemporary view that to cut across an isthmus and unite two seas was not only a crime but a heresy.

On 21 February 1827, two hundred and sixty years later, Eckermann recorded the following reflection by Goethe five years before the poet's death:

> It is quite indispensable to the United States that they should create a passage bringing the Gulf of Mexico and the Pacific into communication and I feel sure that they will do so. I should like to see it happen, but I shall not be there. I should also like to see the Rhine and the Danube connected, but this enterprise

too is so gigantic that I doubt if it will be achieved. . . . And finally I should like to see England in possession of a canal cut across the Suez isthmus. I wish I could witness the completion of these three great works, which would be really worth the bother of living fifty years longer.

Within a few years of this utterance a young French diplomat named Ferdinand de Lesseps, newly appointed to a post in Egypt, was pondering a memorandum which set forth the arguments for and against a canal linking the Mediterranean to the Red Sea through the isthmus. It had been written by Jean-Baptiste Lepère, the engineer who accompanied Napoleon's expedition to Egypt in 1789 and who carried out a survey for a canal intended to provide the French with a short trade route to India. Napoleon flung open the doors of the land of pyramids and sphinxes, and archaeologists, historians and philologists had followed. De Lesseps, who remained in Egypt from 1832 until 1838 and acquired a very thorough knowledge of the country and its people, became interested in the antiquities of Egypt and followed up his reading of Lepère's report by studying the history of canals which had connected the Nile to the Red Sea in ancient times.

It has been inferred from an inscription at Karnak that in the time of the pharaohs Seti I and Rameses II, fourteenth to thirteenth centuries B.C., a canal was dug connecting an eastern arm of the Nile through Wadi Tamilat to Lake Timsah, north of the Bitter Lakes, whence a trade route was established to the head of the Red Sea, which was then nearer to the lakes than it is today. The canal left unfinished by Necho II about 600 B.C. has already been mentioned; according to Herodotus Necho abandoned this work because an oracle warned him that he was 'labouring for the barbarian'.

To some extent the oracle was right. The Egyptians could certainly have used this canal to pass their fleet from the one sea to the other, and Necho, who organized the naval expedition which first circumnavigated Africa, probably had some inkling of the part to be played one day by such a water link. Nevertheless the Assyrians, the Persians and other Asiatic invaders would have made use of it in order to establish themselves firmly in Egypt. Necho's real reason for giving up was similar to that underlying Philip II's hostility to the digging of a canal in Panama.

Darius, King of Persia, about a century later resumed the work relinquished under Necho, and the Ptolemies made various improvements, but by Cleopatra's reign the branch of the Nile which had provided the Mediterranean access had silted up, and the canal went out of use. Trajan reputedly repaired part of it and had another channel, the *Amnis Trajanus*, excavated between it and Old Cairo. The Arab conquerors of Egypt in the seventh century restored the canal, but subsequently the waterway seems to have become wholly or partly unnavigable. After the opening of the sea route to the Orient by way of the Cape of Good Hope the Venetians, whose trade had suffered, thought of cutting a canal through the isthmus, and the German philosopher Leibniz urged Louis XIV of France to embark on the same undertaking. About 1770 the Mameluke ruler of Egypt, Ali Bey, also favoured the construction of a canal, but only with the arrival of Napoleon and Lepère was anything positive attempted.

To Lepère the line of the future canal was indicated by the depression occupied by the two Bitter Lakes within the seventy-mile span of this isthmus. But Napoleon's Egyptian adventure was of short duration, which explains the mistakes which abound in Lepère's memorandum. He believed, for instance, that the level of the Red Sea was higher than that of the Mediterranean by thirty feet, making direct communication possible only by the use of a flight of locks, and therefore advised that the example of the ancient Egyptians should be copied and a route chosen which passed into the valley of the Nile.

When Ferdinand de Lesseps first read Lepère's memorandum the last thing he suspected was that this work was to be his life's career. The idea certainly excited his interest in spite of Lepère's doubts. For eleven years, however, de Lesseps held important diplomatic posts in various European countries until, in 1849, disagreeing with government policy, he retired to live in the country in France. Here he had time to think about plans for a canal through the isthmus and to study all aspects of trade between East and West. Meanwhile, engineers surveying for a scheme to build a canal 250 miles long from Suez to Alexandria via Cairo had established that there was no difference in the levels of the Mediterranean and the Red Seas.

Events in Egypt now took a hand. The country, as part of the Ottoman Empire, was ruled by a governor who, when de Lesseps was first in Egypt, was Mehemet Ali, 'Founder of modern Egypt'; he died in 1849. De Lesseps became very friendly with one of Ali's younger sons, Mohammed Saïd, a friendship renewed in 1852 when the latter was in temporary exile in Paris during the rule of Abbas Pasha. When Saïd became Governor in 1854 he responded to de Lesseps' letter of congratulation by inviting him to Egypt. Choosing his moment carefully, de Lesseps put the proposal for a maritime canal through the isthmus before Saïd Pasha, who was enthusiastic, and granted de Lesseps a concession for the undertaking. Important among its provisions were that shares in the company to be formed would be available to investors of all nations, that the concession would expire ninety-nine years after the completion of the canal, and that ships of all countries would be treated equally. De Lesseps gave great importance to the international character of the enterprise. The company was also to build a fresh-water canal from the Nile to Lake Timsah with branches to the Suez and Mediterranean ends of the maritime canal.

For the next few years de Lesseps worked hard to raise the capital and to win the support of governments and leading men in many countries. His diplomatic training and contacts stood him in good stead. Only the British Government offered strenuous opposition, suspicious that the French aimed to dominate Egypt—despite the fact that at that very time France and Britain were allies in the Crimean War. The British Government feared that disruption of the Ottoman Empire, whether the threat came from Russia or from the ambitious Napoleon III, would endanger the overland route to India and British influence in the East. It was a short-sighted view which many eminent men in the country did not share, and the most devious British diplomatic moves intended to prevent the building of the canal, which continued for more than a decade, were ultimately thwarted. De Lesseps gained firm support in his own country and from the Emperor Napoleon, and also from the Austrian Chancellor, Metternich. (Not until 1875, when Disraeli bought the Khedive Ismail Pasha's shares in the company, did Britain have any say in the affairs of the Canal. The Suez Canal Company remained the proprietors until President Nasser, anticipating the expiry of the concession by twelve years, nationalized the Canal in 1956.)

One of the first things de Lesseps did was to set up an international commission of eminent engineers who met in Paris in 1855, applauded the scheme and appointed a sub-commission to study the land in Egypt. This it did thoroughly and promptly, reporting early in 1856 that 'the direct route offers every facility for the execution of the canal itself . . . and presents no more than ordinary difficulties for the creation of two ports. . . .' It was estimated that the cost would not exceed £8 million. Here was confirmation of the feasibility of a maritime canal by a body of professional men representative not of one country but of all the European powers.

By the end of 1858 de Lesseps' efforts as propagandist had resulted in the raising of a substantial part of the capital, and although the agreement of the Sultan of Turkey to the concession had still not been obtained (largely due to British pressure), on 25 April 1859 Ferdinand de Lesseps 'gave the first blow with the pickaxe, and turned the first spadeful of earth' on the site of the future Port Said. Twenty-five thousand men, largely contingents of forced labour from all the provinces of Egypt, were soon at work. Although some machinery and dredgers were used the greater part of the immense task of excavating thousands of tons of soil was done by hand in the early years. Since there was no drinking water available in the stretch of desert between the seas, supplies for the vast labour force had to be transported by a large number of camels at a cost of three million francs a year, until the Sweet-water Canal, following for much of its course the line of Necho's canal through Wadi Tamilat, reached Lake Timsah in 1862.

In November that same year the first waters from the Mediterranean were allowed to flow through the excavated, though not completed, channel to Lake Timsah. In 1863 Mohammed Saïd died, and although his successor, Ismail Pasha, was favourable towards the Canal Company, approval from the Sultan was still lacking. Under British pressure objections to the use of forced labour (which had officially been banned throughout the Ottoman Empire) and to the amount of land conceded to the Company were now raised in Constantinople. With Napoleon III as arbitrator, new terms were agreed, the most important change being that henceforth hired labour must be employed. Although the Company received substantial indemnities from the Egyptian government, this condition increased the costs and its financial resources were soon strained. From 1864 about half the labour force was European. An outbreak of cholera in 1865 brought further difficulties. Indirectly, by compelling the company to use more, and more powerful, machinery these factors probably hastened completion of the canal and its terminal ports. After the Sultan's authorization had finally been granted, in 1866, work went ahead more rapidly.

The opening of the canal was the occasion for great ceremonies. At considerable expense the Khedive entertained important guests from many countries, among them the Empress Eugénie of France and the Crown Prince of Prussia—though their meeting did not prevent the outbreak of the Franco-Prussian War eight months later. On the morning of 17 November 1869, a fleet of forty ships headed by the French vessel carrying the Empress and Ferdinand de Lesseps entered the canal at Port Said and passed majestically through to Ismailia in twelve hours—a grounded Egyptian frigate being removed only just in time. The fleet steamed through to Port Suez three days later.

The Company weathered its financial difficulties and, although construction costs had soared to more than twice the estimated £8 million, within five years began to make a profit. The Suez Canal initiated a new era in relations between Europe and Asia. The sea route to India no longer passed by the Cape of Good Hope. From ports such as London or Hamburg the route to Bombay had been shortened by five thousand miles. From the Mediterranean ports the distance saved was even greater. Further, East Africa now entered the orbit of Europe, and the great powers were already casting envious eyes upon it.

Ferdinand de Lesseps, acclaimed throughout the world, enjoyed his triumph in his château of La Chesnaie, built by Charles VII of France for his mistress Agnès Sorel. He was soon to be torn away by a new and grandiose adventure.

My friends advised me against it [he wrote later], they recommended me to retire after Suez. But a general who has once gained a battle never refused to engage in another.

The new battle in which de Lesseps intended to engage was going to take place in the New World and, more precisely, in that part of Central America where, three centuries earlier, Philip of Spain had forbidden the digging of a canal under pain of death.

CHAPTER FOUR

THE SCANDAL OF PANAMA

THE FIRST notion of a future Panama Canal arose soon after the day in 1513 when, after crossing the tongue of land between the two oceans, Vasco Nuñez de Balboa reached the waters of the Pacific. One of his companions, Alvaro Saavedra, convinced that there was no natural link between the Pacific and the Atlantic, proposed to the Emperor Charles V the construction of a ship canal.

Another proposal was made a few years later by Hernando Cortes: the destroyer of the Aztec kingdom recommended cutting through the isthmus of Tehuantepec in southern Mexico. Other plans of Spanish origin dealt with possible canals through Nicaragua and from the Gulf of Darien. In 1550 Antonio Galvao, a Portuguese, published a book intended to demonstrate that the land bridge between the continents could be pierced at any of those points. In 1771 the Spanish Government ordered a survey to be made for a canal route across the Tehuantepec Isthmus, but decided this was impracticable. Another Spanish expedition in 1779 explored the Nicaraguan route, and in the following year, Britain and Spain being at war, a naval expedition under Nelson landed in Nicaragua. Nelson reported favourably on the possibility of building a canal which would effectively divide Spain's American empire, but fever almost wiped out the members of the expedition and nearly killed Nelson. Early in the nineteenth century Alexander von Humboldt suggested a number of routes which he considered worth study. Simón Bolívar, liberator of Colombia, favoured the Isthmus of Panama, which was then part of his newly independent country. Coincidentally with the emergence of the independent republics of Central and South America the United States proclaimed in 1823 the Monroe Doctrine, a warning in effect to the European powers, 'hands off the Americas'. European interest in an inter-oceanic canal did not wane, however; among those who produced plans was Louis Napoleon, the future Napoleon III, who used his enforced leisure while a prisoner following his abortive attempt to gain the French throne in 1840 to study the subject; he favoured the Nicaragua route, declaring that a canal across the Isthmus of Panama would cross 'a country which was marshy, unwholesome, desolate and uninhabitable'.

When the United States occupied the former Mexican territory of California in 1847 the need for improved communications across the isthmus—which involved twenty miles of mule-train transport between the navigable limit of the Chagres River and Panama City—became increasingly obvious. Accordingly, enterprising Americans surveyed a route for a Panama railroad and obtained a concession from the government of Colombia in 1848; but because the California gold rush forced up prices a new contract had to be signed in 1850, one clause of which gave the American company a monopoly of transport, including any future navigable waterway, in the Panama isthmus. A route for a Nicaraguan canal was investigated in the same year. Great Britain meanwhile had become alarmed at the extension of United States influence in Central America, and her fears resulted in the signing of the Clayton-Bulwer Treaty of 1850, which recognized the right of the United States to build a neutral canal while both countries undertook not to obtain exclusive control of it. But American financial and engineering resources available for inter-ocean transport were fully engaged for the next five years in the building of the Panama railroad. This great feat of engineering was carried out under immense difficulties, and while the claim that every sleeper of its 48-mile length represented a life lost was a gross exaggeration, malaria, yellow fever and the general conditions in this tropical region took a heavy toll of the men working on it. The building of the Panama railroad had many useful lessons for the future canal builders; some of them they chose to ignore.

After the Civil War American interest in a canal revived and exploratory expeditions were carried out under naval officers, but economic difficulties in the later 1870s caused all such projects to be dropped. Meanwhile the opening of the Suez Canal had stimulated European interest, and an international geographical congress meeting at Antwerp in 1871 considered in some detail a plan for a Panama Canal put forward by Antoine de Gogorza; the congress of 1875 met in Paris and was presided over by Ferdinand de Lesseps, who advocated a sea-level canal to be financed by shareholders in a Panama Canal company rather than by governments. France was eager to find an enterprise to restore the prestige lost in her humiliating defeat in the Franco-Prussian War. Who better to initiate such a project than the victor of Suez? The Congress established a society to undertake expeditions to Nicaragua and Panama, led by a French naval lieutenant, Lucien-Napoleon Bonaparte-Wyse, great-nephew of Napoleon I. In 1878 Bonaparte-Wyse returned to France with a plan for a canal following very closely the line of the Panama railroad and envisaging a long tunnel through the central highlands of the isthmus—and a concession from the government of Colombia.

In 1879 de Lesseps called an international Congress of engineers, geographers, industrialists and others representing many nations, including China, to consider an inter-oceanic canal. De Lesseps was now aged 73 and as persuasive as ever; but perhaps his very success in overcoming the obstacles to the Suez Canal and the esteem in which he had been held for a decade blinded him to the fact that the problems to be faced in a tropical zone of heavy rainfall, thick jungle and difficult subsoil, and rising several hundred feet above sea level, in a virtually uninhabited area of a young country distant from the seat of government and lacking almost all facilities, were very different from those he had encountered in Egypt. There was an air of inevitability about the Congress's verdict, reached after two weeks of thorough discussion and in the face of opposition from several notable engineers, that a sea-level canal with neither locks nor tunnel, but with a deep cutting down to sea level through the Culebra highlands and a dam to control the Chagres river, was possible. The cost was estimated at £44 millions.

De Lesseps then set about forming the Universal Inter-Oceanic Canal Company and raising capital, but public response was less than he had expected. Late in 1879, therefore, he travelled with a technical commission to the isthmus. In Panama he received a hero's welcome and in January 1880 formally inaugurated work on the canal. The technical experts estimated that the engineering costs would be greater than those forecast; de Lesseps, in optimistic mood, calculated that they would be some £10 million less. His pronouncements about the cost of the canal and the time it would take to complete became increasingly distant from reality. He was hospitably entertained in the United States and seems to have persuaded himself that he had overcome opposition there, but the American government remained hostile to the idea of a canal under European control. Moving on to England (where he stated that the work could be completed in six years), Belgium and Holland,

and thence back to his own country, he undertook a strenuous tour of French cities. By the end of the year the company had raised about twice the capital, £24 million (600 million francs), that had been its initial target, chiefly from small shareholders in France. However, large sums were expended on publicity, on placating hostile sections of the press, on bankers' commissions, and the concession obtained by Bonaparte-Wyse was bought for 10 million francs. The concession in itself was worthless because of the Panama Railroad Company's monopoly, and it cost the Canal Company about £5 million to obtain control of the Railroad Company; the railway, however, was an asset for the movement of men and materials. But even had its affairs been properly managed, the Canal Company never had sufficient capital for the task it had undertaken, the immensity of which the directors consistently underestimated.

The first contractors' men moved into Panama in 1881 and the French tragedy began. Although progress was made in dredging and excavating the deep cut through Culebra, the story became one of successive disasters: landslides caused by the tropical rainfall and the nature of the soil not only ruined the excavations but also engulfed expensive machinery; an earthquake caused enormous damage at Colón and Panama City as well as to the railway; there were gross extravagance and almost unbelievable inefficiency on the part of some of the contractors; there were strikes, political unrest and open insurrection. Above all, yellow fever, malaria, smallpox, typhus and other diseases killed thousands of men, many of whom were recruited in Jamaica and other Caribbean islands. No one at the time realized the part played by mosquitoes in spreading both malaria and yellow fever, and although good hospital services were set up by the Canal Company there was no effective defence against those diseases. Conditions in the town of Panama, moreover, verged on squalor; Colón, ironically in a land of phenomenal rainfall, lacked a supply of clean water.

The Company was forced to raise more and more capital. In 1885 it resorted to the idea of borrowing 600 million francs on lottery bonds. This required government approval, and an engineer sent to the isthmus reported that substantial alterations to the plans were needed if the undertaking were to be completed. De Lesseps had at last to abandon his insistence upon a sea-level canal and accept a scheme for locks. The engineer Gustave Eiffel, then erecting his tower in Paris, was called in, and he designed the locks; but this change of plan came too late. No expedients could now save the Company, and at the end of 1888 liquidators were appointed. Efforts to retrieve the situation dragged on but culminated in a major financial scandal; thousands of small shareholders were ruined and an investigation was demanded, which resulted in 1892 in the prosecution of Ferdinand de Lesseps, his son Charles and other directors of the Canal Company, and Gustave Eiffel, for fraud and embezzlement. The trials revealed a complicated history of corruption and bribery at high levels, involving at least one Minister, which shocked France. In 1893 Ferdinand de Lesseps was sentenced to five years' imprisonment, his son, other directors and Eiffel to two years, as well as fines; the ex-minister, Baïhaut, was subsequently sentenced to five years' imprisonment and a heavy fine and also to loss of civil rights. Ferdinand was now aged eighty-eight and had been too ill even to attend his trial; sunk in a melancholy stupor, he probably never fully understood its outcome and he died at Chesnaie in 1894. He retained to the end the sympathy and affection of many Frenchmen who believed him guilty of no more than 'a reckless disregard of the practical difficulties' and remembered the glory his enterprise had brought to France in earlier years.

On the isthmus great distress had been caused by the collapse of the undertaking and many destitute labourers had to be repatriated. In 1894, however, the liquidators created a New Panama Canal Company, which took over the remaining assets of the old company and reorganized the work. Since 1887 the contract for the 8-mile cut through the Culebra Highlands had been held by Philippe Bunau-Varilla, an able young French engineer who from 1884 to 1886 had acted as Director General in the isthmus, and under his direction work on the Culebra Cut had made good progress. He now devoted all his energies to keeping the Panama Canal project alive. Bonaparte-Wyse had succeeded in renewing the Colombian concession, which stipulated that excavation must be carried on, and by 1897 between three and four thousand men were once more at work. But the company's financial problems were not solved.

Meanwhile the United States government, alarmed at the situation in Panama, in 1889 incorporated the Maritime Canal Company of Nicaragua. This proposed canal would have been 170 miles long, including a passage of 56 miles through Lake Nicaragua and making use of rivers, but involving expensive locks and harbour works. Preliminary work was started but abandoned in 1893 when the construction company failed. Nevertheless, the United States was still eager to see an isthmian canal under full American control, and a new agreement with Great Britain, modifying the Clayton-Bulwer treaty, was signed in 1901. Matters were brought to a head by the Spanish-American War of 1898, after which the United States found itself a colonial power with possessions in the Caribbean and the Pacific. In 1899 the Isthmian Canal Commission was set up, which reported on both the Nicaragua and Panama routes and recommended the former. The New Panama Canal Company, still in financial difficulties, was now prepared to sell its assets; Philippe Bunau-Varilla was active in furthering this end and thus saving from abandonment the years of French endeavour. In his book on the Panama Canal he relates that among the stratagems he used was that of buying sheets of Nicaraguan stamps which showed active volcanoes and sending them to United States Senators, to underline the advantage of the Panama route in this respect, for Nicaragua has many volcanoes and the proposed canal route was more susceptible to earthquakes than Panama. With the prospect of buying the French workings and assets for $40 million, the Canal Commission was prepared to recommend this step to the American government, which acted accordingly and in 1903 signed a treaty with Colombia embodying the transfer of rights. The Colombian senate, however, refused to ratify the treaty, hoping for better terms.

Bunau-Varilla was not to be thwarted. Panama was in a state of political discontent and the French engineer seized the opportunity to instigate a seccession movement from Colombia. Gunboats were dispatched by the government in Bogotá to Colón, but the United States, ostensibly to protect American interests, also sent a gunboat; and since the Canal Company's assets included the Panama Railroad they were able to prevent the passage of Colombian troops across the isthmus to Panama City. The bloodless revolution was soon over, and within a month Bunau-Varilla, acting as Panamanian minister, negotiated a treaty giving the United States rights over the 'Canal Zone', a strip of territory ten miles wide across the isthmus, excluding Colón and Panama City. President Theodore Roosevelt, who had determined that the building of the canal should become a notable achievement of his administration, immediately set up a Canal Commission, which in 1904 appointed John F. Wallace chief engineer.

A limited amount of excavation was still being carried out in the Culebra Cut, but there was an immense amount of preliminary work and planning to be done before the Americans could start on actual construction. An immediate problem was that of sanitation and control of disease. In the 1890s Sir Ronald Ross had established the link between mosquitoes and malaria; Walter Reed of the American Army in Cuba after the Spanish-American War had proved that the same was true of yellow fever, and that control was possible. The measures introduced to the Panama isthmus by Colonel William Gorgas, over which he had to be almost ruthless, contributed a great deal to the eventual success of the American enterprise.

John Wallace was frustrated by administrative difficulties and resigned in 1905; he was succeeded by John F. Stevens, who remained until March 1907. Both these men had produced splendid results so that a first-class organization existed when, at the instigation of President Roosevelt, an Army officer was put in control. This man was Lieutenant Colonel George Washington Goethals, who was vested with almost dictatorial powers. With ample resources in men, money and machines he drove the work forward and overcame the technical and administrative problems, which were many. Earth and rock excavated from the Culebra were used in building the Gatun Dam, itself a massive structure which created the Gatun Lake; the double sets of three locks at either end, which overcame the 85-foot difference between the canal and sea level, together with breakwaters, harbour works and a host of other undertakings, were completed.

On 3 August 1914 the first ocean-going ship, the *Cristobal* belonging to the Panama Railroad, entered the Gatun Locks from the Atlantic and was towed through by electric locomotives; she crossed the lake and passed through the Culebra Cut—renamed Gaillard Cut after one of the Army engineers—under her own steam and reached the Pedro Miguel Lock, the first on the Pacific side. Beyond this lock was the mile-wide Miraflores Lake (also artificially created) to be crossed, and then the two Miraflores Locks and descent to sea level and the Pacific Ocean. On board the *Cristobal* for this 'rehearsal' of the official opening was Philippe Bunau-Varilla; on the same day that he witnessed the final fulfilment of a French dream he learned that his country was once again at war with Germany. The passage of the *Cristobal* revealed difficulties with the locking procedures; but all went smoothly for the formal opening twelve days later, when the larger vessel *Ancon*, with the President of Panama and many officials aboard, entered the Gatun Locks at 8 o'clock in the morning and reached sea level in the Pacific soon after 3 o'clock. Colonel Goethals chose to be among the thousands of spectators who watched this inaugural voyage from the canal banks.

The completion of the canal had a dramatic effect in shortening the sea routes between East and West. Its defence in time of war has been of vital consequence to the United States, and the vulnerability of the locks to precision bombing has revived interest in proposals for a sea-level canal, which would not be beyond the capabilities of modern excavating and dredging techniques. Such a canal might well be cut across the Panamanian Isthmus, though the Nicaragua and other routes have all been given consideration in the 1960s. Modifications to the Treaty of 1903, giving Panama greater jurisdiction over the canal zone, improve prospects of co-operation between the two countries. Whatever the future of inter-oceanic waterways, let us hope that they will promote international understanding rather than become a cause of international strife.

CHAPTER FIVE

'ROLL OBEDIENT RIVERS THROUGH THE LAND'

'THE TENNESSEE VALLEY consists for the most part of plantations in a state of semi-decay and plantations of which the ruin is total and complete.' Thus wrote a British observer shortly after the American Civil War, and his words applied almost throughout the varied terrain which the great river traverses, from the small hill farms of the east to the cotton plantations along the loop of the valley passing through Alabama. The State of Tennessee had been much fought over, its manpower depleted, and recovery was slow.

A steady stream of settlers, mainly from the east, had entered the territory after the War of Independence. They were long in conflict with the Indian tribes, and eventually drove them from their favourite hunting grounds. Indiscriminate tree-felling and over-cropping of the land, followed by years of devastation, neglect and the continued impoverishment of the farmers, resulted in areas of eroded soil on the uplands, while many of the river valleys were subject to flooding and in the south-west of the State especially there were malarial swamps. The mineral resources had scarcely been tapped and there was little manufacturing industry. The chief outlet for produce was by way of the rivers to the Mississippi, but navigation on the Tennessee, even for flat-bottomed boats, was hindered at a point called Muscle Shoals where the river descended 134 feet in a stretch of 37 miles; in spite of early attempts to improve the waterway it remained impassable to steamboats.

George Goethals obtained much of his practical experience of water engineering and canal construction, which he was later to put to such good use in Panama, when he was engaged on work at the Muscle Shoals Canal and other river improvements in the 1880s and 1890s. Then during the First World War a decision was taken to build at Muscle Shoals a plant to produce nitrates for explosives (and subsequently for fertilizers), and a large dam to supply power. In the post-war years the project proved uneconomic and its future became a matter of controversy until, under the New Deal policy of President Franklin Roosevelt, the Tennessee Valley Authority—T.V.A.—was set up in 1933.

The Tennessee River is 652 miles long; but with its numerous tributaries its 'valley' covers an area of over 40,000 square miles—four-fifths the size of England. Here in 1933 lived fewer than three million people, whose standard of living generally was low. While there were still extensive forests, about a million acres of former agricultural land were badly eroded and had been abandoned; the sporadic rising of the Tennessee contributed to flooding along the lower Mississippi, and the irregularity of its flow made it unsatisfactory for power production. Taking a comprehensive view, President Roosevelt saw the T.V.A. as a public corporation 'charged with the broadest duty of planning for the proper use, conservation, and development of the natural resources of the Tennessee River drainage basin. . . .'

Direction of this bold programme of regional development was placed in the hands of three men: Arthur E. Morgan, an experienced engineer and first Chairman; Harcourt A. Morgan, President of the University of Tennessee, who became Chairman in 1938; and

David E. Lilienthal, a lawyer with extensive administrative experience, who succeeded as Chairman from 1938 to 1946. T.V.A. met considerable opposition on many counts: there were those who feared it as introducing socialism, or even communism, so abhorrent to the United States; there was conflict with the existing power companies and other interests; and the building of dams and creation of reservoirs inevitably meant displacing many people from their farms and homes.

However, flexibility of organization, generous help towards resettlement and willingness to co-operate with local authorities, plus the extra stimulus provided by the demands of the Second World War, finally won the day. The work carried out by T.V.A. has many aspects. The twenty-eight dams, either built by T.V.A. or taken over and incorporated into the system, with their hydro-electricity installations and storage lakes are the most obvious; but, as C. Herman Pritchett wrote in *The Tennessee Valley Authority* (1943), 'the battle for water control is lost before it is begun if the heavy rains characteristic of the Tennessee Valley fall on hillsides stripped of their forest cover. . . . Water control is consequently an equation to be solved both on the land and in the river.' Flood control and the provision of a 9-foot-wide navigable waterway from Paducah, where the Tennessee joins the River Ohio, 630 miles to Knoxville, have done much to restore a healthy balance to the region; but T.V.A. has also concerned itself with afforestation, with the development of fertilizers and the demonstration of their proper use for soil improvement, and with other aspects of research and experiment. The tremendous output of electrical power has attracted a variety of industry; and it is perhaps a little ironical that it was the success of this vast exercise in conservation and development that made Oak Ridge, Tennessee, the home of the National Laboratory of the United States Atomic Energy Commission, of which David Lilienthal was Chairman from 1946 to 1950.

The particular problems offered by the Tennessee valley are not repeated elsewhere; they and the methods employed to solve them make the T.V.A. unique. Nevertheless, there are other large-scale schemes for river improvement and irrigation in the United States which, less controversial in their administration, have received less attention. The Central Valley Project in California, which went into operation in 1951, is one example. The Sacramento river, which goes through the valley from north to south before turning west to enter San Francisco Bay, has a more than ample flow and formerly caused flooding, especially in its upper reaches where over-grazing had left denuded slopes. On the other hand the waters of the San Joaquin river, flowing south to north before entering the bay, are too slight to provide irrigation for the drier southern part of the valley. As a result of the project the waters of the Sacramento are now stored in the lake created behind the Shasta Dam and fed as needed by way of the Delta-Mendola Canal into the lower San Joaquin valley; the upper San Joaquin valley is irrigated by the waters of its river stored and controlled by the Friant Dam. A complex of other dams, canals and tunnels protects the resources and provides power, irrigation, navigation and flood control for this very productive area of over six million acres, and additional dams and canals are due for completion in the 1970s. The whole project is directed from one control centre in Sacramento.

In the extreme south of California the waters of the Colorado river are carried by the 80-mile All-American Canal, completed in 1940, and by its 123-mile-long branch the Coachella Canal, finished eight years later, to irrigate an arid area of over half a million acres in the Imperial and Coachella valleys. From Lake Havasu behind the Parker Dam higher up the river water is pumped into the Colorado River Aqueduct and carried 242 miles across mountains to provide a reliable water supply to Los Angeles and other towns near the coast. Control and utilization of the Colorado river for the benefit of the south-west United States really began in the 1930s with the building of the great Hoover Dam, Arizona, and the transformation of the valley above it into Lake Mead, over a hundred miles long; where it enters the lake the Colorado is now building a new delta.

But in spite of these and other schemes the increasing demand for water, especially by industry, has led scientists to forecast a water shortage in the United States before the end of the century. Some startling proposals have been put forward, including one for an immense dam in Alaska to turn the Yukon Flats into a lake over ten thousand miles square, and another to redirect numerous Canadian rivers. Such plans and the tremendous effect they would have in altering the ecology of the whole continent have alarmed conservationists and hydrologists, and in the future American planning for water control will have to be tackled, with the co-operation of Canada and Mexico, on a continental rather than a regional scale.

In the vast Euro-Asian territory which comprises the U.S.S.R. there are innumerable rivers and watercourses which, if fully utilized, could produce superabundant hydro-electric power, navigable waterways and irrigation. Since prehistoric times the larger rivers have provided the chief routes by which various peoples penetrated the contrasting regions of forest, steppe, frozen tundra, swamp and desert. In European Russia especially the 'river-roads' provided the north-to-south trade routes; it was by the way of the Dnieper, for example, that Scandinavians, the Varangians, in the ninth century reached the Black Sea and mastery of the trade with Byzantium. Pre-eminent however is the Volga, which with its 2,300-mile course from north of Moscow to the Caspian Sea is Europe's longest river.

For centuries thousands of men were employed along the Volga hauling the boats through reaches too shallow for normal navigation. Their rhythmic, rather mournful songs have been regarded in the rest of Europe as a typical expression of the Slav mentality. It is understandable that the westward-looking tsar Peter the Great, who took the first steps towards modernizing Russia in the early eighteenth century, should have turned his attention to water communications and produced a scheme for a canal to connect the Volga to the Don and hence to the Black Sea. For three years serfs and soldiers laboured on this undertaking, but there were not only natural obstacles to be overcome; resistance to change, inadequate means and political intrigue brought about its abandonment. Although plans were revived at intervals it was not until 1952 that the Volga-Don Canal, sixty-three miles long and with thirteen locks, was opened.

Another of Peter the Great's projects, the linking of his newly founded city of St Petersburg (Leningrad) by way of the River Neva and canals passing south of Lake Ladoga to the complicated network of waterways east of the lake, came to earlier fruition, in 1741, although not in his lifetime. As part of larger schemes this contributes to the elaborate system which now connects the White Sea to the Baltic and both to the Caspian and Black Seas, while the building of the Moscow-Volga canal in the 1930s gave the capital a direct link to the main water highway.

The volume of traffic carried on the Volga is enormous. The building of hydro-electric plant (as on many other rivers in the Soviet Union) has further enhanced its importance, but brought fresh problems. The increased evaporation from the reservoirs created by the dams, and the amount of water used (and its pollution) by new industrial development, have so reduced the volume of flow that other rivers have had to be diverted into the Volga, while the level of the Caspian Sea has been steadily lowered. Unchecked, this result could endanger the effective operation of the scheme for desalination plants allied to a nuclear power station at Fort Shevchenko on the Caspian.

East of the Urals new industrial towns which utilize the resources of the great north-flowing rivers, such as the Ob, the Irtysh and the Yenisey, which traverse Siberia, as well as around Lake Baykal, have been rapidly developed in recent years. But geologists have warned that if demands for power and water continue to grow at the present rate even Siberia could experience a serious shortage of fresh water within the next twenty years. In addition, pollution has seriously affected the numbers of fish and all forms of natural life in the rivers and streams.

Clearly, there are immense possibilities for this vast but hitherto sparsely populated region, even though for a great part of it the climate is harsh. But to achieve a balance between reasonable exploitation and conservation of its many resources is for the Soviet Union a challenge of a greater scale than that facing any other single country. Fortunately, criticism of waste and abuse has been outspoken; there is at least awareness of the problem and its dangers.

CHAPTER SIX

'GOD MADE HEAVEN AND EARTH,
BUT THE DUTCH MADE HOLLAND'

EVER since the close of the last Ice Age the coastline of northern Europe has been the scene of continuous change in the complicated story of rising and sinking land, encroaching sea and delta-building rivers. Nowhere, in historical times at least, has the balance between land and water been more precarious than in the Netherlands. In Roman times the depression later occupied by the Zuider Zee held a large fresh-water lake, Lake Flevo, which was fed by several rivers and had an outfall northwards beyond the present West Frisian Islands. To the south the Rhine, the Maas and the Scheldt branched through their alluvial land to reach the sea well to the west of later limits. Along much of the coast sand dunes protected the low-lying hinterland.

Experience had early taught the hardy inhabitants of that inhospitable terrain to build protective dikes for their settlements and towns, but remorselessly the sea gained ground. In 1170, on All Saints' Day, a disastrous high tide overwhelmed the coast, creating and cutting off the chain of the Frisian Islands and making the Zuider Zee a great inlet of the North Sea. In the delta area portions of land were cut off to become islands such as Walcheren. The people fought back, in the succeeding centuries bringing to the struggle a furious zeal. Again and again the sea advanced; again and again the Dutch renewed the dikes and drained the land, establishing their fame as water engineers.

Early in the seventeenth century Jan Adriaanzoon Leeghwater proposed the draining of the Haarlem Lake by means of 160 windmills—an ambitious project not actually carried out until 1840–53, when steam pumping stations restored to agricultural use an area of about seventy square miles west of the Zuider Zee which had been inundated in the sixteenth century. In 1667 Hendrik Stevin suggested the building of a dam to exclude the North Sea from the Zuider Zee, but such an undertaking was at that time beyond the imagination and the capabilities even of the Dutch.

Sea encroachments did not affect only those areas actually lying under water. As the tides carried sea water up the rivers an increasing proportion of land was ruined by salt, wells were affected and brackish marshes extended in area. Sand blocked harbours and canals, and the silting of Amsterdam's access to the Zuider Zee would have destroyed that city's importance as a port had not the North Sea Canal been built in 1876. But this and Rotterdam's 'New Waterway' to the Hook, constructed in the same period, in turn added to the salinity, for the outward flow of the rivers never completely counteracted the tidal infiltration of salt water.

By the late nineteenth century technology had made great advances compared with the position two hundred years earlier. Between 1887 and 1891 the engineer Cornelius Lely, then in his thirties, drew up plans for two dams to enclose the Zuider Zee—one across the arm of the sea 1½ miles wide between the island of Wieringen and the

Province of North Holland, the other a barrier dam some twenty miles long between Wieringen and Friesland. Lely's plan was for the reclamation of the greater part of the land, leaving about one third of the former sea to become a freshwater lake, fed by the River IJssel (a branch of the Rhine), which could be used to irrigate and desalinate the soil in adjoining areas. A road built along the Barrier Dam, moreover, would provide a direct route between the two provinces for the first time since the twelfth century.

Lely, a man of the same stamp as Vermuyden, persistently urged his proposals. But not until after further extensive flooding in 1916 did the Dutch Parliament authorize the undertaking, and work began in the 1920s. Between 1926 and 1932 the great Barrier Dam was constructed in the open sea, of boulder clay over willow 'mattresses' and protected with stone and brick. With the closing of the last gap the impoldering of the land could start. Within four years the former Zuider Zee, which had covered an area of over two thousand square miles, had been converted into the freshwater IJssel Meer. Wieringen ceased to exist as an island and became part of the north-west polder, which was supporting farms by 1940. The north-east polder, 120,000 acres, was reclaimed by 1942, but deliberate flooding during the war ruined much land which had been won with such great effort. The Dutch, however, vigorously renewed the work and by 1961 a further polder of 135,000 acres had been added. The completion of this gigantic plan of reclamation will add to the Netherlands a total of more than half a million acres of fertile land and a new province, Flevoland, with its capital Lelystad, a new town named in honour of the engineer who envisaged the scheme.

Impoldering starts with the building of encircling dikes, usually based on a 'mattress' of willow bundles woven on to a grid of stakes, about a yard thick. This mattress is floated into position and then weighted with stones and sunk to the bottom; such a foundation resists the scouring action of moving water. With the completion of the dikes pumping begins, and as the former sea bed emerges ditches are dug to hasten the drainage. With long experience the Dutch have evolved a programme of planting different types of vegetation in succession for the full transformation of the water-logged, saline soil to good agricultural land in about four years. The patient care which thus creates new soil is continued in the methods by which it is later farmed, and rewarded with good crops.

The Barrier Dam withstood well the surge tide which on 1 February 1953 smashed through the sea defences and flooded half a million acres of land in the delta area, killing nearly two thousand people, making more than seventy thousand homeless and drowning uncounted livestock. This colossal disaster called for a 'never again' remedy on an unprecedented scale. The government was prompt to set up a Delta Commission, and from its studies came the Delta Project.

In essence this plan is for flood control and the storage and redistribution of fresh water. All the sea inlets from the Western Scheldt in the south to the Rotterdam Waterway in the north will be closed by dams between the islands of Zeeland Province, shortening the coastline by about 440 miles and providing defence for the land behind them against the worst attacks that gale-driven waters of the North Sea can conceivably hurl at them. Additionally, roads on top of these and secondary dams will provide communication between the islands and some new land will be reclaimed.

The engineering problems are immense but the project has kept pace with its schedule, which calls for completion in 1978 with the damming of the Eastern Scheldt. Various methods of construction have been adopted, according to the needs of particular sites; these include the laying of asphalt under water and also the use of nylon 'carpeting' unrolled from a trolley towed along the sea bed, on which to found the mass of the dike. The latter procedure replaces the older technique of using willow mattresses, which absorbs too much time and labour for use on such a scale. Temporary artificial islands have been created to enable the engineers to construct the sluice gates and assemble the intricate machinery for their control. The Haringvliet Dam, one of the key structures of the whole complex since it is astride the chief outlet for the Rivers Maas and Waal (a branch of the Rhine), has seventeen sets of gates each 185 feet long. One pier in three has a culvert to allow fish, especially eels, to pass up and down the rivers.

With the Delta Project well advanced engineers have been looking further ahead to an even more ambitious scheme. This is no less than the linking of the Frisian Islands to form a continuous dike enclosing that part of the Zuider Zee, now called the Wadden Zee, which is on the seaward side of the Great Barrier Dam. Such an undertaking would demand whatever new engineering techniques the rest of this century may have to offer.

In a world both wantonly wasteful of its resources and intent upon new and more terrible methods of destruction, the achievements of the Dutch are noble landmarks along the road of engineering science and human progress. Peacefully and without fuss they have defended and reclaimed land from its immemorial foe, water, bridling its strength and schooling it in what Keats counted its prime duty to man:

> The moving waters at their priestlike task
> Of pure ablution round earth's human shores.

INDEX